Persistence and *Flexibility*

SUNY Series in Anthropology and Judaic Studies
Walter P. Zenner, Editor

Persistence
and
Flexibility

Anthropological Perspectives
on the American Jewish Experience

Edited by Walter P. Zenner

State University of New York Press

Published by
State University of New York Press, Albany

For information, address State University of New York
Press, State University Plaza, Albany, N.Y., 12246

Library of Congress Cataloging-in-Publication Data

Persistence and flexibility: anthropological perspectives on the
    American Jewish experience / Walter P. Zenner, editor.
        p. cm.—(SUNY series in anthropology and Judaic studies)
    Includes index.
    1. Jews—United States—Identity. 2. Jews—United States—Social
life and customs. 3. Immigrants—United States. 4. United States—
Ethnic relations. I. Zenner, Walter P. II. Series.
E184.J5P366   1988
305.8'924'073—dc19   87-24465
ISBN 0-88706-748-4.   ISBN 0-88706-750-6 (pbk.)   CIP

10   9   8   7   6   5   4   3   2   1

To my parents
Justin Zenner and Hertha Speyer Zenner
of blessed memory

Contents

Preface   ix

Introduction   1

  1 *The Cultural Anthropology of American Jewry*   3
      Walter P. Zenner and Janet S. Belcove-Shalin

Part I   IDENTITIES AND IDENTIFICATION   39

  2 *Stigma, Identity and Sephardic-Ashkenazic Relations in*
     Indianapolis   41
      Jack Glazier

  3 *American Yemenite Jewish Interethnic Strategies*   63
      Dina Dahbany-Miraglia

  4 *Jewish in the USSR, Russian in the USA*   79
      Fran Markowitz

  5 *Learning to Be a Part-Time Jew*   96
      David Schoem

  6 *Integration into the Group and Sacred Uniqueness:*
     Analysis of an Adult Bat Mitzvah   117
      Stuart Schoenfeld

Part II ARENAS OF JEWISH LIFE   137

  7 *A Home Away from Home: Participation in Jewish*
     Immigrant Associations in America   139
      Hannah Kliger

  8 *Family, Kinship, and Ethnicity: Strategies for Social*
     Mobility   165
      Myrna Silverman

9 *The Hasidim of North America: A Review of the
   Literature*   183
      Janet S. Belcove-Shalin

10 *Separatist Orthodoxy's Attitudes Toward Community:
    The Breuer Community in Germany and America*   208
       Steven Lowenstein

11 *That Is the Pillar of Rachel's Grave Unto This Day:
    An Ethnoarchaeological Comparison of Two Jewish
    Cemeteries in Lincoln, Nebraska*   223
       David Mayer Gradwohl and
       Hanna Rosenberg Gradwohl

12 *Jews and Judaica: Who Owns and Buys What?*   260
       Samuel Heilman

Glossary   281

Contributors   291

Index   295

Preface

When I first taught a course on the ethnology of American Jews around 1976, I found it difficult to find adequate readings for my students. There were ample historical works, including some stressing the social dimensions. Sociological studies, based primarily on material derived from questionnaires, and journalistic accounts were numerous enough. It was, however, hard to find books which represented the diversity of Jewish populations in North America, and works which represented the rich textures of the fabric of North American Jewish life.

Shortly thereafter the situation altered. In recent years more and more book-length studies of various American Jewish communities and subgroups have appeared, beginning with Mintz's book on Hasidic tales and life, Mitchell's study of family clubs, the works of Kugelmass and Myerhoff, as well as Furman's monograph on the expression of Jewish identity in a Reform temple. These and other comparable works, however, necessitated buying several books at a time.

In 1985, several publishers broached the ideas of having a series on Anthropology and Jewish Studies, which eventually came to fruition. In conjunction with this, we had the idea of including in such a series a volume representing the cultural anthropological study of Jewry on this continent. This volume is the fruit of that endeavor.

Putting together such a collection is a work entailing many frustrations, but it would be impossible without the cooperation of a large group of people. First of all, I would like to thank the contributors to this volume. They responded expeditiously to my call for papers and they adhered with reasonable faithfulness to my guidelines and my pleas for brevity. They met their deadlines with an alacrity rare in academic scholarship. I am especially appreciative of Janet Belcove-Shalin's aid in the revision of the introductory chapter during a difficult and busy period of her life. While she was completing a dissertation and getting ready for a baby, she set aside time to work on a final draft of this chapter, combining some passages from her original draft of the review of literature on the Hasidim and interpolating these in my original draft of the introduction and in filling out and changing the introduction. She was a full co-author in this endeavor.

I also would like to thank William Eastman, Rosalie M. Robertson, and Judith Block for their help and support. They have truly made the production of this book possible. The various "anonymous" reviewers deserve much credit for both supporting this project and for forcing us to refine our work, adding to its appeal for scholar and public alike. Linda Zenner has over the years given me help and support in my scholarly activities.

I am dedicating this book to the memory of my parents Justin Zenner and Hertha Speyer Zenner. Even though they died long before I ever thought about an ethnology of American Jewry, they made it possible. By their heroic efforts in successfully immigrating to the United States in 1939 and in introducing me to this society, they helped make me an American Jew.

Walter P. Zenner

October 1987
Tishri 5748

Introduction

1 The Cultural Anthropology of American Jewry

Walter P. Zenner and
Janet S. Belcove-Shalin

The anthropological study of American Jewry may sound to some like an oxymoron. Are not anthropologists supposed to journey to the remote corners of the earth and brave inhospitable terrain in search of the secrets of cultural life? Jews, by contrast, have been the quintessential urban dwellers, since the coming of the modern age, and as such, were unlikely candidates for ethnographic research. It is only in recent times that anthropologists began to set their sights on people and places in urban, western environments, which explains why the ethnography of Jewish life is a relatively new field, with roots extending no further than the late 1940's and with numerous gaps still waiting to be filled. The present collection of essays marks the boundaries of the emerging field of Jewish ethnography, elucidates various methods in which social scientists interested in Judaism approach their subject, and makes a modest contribution to our knowledge of modern Jewish culture.

Since anthropology made its appearance as a discipline on this continent, anthropologists have made contributions to the study of North American society. In the early days, they did this primarily through the ethnological studies of American Indians and through physical anthropological research. By the 1950s, there were enough studies in all branches of anthropology so that a special issue of the *American Anthropologist,* the leading journal in the field, was devoted to the "The U.S.A. as Anthropologists See It" (1955).

One of the articles in that special issue, written by Melford Spiro, is on the subject of the "acculturation of American ethnic groups." Spiro notes the dearth of interest shown by anthropologists in the conflict of cultures at their own doorstep: "Apparently we prefer more exotic locales for our researches than South Boston or the West Bronx" (1955:1242). While he cites a number of studies dealing with "minority-groups," "race-relations," and what sociologists call "intergroup" relations, he is quick to point out that few ethnographers have actually tackled an anthropological analysis of culture and culture change. Spiro's review of the scant literature on ethnic groups

3

of European and Asian origin includes six publications devoted to the Jewish community. The most common theme he traces in these publications is the endogamy of the Jewish community which persists despite a high rate of acculturation.

At the time in which this article was written, anthropology was in a rapid state of transition. Before World War II, hardly any ethnographic research was being done in communities which were not rural, kin-based, and non-western. Subsequently, cultural anthropology began to turn to the metropolitan areas of the world, including the United States. The reasons for this change of direction (and heart) are complex. For one thing, anthropologists were following to the cities the tribal and peasant peoples whom they had previously researched. In part, they studied populations in the United States when they were inaccessible abroad, as in the case of the "cultures at a distance" research led by Ruth Benedict and Margaret Mead during the Second World War and its aftermath. For some, the focus on American urban communities was a way of reflecting on one's past. Others took it as a preliminary step toward overseas research.

A case in point is the research interests of one of the authors. As an undergraduate anthropology major and graduate student Zenner wrote an ethnographic account of a youth group to which he belonged, a family genealogy, a paper on the "transfer of status" by German Jewish refugees in the United States, and conducted a series of interviews with his father about the German Jewish situation before Hitler. His first funded research project was a study of Syrian Jews in Brooklyn in 1958 (Zenner 1970, 1983). Similarly, his colleague, Plotnicov, first published on New York City Jewish families (1968a, 1968b) before he went on to work in Nigeria, while another contemporary, E. Leyton, studied an extended family in Canada (1970) prior to his doctoral research in the north of Ireland.

Even before anthropologists turned their focus to American populations, Jews had been a group under-studied by social scientists. The dearth of Jewish scholarship was noted as early as the 1920s by Robert Park, one of the founding fathers of American sociology and the leader of the Chicago school, who urged his Jewish students to do research in their native communities. His exhortations were met with such little success,[1] that several decades later American social science was still a field in which there were "no full-length studies of Jewish personality, no full-length studies of the Jewish family, no full-length studies of a Jewish community" (Glazer 1950:277), as well as the field with "many Jewish sociologists and . . . few sociologists of the Jews" (Lipset 1955:177; see also Fishman 1958). The reasons for this neglect are both institutional and individual. For one thing, foundations devoted to furthering Jewish scholarship have been traditionally dominated by the representatives of the humanities who viewed their upstart social science colleagues with a good deal of skepticism. A bias against the methods and goals of the social sciences is evident by the fact that even today, few social science projects dealing with Judaism are funded. As a result, a number of academics have been unwilling to commit themselves to an area of scholarship that is financially thwarted from the start. On a more personal level, the prospect of studying fellow Jews was clearly unattractive to Jewish social scientists. The typical Jewish sociologist of this time was often a first generation born American who had drifted away from the ways of his "greenhorn" parents. The universalistic nature of social science appealed to him precisely because he could escape the parochial constrictions of his faith (Lipset 1955, 1963). When he did consider research among Jews, it was most likely to be a study of the assimilation and acculturation of orthodox immigrant communities. For such a researcher, the only appreciable value of orthodoxy was that it "functioned as a cultural constant in the life of the disoriented newcomer, as a place of haven in the stormy new environment" (Sklare 1955:44).[2]

The premise that Orthodox Judaism in America is a cultural artifact doomed to extinction is evident in the Columbia University Research Project on Contemporary Cultures. Initiated by Ruth Benedict in 1947, this project focused on cultures at a distance, to be researched through space and time. One cultural area of interest was East European Jewry, recently decimated by the events of the Second World War. Despite the regional differences between these individuals, the purpose of the study was to delineate the patterns of "shtetl" culture, to "capture the core of continuity running through the Jewish culture of Eastern Europe rather than the details in which localities and regions differed" (Zborowski and Herzog 1952:23). This project spawned a number of articles and monographs, the more important of which are Bienenstok (1950, 1952), Joffe (1948–1949), Landes and Zborowski (1950), Zborowski and Herzog (1952), and Zborowski (1949). Its shtetl model of East European Jewish culture was to become the foundation for later psycho-cultural work on American Ashkenazic Jews.[3] Hardly any other paradigm has since then exerted as much influence on scholars reconstructing the past and present of Ashkenazic Jews (Howe 1976 and Fredda M. Herz and Elliott M. Rosen 1982).[4]

The basic premise underlying this research program, however, did not withstand the test of time. Social scientists' perception of orthodoxy changed measurably when it became abundantly clear that the Orthodox community had not assimilated and was in fact flourishing. This revitalization owed much to the sizable influx of immigrants in the aftermath of World War II, which for the first time included prominent Jewish leaders and entire communities. It was subsequently enhanced in the 1970s and 1980s, a time of religious awareness throughout the country, where side by side with the regeneration of Christian fundamentalism was a growing number of *baalai tshuvah*—non-traditional Jews seeking an Orthodox way of life. The realization that orthodoxy was here to stay along with the new-found interest in traditional and novel forms of religious expression representative of the other branches of Judaism, and reinforced by the rise of ethnic consciousness among the general public in the late 1960s and 1970s which finally pushed "ethnic" social scientists to study "their own," spurred the researchers' interest in Jewish communities.[5]

In time, others besides social scientists cultivated an interest in American Jewish ethnography. Especially after the popularization of anthropological concepts by Margaret Mead, Ruth Benedict, and their contemporaries, professionals inside and outside of academia made use of such notions as "culture." Social historians, folklorists, psychologists, and journalists, they have all added considerably to our understanding of what it means to be Jewish in America.

A key element in this understanding of culture and conceptualization derives from its non-judgmental approach to actual behavior. The distinctions made by cultural anthropology between "ideal culture" and "real culture" parallel the dichotomy between scriptural religion and folk religion found in many writings of comparative religionists. In the past, many scholars looked on the actual practices as corrupt forms of the former. For the most part, anthropologists eschewed such normative evaluations. Whether we speak about "overt" and "covert" culture, "values and norms," "great traditions and little traditions," or "ideology and practice," we are dealing with this split. The "real culture," the practices of a folk, are as valid an expression of a tradition as are the dicta of its prophets.

This approach, which is a clear link between the functionalists and configurationists of the 1930s and the symbolic and materialist anthropologists of the 1980s, is very much a product of the fieldwork experience. Unlike most other scholars, cultural anthropologists are expected to live near and/or with the subjects of their research. They are expected to observe their daily and festive practices while sharing these experiences. The ambiguities of "participation/observation" which underlie anthropological methodology makes anthropologists, as one ethnographer has called us, "marginal natives" (Freilich 1977). It is an approach which involves both involvement and objectivity, observation, and insight based on experience.

This review covers the research of anthropologists and other social scientists whose prime focus is on cultural phenomena and who tend to favor participation/observation as the key research strategy. The review is divided into nine categories. The first one deals with a theoretical perspective: (1) Ethnographic studies as well as other social scientific research are linked with the idea of cultural evolution in the *Modernization Perspective*. (2) In the *Importance of Numbers*, ethnographic research augments the demographic and geographic studies of quantitatively oriented scholars. (3) The economic base is analyzed in the *Jewish Occupational Structure* and (4) *Jews as Consumers*. (5) Political life is examined in the *Political Culture of American Jews*. (6) Research on kin and interpersonal relations is presented in *Family, Self, and Interpersonal Relations*. (7) The growing number of ethnographies on worship and belief are highlighted in *Synagogues and Communal Ritual*. (8) Issues of participation and observation by "native anthropologists" are discussed in *Insiders and Outsiders*. (9) The final section, which casts light on the future of American Jewry—the prospects for its survival, assimilation, and accommodation—is titled *Persistence and Flexibility*.

The Modernization Perspective

Cultural anthropologists share with their colleagues in other disciplines certain general theories about human beings in modern society. Sometimes these theories are tested; at other times, they serve as "paradigms" or a set of shared assumptions. The term "theory" is typically used to indicate an approach rather than a tightly knit set of assumptions, explanations, and hypotheses. One of the most common of these theories employed in many studies of North American and other modern Jewries is that of modernization. Modernization theory is a variant of the conception of a universal or unilinear evolution of human societies from simple to complex. Such theories assume that ultimately all human societies will progress along a single path, or be engulfed by the strongest way of life.

Modernization is generally seen as consisting of the domination of science, fuel-powered mechanization and automation, and an increasing secularization and individuality on the one hand, and the influence of large corporations, government, and the mass media on the other. Implicit in this perspective is a sharp differentiation between traditional folk societies basaed on I–you relationships and modern societies based on I–it relationships, for both humans and other creatures.

This paradigm is used explicitly or implicitly by various social scientists writing on North American and European Jewry (Sharot 1976 and Elazar 1976). Steven Cohen (1983), for one, unqualifiedly calls his study American Modernity and Jewish Identity. A number of critics, however, have challenged this paradigm. Hope Leichter and William Mitchell (1967) attacked the idea that the loss of extended kin ties was inevitable in a modern urban setting in their study of New York City Jews and social workers and in Mitchell's subsequent study of Jewish family clubs in the same city (Mitchell 1978). This has been part of a general critique of the evolutionistic view of the decline of close kinship ties in industrial societies.

Such criticisms have also been made by students of East Asian societies. Japan, in particular, has demonstrated that it is possible to adopt an industrial technology without necessarily accepting a Western way of life in all of its respects. Thus the connections between modernism and a particular culture may be accidental. When Mark Glazer (1973) adopted from Francis L. K. Hsu this perspective for his comparative study of Ashkenazic Jews of metropolitan Chicago and the Sephardic Jews of Istanbul, he implicitly adopted this critique of modernization theory.

The thesis that assimilation (behavioral, structural, and identificational) and secularization is inevitable is a corollary of the assumption that uniformity and individualization are the natural outcomes of progress. Except for a stress on pluralism by such figures as Novak, Greeley, and other exponents of the new ethnicity, most social scientists and thinkers have suggested a movement toward assimilation on the part of those who immigrate to the United States. If there are exceptions, they are due to institutional and ideological factors, particularly racism (see Steinberg 1982). This emphasis has been criticized by several anthropologists who point out the resilience of groups bearing particular cultures.[6]

Edward Spicer has developed a concept using a qualitative comparative approach, which he has variously labeled "persistent cultural system" or "persistent identity system," or more simply "persistent peoples" (Spicer 1971; 1980:333–362). Like Frederik Barth (1969) and Milton Gordon (1964) he has separated ethnic identity from the cultural content connected to a particular group. Spicer's concern is with the cultural content insofar as it helps to maintain group identity in the face of such disturbances as dispersion and persecution. He names the "persistent peoples" who have been stubborn in their refusal to assimilate. These include North and Central American peoples like the Maya, the Yaqui, the Navajo and others such as the Jews, the Catalans, the Irish, and the Welsh. Each community maintains a core culture, including a system of communication, and shares certain moral values as well as a degree of political organization for achieving group policy. All of these communities are minority groups dominated by outside forces. While all these persistent groups declare their own symbols of identity, each one showed flexibility in changing important aspects of its culture over time. In some cases, there has been linguistic change, which is quite evident among the Jews, while others have changed their religion. Despite their flexibility, however, each group has maintained a stance of opposition to the dominant groups and surrounding environments and a defiance of forced assimilation, manifested in open political revolts. Even at their lowest point, such groups have maintained a semblance of order, perhaps in the form of what Abner Cohen (1974:65–118) has called an "invisible organization."[7]

In applying this model to American Jews, the question may be asked if American Jewry maintains a sufficient "opposition" to the majority culture. The argument of many Jewish survivalists is that it does not (Liebman 1973; Duker 1950).

Much of what Spicer writes follows a standard sociological analysis. What is particularly valuable in his work is its comparative perspective. Rather than seeing Jewish survival and differentiation as an isolated phenomenon, he shows how Jews fare compared to other groups. Along with other critics of the modernization approach, Spicer provides an alternative to looking at Jewish assimilation as inevitable.

Certain aspects of the modernization perspective can thus be seen as flawed. Earlier claims notwithstanding, modern society is not and will not be homogeneous. Ethnic and ideological/religious differentiation will persist. Individualism which was thought to be an inevitable concomitant of social evolution, may in fact be the product of a particular cultural tradition. Indeed, technology that fosters homogenization can also be instrumental in maintaining differences. Observance of the dietary laws, for instance, is made easier by the freezer, since Jews living far from big metropolitan areas can buy and store kosher meat, even if there is no *shohet* within a hundred or more miles. Ease in communication and transportation may make small Orthodox communities feel less isolated than they had in the past (cf. E. Rosenthal 1980). Clearly the prevailing notion that technological and social evolution is unidirectional must be modified.

The Importance of Numbers

Social scientists constantly ask questions such as how many people are in a particular group and what percentage of them are active members. The concern with cultural evolution discussed above is intimately related to the increase in population and the growing complexity of technology and social organization. One of the major fields within the sociology of Jewry is demography, which keeps a watchful eye on the ebb and flow of Jewish populations, especially in the context of intermarriage and conversion. The latter are of primary concern for Jewish social agencies providing services to the young, the old, the affluent, and the poor. Since anthropologists in the United States have historically focused on the functioning of small groups in the context of urban society, the broader picture involving the population as a whole is generally missing (although there are some notable exceptions: see Heilman, and Gradwohl & Gradwohl below). It is undeniable, however, that the cultural dynamics described by anthropologists and historians very much depend on how many people in a given place are engaged in a particular set of activities. One cannot assume that simply because the number of Jews is small in proportion to a large Gentile population that the Jews will be overwhelmed culturally. For instance, a small concentrated intentional community in a rural setting may be able to keep out unwanted influences. Similarly, the assumption that minorities in urban areas, because of their numbers, will tend to lose their identity and culture may or may not be true.[8]

Numbers do matter. The question, though, is how their impact can be measured. Claude Fischer (1975) has pointed to a large body of work showing that ethnic and religious institutions remain viable and may actually thrive in urban settings. They may do so alongside such counter-cultural bodies and networks as bohemias, gay bars, red-light districts, criminal syndicates, and skid rows. In the metropolis, one finds subcultures of poverty, affluence, and opulence, which may include peoples of vastly different backgrounds. It is not simply a matter of proportions in the population, Fischer declares, but absolute numbers. A ballet club of ten in a village of 100 people is a larger proportion than 1,000 fans in a city of a million, but an audience of 1,000 can support more ballet performances. Each of the relatively small concentrations of peoples in a large city, therefore, can be sufficient to sustain various subcultural activities.

While formulated at a macro-societal level, the critical mass view of subcultures is useful in examining the persistence and strength of Jewish institutions in American society at a small group level. Both in historical and contemporary perspective, we find that where American Jews are small in number, Jewish institutions are weak. This was characteristic of the period from 1654 to 1840 and it has been the case where Jews live in small towns, especially in the South and the West. Jewish subcultures have been more vibrant in the very large metropolitan concentrations of Jews, especially in the metropolitan New York City area, the Boston-Washington corridor as a whole, and in such centers as Toronto, Chicago, and Los Angeles. The time dimension is also of significance. Jewish communities which are growing or declining rapidly often have weak synagogues and other institutions. Communities suffering urban flight are often characterized by the closing or mergers of synagogues, while some Jewish communities settling in the suburbs of the Sunbelt have so far failed to establish synagogues or schools.[9]

The elaboration of subcultures within the Jewish community is also most characteristic of very large cities and population concentrations. In small communities one may find only one synagogue or perhaps two. These synagogues do not generally represent denominational extremes within Judaism; separate, secular, gay, or ultra-orthodox congregations are by and large nonexistent. While small, cohesive followings of certain Hasidic *rebbes* have formed homogeneous communities outside cities, even these are within commuting distance of large cities. This is especially characteristic of New York City and its environs. Sephardim, Yemenites, German Jews with different political and religious orientations, Hasidim, Communists, Soviet emigres, and many other groups have flourished there. Some of these groups, although tiny in percentage terms, rival the size of small town populations (for example the German Separatist-Orthodox: see Lowenstein below).

A mention should be made here of Jewish laws that make metropolitan areas congenial to the more Orthodox. Urban concentrations facilitate the establishment and maintenance of kosher butchers and food stores, yeshivot, mikvehs, and the like. Communication with and among the learned is facilitated by proximity in a city. This is not to say that modern technology has not added new wrinkles. Telephones and television, as well as refrigeration, have made possible the dispersion of even observant Jews in a way unknown a century ago. The extent of the change, however, need not be exaggerated. Jewish education, which cannot function without some face-to-face contact, puts a limit on how far observant Jews could venture outside the established territory of Jewish life.

The Jewish Occupational Structure

While the general social theories which deal with Jews and Judaism include Jewish economic behavior under their purview, there are relatively few anthropological studies of "Jewish" occupations.[10] This is due, in part, to the ethnographers' traditional preference for the folk rather than the elite.[11] Eventually, we must rely on historians, journalists, and others for descriptions of upper class Jews. How the people observed fit into the overall structure of American economic life can be understood only through macroscopic studies.

The occupational structure of Jews, in the United States and elsewhere, was summarized by Simon Kuznets (1960; 1972). As this author shows, there are considerable differences between Jews and Gentiles when it comes to the industrial sector. In the past, Jewish workers were employed mainly in light industries, such as cigar-making and garment finishing, rather than in coal mining or steel-making.

There are several descriptive studies of Jewish occupations written by historians, journalists, and social scientists. Irving Howe (1976) describes the garment industry, including factories and sweat shops, which played a crucial role in the lives of East European immigrants in New York City at the turn of the century. In many ways, this industry was the heart of a Jewish enclave economy. On a smaller scale, the international trade and processing of diamonds form another occupational niche where Jews, including Hasidim, have done very well. While the "diamond district" around 47th Street and Broadway in New York is one branch of this trade, it is really much more international, with links that go from Johannesburg to Tel Aviv, Amsterdam, and Antwerp. While dominated by Jews at various points, the field is also favored by other groups (e.g. Lebanese Muslims in Sierra Leone).[12] The scrap industry began with Jews trading in second hand goods, and has been celebrated in song and literature, forming a part of the Jewish stereotype and noted in the film "Lies My Father Told Me" and Barbra Streisand's rendition of "Second Hand Rose." This industry is well described by Joseph Fauman (1941) in its pre-World War II phase. Even then, scrap metal yards in the United States were marked by Jewish proprietors with Black employees. In more recent years, this industry has changed somewhat with the appearance of younger, "non-ethnically marked" entrepreneurs with environmentalist ideas who view it in terms of recycling.[13]

Peddling in both urban and rural areas continued to be important for large numbers of immigrants, both Jewish and non-Jewish, well into the 1920s. This activity was especially important for the spread of Central European Jews from the Eastern Seaboard during the mid-nineteenth century, and continued to be significant for East European Jews and for Syrians, both Jewish and Christian.[14]

There are some ethnographic descriptions of specialized groups, particularly Hungarian Hasidim and Syrian Jews. The former, at least in the early 1960s, had begun to specialize in providing ultra-kosher products for other Orthodox Jews (Poll 1961). The latter, beginning with the peddling and importation of table linen, had moved into the importation of infant wear and electronic equipment, and retailed them through a variety of channels, including "tourist bazaars," discount stores, and the like (Zenner 1982; Sutton 1979).

Jobs in corporate and governmental bureaucracies based on merit are quite different from the enterprises dependent on familial and ethnic solidarity. In the "meritocratic" settings, information about job openings, for instance, is as important as direct favoritism. While nepotism is not unknown in such bureaucracies, it is not a norm the way it is in family firms. In government civil service, corporations, and academia, there are significant numbers of Jews who have used the merit system. The effect of this kind of occupational change on the American Jewish community is not yet clear (Zenner 1978; 1980).

Much Jewish economic activity is related to ethnic solidarity, usually between family members, extended kin and/or people who come from the same town. This comes out in the writings on the Jewish upper class which have often focused on personal and business relationships within such families. These include sketches of German, Sephardic, and East European elites, the Ochs-Sulzberger clan and the New York Times, and an account of the families who own department stores throughout the United States. These accounts are often gossipy, such as a recent book on the demise of the once-proud, and originally Jewish firm, Lehman Brothers. In Auletta's book, a tension is revealed between "old money," represented by German Jews, WASPs, and an assimilating Greek American and "new money," represented by a New York East European Jew.[15] Such conflicts still pervade high finance, whether that of the establishment or of parvenus.

For the most part, the upper classes are inaccessible to the probings of ethnographers. There are, however, some social anthropological studies of middle class families in business. Elliott Leyton has published a study, showing how a Jewish family became dispersed in southern Canada on account of its business ventures (Leyton 1970). In their analysis of extended kin in New York City, Leichter and Mitchell illustrate the negative effects of family-owned businesses on Jewish families in New York City. In a family business, one always brings work-related worries home, precisely because these are familial in character (Leichter and Mitchell 1967:135–145). On the other hand, Silverman (below) stresses how families help their members in achieving social mobility.

The world of work deserves more attention from ethnographers of American Jewry than it has received, particularly since most students of American life have found that a career is a major focus for most middle class Americans. This observation is especially true of Jews; witness the large numbers of Jewish men and women in graduate programs and professional schools. The desire for a white collar job and the pride taken in it has even become a part of Jewish lore. Who, for example, has not heard the familiar boast, "my son, the doctor"? As all aspects of Jewish life in North America are integrally affected by this concern with professional status, an understanding of the economic base will go a long way in shedding light on this community.

Jews As Consumers

Economic studies of Jews usually limit their roles to that of producers and middlemen, to workers and capitalists. Yet much attention has also been given to Jews as consumers.[16] Indeed, the field of market research from which so much social scientific methodology stems is consumer oriented. While production and investment are considered rational activities, a great deal of irrationality is allowed the consumer. Only a few studies deal directly with preferences in buying. Indirectly, however, one can learn about patterns of consumption from projects devoted to Jewish ceremonies such as sedarim, weddings, bar mitzvahs, foods, funerals, and the like. Thus, Heilman delineates the ways in which different kinds of Jews purchase articles of Judaic value for both ritual and aesthetic reasons, and the Gradwohls show how Jews have prepared for their deaths in an ethnoarchaeological study of Jewish cemeteries. The folklorists, more than the anthropologist, have pioneered the research of Jews as consumers.

Two studies exemplifying this point deal with occupations serving a Jewish clientele; one of them involves the butcher shop, and the other, the caterer. In the former study, an attempt was made to show how Jewish women bargain in the butcher shop (Dressler 1971). In the latter, the work of the caterer is described and analyzed (Prosterman 1984). Heilman's analysis (below) of Judaica shops and their clientele offers another dimension of this kind of study and links it integrally to symbolic studies.

The Political Culture of American Jewry

Studies of American Jewish political culture, particularly as expressed in voting behavior, have been the subject of many articles and books by journalists, sociologists, and political scientists. Typically, the discussions revolve around the concept of culture, even though cultural anthropologists have not, as a group, contributed much to this research. Most of these works seek to explain why Jews have remained part of a liberal coalition in the United States, even though they have become one of the most affluent groups in American society. Related to this issue is an interest in the pro-Israel lobby in Washington and the somewhat successful efforts to woo significant numbers of Jewish voters to the conservative side (Fuchs 1956; Lipset 1963; Whitfield 1984; Cohn 1958). Isaacs, a journalist, has described Jewish involvement at the upper echelons of American politics, including congressional staff aides, high government officials, financial contributors, and lobbyists.

The major cleavage which is discerned by political scientists and journalists between liberal and conservative Jews is certainly mirrored in the anthropological studies, although the association of liberalism with assimilationism and conservatism with Zionism or Orthodoxy, which seems to be in style today, seems to us too simple. Many of the anti-Zionist Reform Jews of the early twentieth century were staunch Republicans, while the American Jewish Congress, founded by Rabbi Stephen Wise, was in its early days a pro-Zionist, liberal organization, which continues to this day to make its stance in favor of a wall between church and state. Liberals have formed a coalition with conservatives in Berkeley, California, where radicals dominate, while radicals have been known to support liberals against conservatives elsewhere. As shown in a study of how Southern Jews of the same congregation reacted to a synagogue bombing in 1958, Lowi (1961) found a deep division between the native Southerners, who wished to maintain a low profile, and more recent migrants from the North, who as activists, wished to offer a reward. Neither group had much independent power in the community, but each entertained an idea that the behavior of the other endangered the community (Lowi 1964).

In Canadian politics, especially in the province of Quebec, these divisions take on a very different meaning. Shaffir (1983) has shown how Hasidic leaders found it easier to accommodate to the imposition of French as the primary language of instruction than did mainstream Anglophone Jews, since instruction in either French or English was peripheral to their goals of teaching *yiddishkeit* (orthodox Jewishness in this context). This struggle is paralleled by that of the Francophone North African Jews with the dominant Anglophone Ashkenazic Jewish community where the North African French heritage favorably disposed them toward the Catholic Quebecois, even to the point of fostering intermarriage (Lasry 1981). In neither case do explanations in terms of conservatism or liberalism contribute much.

There have been several anthropological studies of community conflicts and radical groups. Among them is Maibaum's description (1971) of the struggle between a left-wing radical Union of Jewish Students and the "establishment" Hillel society in Berkeley, California, during the turbulent 1960s. Another is Dolgin's study of the early days of Meir Kahane's Jewish Defense League, which focused on the organizing symbols of that organization (Dolgin 1977). The Jewish Defense League, she points out, grew out of urban community conflicts in the late 1960s and early 1970s, which pitted lower middle class Jews against upwardly mobile blacks, as well as against liberal and radical Jews who sympathized with the lower-class minorities. In New York City in particular, such conflicts often involved a struggle between the "locals" of the neighborhood and "cosmopolitan" Jewish academics and civil servants. Gradually some Jewish organizations developed coalitions for protecting their own interests either in conjunction with their neighbors or in opposition to them.[17] Often the struggles are between groups with quite different, but legitimate, vested interests (such as middle class Forest Hills residents seeking to preserve their security at home versus welfare recipients desperately in need of better housing), but the fights are often posed in terms of larger symbols (e.g., the community vs. City Hall, racial bigots vs. anti-Semites, Third World vs. Zionism).[18] Although Jews inevitably see themselves as a minority, in New York City and in other large metropolitan areas, they operate as part of the country's white majority. The mixture of "majority group politics" with a "minority psychology" is an important factor in Jewish political behavior where there are large centers of Jews. The situation is quite different in other parts of the United States where Jews are less concentrated (Lowi 1961: Glazier below).

The "local"/"cosmopolitan" dichotomy is explicit in Donna Arzt's (1986) study of the different cultural and political orientations of the typically assimilationist "public interest" lawyers and that of the more traditional Jews who tend toward private practice. The author rejects the thesis that the source of Jewish liberalism is embedded in Jewish tradition. Implicit in much of this discussion is a running debate about where Jewish interests lie and whether the Jewish establishment and upper class betray these interests for the sake of their own class or personal concerns.[19]

A full-scale study of political culture must include political socialization and the manipulation of symbols as weapons in conflict. Arzt's study of lawyers suggest some ways in which political socialization might affect a social group (in that case, the public interest lawyers), while Shuldiner (1984) has supplied life histories for aged Jewish working-class radicals. Shaffir's study of Hasidim in Quebec and Lowenstein's article on the separatist-Orthodox of Washington Heights (see below) illustrate the historical depth of these groups' political orientations. Showing how the context of debate and conflict resonates with potent symbols drawn from the past is one of the tasks which will help political anthropologists put flesh on the bones of quantitative students of power.

Family, Self, and Interpersonal Relationships

During the 1950s and 1960s, family and kinship were focal areas in cultural anthropology in general and in the study of American Jews in particular. The studies of Zborowski and his colleagues (Zborowski and Herzog 1952; Landes and Zborowski 1950; Wolfenstein 1958; Zborowski 1969), by Snyder (1958), and by Leichter and Mitchell (1967; Mitchell 1978) are representative of this interest. We have noted much of this above. More recently, the concern with kinship, child-rearing, emotional development, and the like has diminished in anthropology, although such interests are still prominent in social history and in social work.[20]

Despite the failure to follow-up on the earlier work, some current studies do, in fact, address the issues of family life. Studies of aging, poverty, and rituals all contain material relevant to an understanding of Jewish kinship. For instance, the elderly in Venice California and in the South Bronx of New York live apart from their children and for the most part are widowed. Even if they do have kin in the metropolitan area, they nonetheless choose to live separately (Myeroff 1979; Kugelmass 1986). Passover seders, bar and bat mitzvahs, and weddings are family assemblages in which the dynamics of kinship can be amply illustrated. Tensions between kin may often be accentuated on such occasions, when one can see who is invited and who is not (see Frankel 1980; Leichter and Mitchell 1967:127–159;

Myerhoff 1984; Schoenfeld below). Spotting such tensions is important, because they can help explain discontinuities in Jewish family life. On the other hand, Epstein (1978:139–156) sees one facet of ethnic persistence in a particular kin tie—that of grandparents and grandchildren. This was detected in his studies of American Jews, as well as in his research of the Zambian Copperbelt and Melanesian societies.

The effort at reproducing the warmth of home and family is found in various contexts. Some examples are the *landsmanshaft* as discussed by Kliger (below), Jewish clubs formed by Jews who have moved into new communities (Zenner 1978), and, of course, family clubs (Mitchell 1978). Small synagogues and closely-knit prayer groups *(havurot)* can serve as kin surrogates for a highly mobile population (Weissler 1986; Schoenfeld, below).

Finding those who are like oneself is needed in such reproduction. Plotnicov and Silverman (1978) have shown the ways in which Jews signal their common identity to each other in a variety of settings and what such signalling means in terms of feeling at home with others. Dahbany-Miraglia (below) shows the working of such signalling in the case of Yemeni Jews, who are frequently mistaken for non-Jews of color. Glazier also gives some examples of Jews of non-Ashenazic background who do not fit the self-stereotype of the Ashkenazi (cf. Glazier below; Sutton 1979; Zenner 1983; forthcoming). Markowitz also shows us what happens to Jews who do not live up to others' expectations (below), whereas M. Glazer argues that the individualism of American Jews is achieving priority over loyalty to the family in many areas (1973).

The self-identity of American and other Jews has been the subject of much thought. Terms like "ambivalence" and "self-hatred" are commonly used to describe some of the feelings which Jews have about being "Jewish." The stereotypes of the "Jewish American Princess" (JAP) and the "Jewish mother" are widespread in American Jewish literature (cf. Gilman 1968; Liebman 1973; Baum, Hyman and Michel 1976). The origins and transmission of such ambivalence lie within the family, the peer group and school (Schoem below; Seidler & Ravitz 1955). The attitudes towards Gentiles, Hasidim, Sephardim, German, and Soviet Jews are all affected by how American Jews view themselves and their position in American society. The closely-linked topics of family life, socialization, interpersonal communication, and the symbols of self-identity deserve the continued attention of anthropologists who engage in the ethnography of American Jewry.

Synagogues and Communal Rituals

Of all extra-familial Jewish institutions, the synagogue is still perhaps the most important one. In the United States and Canada, the synagogue has transcended its traditional role as a house of worship. Most children who attend afternoon Hebrew school, for instance, do so in schools affiliated with synagogues. While Jewish day schools are often separate from synagogues, most are affiliated with Orthodox and Conservative synagogue movements. Important rites of passage either take place in synagogues or include rabbis or cantors who are employed by them. This includes bar and bat mitzvah ceremonies, weddings, funerals, and circumcisions. Synagogues may also be used for non-religious social events.

Studies on synagogues and communal rituals are among the best examples of the symbolic approach in anthropology. While the delineation of key symbols has always been present in the study of Jewish communities, more recently it has moved to the forefront, due largely to the application of research by such scholars as Levi-Strauss, Victor Turner, Clifford Geertz, and Mary Douglas. The symbolic approach looks at myth, rituals and symbols insofar as they pertain to ultimate concerns with life and death, the self, and the nature of the universe, rather than with group belonging (ethnicity studies) and cohesiveness (functional studies). This approach reveals the interpretive understandings of a people's system of meaning. Virtually all symbolic studies written on synagogue life use a microscopic lens to examine the interpersonal relations among congregants as they pray, study, argue, gossip, and recreate. From this perspective, synagogue life is regarded as a series of novel interactions and shifting involvements, rather than an age-old static social phenomenon, carved in stone.

In one study Heilman (1973) draws on Erving Goffman's dramaturgical approach to elucidate interactions between members of a modern Orthodox synagogue where he himself was a member. He focuses on the feelings of obligation members have toward one another which serve to ceaselessly initiate, fulfill, and then re-initiate social life. Heilman notes that such activity is instrumental in bonding the membership into a cohesive whole, while serving as a mechanism of social control.

Myerhoff and Kugelmass's bi-coastal studies of the Israel Levin Senior Adult Center in Venice, California[21] and the Intervale Jewish Center of the South Bronx, respectively, are in many respects companion pieces concerned with worship and sociality among elderly Jews. Despite some appreciable differences in emphasis, the works are remarkably similar in tone and theoretical orientation. To varying degrees they draw on Victor Turner's analysis of conflict resolution to see how crises emerge, evolve, and are resolved, all the while generating rearrangements in social relations among their own membership, and between themselves and outsiders. By the same token, each community dramatizes its own notion of what it is and what it hopes to be through various cultural performances, or what Myerhoff terms "definitional ceremonies." Both studies stand out from the rest of the ethnographic literature on the subject for their vivid characterizations of center members. The vitality of these elderly congregants are juxtaposed with their physical decay, and in the case of Kugelmass's book, with the deterioration of the neighborhood, which happens to be one of the worst slums in North America. Both works convey the world view of the membership, and their attempt to rationalize the fact that they remain entrenched rather than flee to the safety of a better neighborhood.

One way in which the above-mentioned studies are noteworthy is that they show how congregants creatively interpret Jewish tradition on an ad hoc basis, often to suit their personal needs. Prell (1978, 1987) and Weiner, on the other hand, demonstrate how different congregations have explicitly institutionalized innovations of Jewish ritual and worship. Prell studies a *havurah* (fellowship), a counterculture type of minyan with an emphasis on sexual equality, quite a radical move for a faith where gender division permeates all areas of religious experience. She examines the constraints tradition places on the drive of its congregation to be gender neutral and the strategies they devise to overcome tradition. Weiner's description of the merger of a Conservative and a Reform synagogue in San Francisco describes both the politics of synagogues and the difficulty of amalgamating two entirely different styles and traditions of worship. By focusing on a conflict between a Conservative cantor and Reform rabbi at a Friday evening service, she spells out the priorities of each branch of Judaism, showing how differences were creatively resolved during the Sabbath.

In recent years a number of studies have explored the havurah movement. One point of emphasis has been its egalitarian spirit. In her analysis of a bar mitzvah celebration, Weissler (1986) describes how the close-knit relations among Dutchtown havurah members have taken on a greater importance than the ties these people have with their own kin.

Though the havurah was traditionally the brainchild of the Conservative Movement, it has cropped up in the other branches of Judaism as well. Furman (1987:85–95) studied one such havurah in a Reform synagogue which is close to the Pittsburgh Platform variety discussed by the Gradwohls (see below). Her work underscores the emotive side of the havurah movement. It is on account of the synagogue's overly formal environment, according to the author, that members formed a havurah to infuse their worship with the warmth and zest they longed for so dearly.

Attention to the synagogue's ritual life has not gone wanting. One recent addition to the analysis of ritual performance is Epstein's study of the Bobover Hasidim's purimshpiyl or Purim play, held in the men's section of the synagogue on the second day of Purim (1977, 1987). Considered by most Jews as a day for the children, not unlike Halloween, Purim has become a particularly important holiday for the Bobovers. Playing on the word *kippurim*, they have elevated this festive holiday to the level of that most solemn one, Yom Kippur. Despite its carnival-like atmosphere, the Bobover Hasidim, through some interesting ritual inversions, have converted Purim into a day of atonement.

Whereas in the past, interest in American Jews was considered to be on the periphery of cultural anthropology, the increasing interest in ritual has been instrumental in bringing studies of synagogues and Jewish communal rites to the central stage of ethnological inquiry. This research is part of our effort to understand the dynamic interactions among the symbols we use to construct reality and human action.

Insiders and Outsiders

Most research on Jews in North America is conducted by scholars who are themselves Jewish. In the past, this fact raised a number of methodological objections. For one, can the researcher studying his own community be objective? With the coming of age of a reflexive ethnographic literature that is devoted to the biases endemic to ethnographic research, however, the critical edge of this objection has been considerably dulled. Still others questioned the native ethnographer's ability to conduct sensitive research in his own community. Termed the "Outsider Doctrine" by Robert Merton (in Heilman 1980), it assumed that an insider's socialization desensitized him to the cultural and social laws and nuances of his own community. This perspective has been soundly laid to rest by a number of studies conducted by Jewish ethnographers, most notably, by the work of Barbara Myerhoff, which offered a penetrating analysis of a Jewish community center for the elderly in Venice, California (1978).

Heilman went further than most in his criticism of the "Outsider Doctrine," turning Merton's notion, in effect, on its head. As a by-product of his own work in a modern Orthodox Jewish synagogue, he resurrects the "Insider Doctrine" (1980) to assert that in a society as complex as Orthodox Judaism, the detached familiarity of the native researcher yields a motherlode of keen observations unintelligible to the uninitiated.

An analysis of native ethnography illustrates that the denominations "insider" and "outsider" are strictly relative. While a Jewish anthropologist studying a Jewish community may appear, to his Gentile colleague, as an insider by virtue of his shared faith, from the vantage point of the informant, the anthropologist may be the representative of a wholly different society. A review of the literature reveals a variety of configurations in which the Jewish anthropologist has the qualities of both insider and outsider, thus challenging a strict insider/outsider dichotomy.

The fieldwork of Zenner (1983) and Stern (1977) are instances of research conducted by Ashkenazic Jews in Sephardic communities. Due to his religious training, Zenner could readily pray in the synagogue of the Syrian Jewish community, despite his need to familiarize himself with the Sephardic/Arabic pronunciation of Hebrew and the unfamiliar melodies of the service. Yet his informants were continually curious to know if he were really a Sephardi, and if not, why he would be interested in studying them. Zenner concluded from his work that although their common faith facilitated access, and he was hardly a Gentile stranger, he nonetheless remained a "Jewish outsider." By contrast, since Stern had "inter-married" into a Sephardic family, his in-laws' community was more than willing to initiate this newcomer into their traditions.

Poll (1962), Shaffir (1985), and Belcove-Shalin (1987) have discussed their research of Hasidic communities in some depth. Of the three, Poll was the most similar to his informants, for he too had attended a Hasidic yeshiva in Hungary. But since his then-current identification was much more "modern," he was shunned by many community members as an *epikoros*, a disbeliever or skeptic. Shaffir reflects upon the ethical dilemmas and methodological problems he encountered in the often painful process of fieldwork. His impressions are drawn from research in a number of startlingly different communities. Belcove-Shalin, who offers a reflexive account of fieldwork among the Hasidim of Boro Park, draws on Goffman's theory of the "presentation of self," and "face-work" in order to illuminate the ways in which both ethnographer and informant arrive at agreed upon definitions of a situation in the course of their encounters.

Although she was regarded by the Hasidim as a stranger, she was tolerated and often welcomed when her behavior conformed to certain roles (e.g. that of the *baalat tshuvah*) sanctioned by them.

The work of Heilman (1976), Sutton (1979), and Dahbany-Miraglia (below) would seem to come closest to "pure" native ethnography. Sutton, a Syrian Jew, and Dahbany-Miraglia, a Yemenite, both studied their own communities in Brooklyn. Heilman, a modern Orthodox Jew, studied life in his synagogue in "Sprawl City." Yet Heilman (1980) has found it necessary to record and analyze the difficulties he encountered in such a familiar environment as his own, ones which are no doubt recognizable to all native ethnographers. One dilemma concerned the question of allegiance. Was he first and foremost an academic or an Orthodox Jew? That is, "Was, for example, the Sabbath to be a rich source of data or a day of rest?" (104) Heilman found that his attempt to scrutinize the familiar with a fresh eye inevitably assured his estrangement from his neighbors. In the end, this insider left his own community an outsider.

Several of the studies in this particular volume were written by present or past residents in the communities considered, including those by Dina Dahbany-Miraglia, Jack Glazier, the Gradwohls, Myrna Silverman and Steven Lowenstein. In all the articles, insights are derived from the shared experiences of observers and observed. This is made especially clear by Hannah Kliger who shows how her own knowledge of Yiddish and background as a child of Holocaust survivors provided her empathy and rapport with the generally elderly members of immigrant associations (see below).

Although few in number, Gentiles have researched Jewish communities. In the 1970s, William Mitchell was encouraged by his professors, Jew and Gentile alike, to study Jewish family clubs. Rather than focus on the obvious dissimilarity of his research with that of his Jewish colleagues, a discussion of the ways in which his fieldwork is comparable might be instructive. As with a Jewish researcher, Mitchell's informants speculated about his background; likewise, they were quick to point out his correct and incorrect behavior; these Jews were amused that any outsider could have an interest in studying their community; the ethnographer was accepted as a "good" one of "them" (in his case, as a "good Gentile"). An analysis, then, of the number of critical similarities shows conclusively how tenuous a strict insider/outsider distinction really is. As all these case studies, and the contributors to this volume indicate, there is, in fact, a broad continuum.

Persistence and Flexibility

What is the picture of American Jewry found in cultural anthropological studies and how does it compare with that of other disciplines? The emphasis in the review by Spiro (1955) was on the acculturation and assimilation of American Jews and other ethnic groups. This had been the main thrust of much of the social science literature. This literature details how Jewish institutions become like those of their neighbors, how Jews behave increasingly like American Gentiles, and it shows how the Jewish group as a separate entity is disintegrating. While theories of acculturation always paid considerable attention to the creativity of peoples whose cultures were under stress, in the American context, it has often been a literature of homogenization. Snyder (1958) found that the Jewish pattern of alcohol consumption and sobriety gave way among second and third generation Americans to Anglo-American drinking patterns. Zborowski (1969) showed that later generations of American-born Jews became more and more like their neighbors in their reactions to emotional pain. Mark Glazer (1973), in contrasting the Jews of Chicago with those of Istanbul, has demonstrated how the value hierarchy of the former has adopted the individualistic priorities that typify American society (also Zenner 1985). This strong impact of North American individualism is shown here, too. For example, Schoem portrays the Hebrew school almost as a rear guard action to maintain Jewish identity in the face of the acceptance of majority culture values which pervade the environment.

This trend toward homogenization was noted as early as the 1940s by the eminent social historian, Abraham Duker, but with a difference. Duker identified the religious trends of Jewish life by highlighting a number of traits which typified the Jewish community: the naming practices, language loyalty, observances of the *mitzvot* (divine commandments), participation by women in the synagogue, and food culture, for example. With an eye toward acculturation, he observed that as Jews and Gentiles come into greater contact, the influence of the dominant culture on Judaism causes a number of these practices to wither away, leading in the direction of inauthentic religious practices, where kitsch has replaced tradition. In spite of the grave scenario he paints, Duker's work was innovative in its attempt to leaven the image of an unyielding trend toward assimilation; he highlights the efforts of rabbis and other professionals to reshape American Jewish culture as well as the culture of the "ignorant" laity. In doing so, he pinpointed a "folk creativity and the desire to maintain as much of Jewish living culture as possible"

(1949; 1950; 1960). In two key respects, Duker's corpus can be seen as a precursor to some of the more recent work on Jewish ritual. There is, in his work, an appreciation for the importance of symbols as a focal point of social interaction, even mobilization. Furthermore, in citing indigenous attempts to wed Jewish tradition to the concerns of modern-day life, he sets the stage for those interactional studies that analyze how particular individuals innovate ritual change.

The "folk creativity" expressed by Duker is the key ingredient in Max Weinreich's analysis of Ashkenazic Jewry in the Middle Ages. This theme is underscored in his classic study, "The Reality of Jewishness versus the Ghetto Myth: The Sociolinguistic Roots of Yiddish," which appears in a volume honoring the structuralist, Roman Jakobson. A prelude to his monumental study, *Geshikhte fun der Yidisher Shprakh* (History of the Yiddish Language), this piece examines Ashkenazic culture (and by contrast, Gentile culture) in the thirteenth century in the Middle-Rhine-Moselle area at the time in which Yiddish had begun to evolve. Weinreich notes that the outward resemblance between Jewish and Gentile cultural patterns is, in fact, merely skin deep. When these culture traits are framed in precepts grounded in Torah-culture, they are distinctively Jewish: "More often than not," he states, "it appears the distance between Jewish and non-Jewish patterns is created not by a difference in the ingredients proper but rather by the way they are interpreted as elements of the given system." (1967 2205)

Weinreich's work is refreshingly contemporary in a number of respects, not the least of which is his differentiation between a symbol's meaning and manifestation, what Ferdinand Saussure referred to as the signified and the signifier, and his insistence on understanding signification as part of a symbolic system. It is not surprising, then, that Weinreich's work has inspired a host of students and forms the basis for a sound understanding of the background of much of American Jewry.

Consistent with many of the insights of Duker and Weinreich are a number of recent ethnographic studies which show how Jewish communities persist in a particularly Jewish way. Social networks of Jews differ from those of other whites, as well as those of Hispanics and blacks (Yancey et al 1985). While Hanukkah has developed as a Jewish counterpart to Christmas, the celebration of bar and bat mitzvahs and of Passover seders is unlike anything found in Christianity, unless it is an imitation of the Jewish custom. Though Jewish worship in America has long imitated Protestant services, the new *havurot* represent ritual innovations along Jewish models. Intimate

Orthodox *minyanim* (prayer quorums) and *shtieblakh* (hasidic prayer rooms) are cropping up in more and more neighborhoods.

The papers in this volume are divided into two groupings. Part I consists of papers dealing with *Identities and Identifications*. Three of the articles gathered under this heading deal with several subgroups who are identified (indeed stigmatized) in particular ways within the United States and within the Jewish minority in particular. The three groups are the Indianapolis Sephardim, the Yemenites, and the more recent Soviet emigres. The other two articles deal with Jewish socialization in North America—an afternoon Hebrew school and an adult bat mitzvah.

Part II, entitled *Arenas of Jewish Life*, contains articles concerned with institutions and communities. These include immigrant associations, middle class families, Judaica gift and book shops, and cemeteries. The remaining two articles deal with a couple of ultra-orthodox communities, one structured around a particular synagogue and the other being a general review of the ethnographies of Hasidic communities.

The articles in this volume show both the stresses and strains suffered by a variety of Jews in North America who seek to accommodate to life on this continent and to preserve a measure of dignity and self-esteem as Jews. They reveal a complex reality engendered by the cultural content examined in this volume. It is hard to reduce this reality to simple linear movements from immigration to assimilation, as earlier social scientists have tried to do. What these studies reveal about Jews is comparable to other findings. Human beings are not simple automata reacting to stimuli from the environment, but they seek to reconstruct their habitats to meet a variety of needs. To this end they use traditions they have learned from their elders and they seek the company of others. Their activity is catalyzed as much by the need to find an ultimate meaning in one's life as by economic necessity.

Notes

1. One of Park's students, Louis Wirth, did go on to do his doctoral research on Jews. His book, *The Ghetto* (1928), was one of the few contributions to the study of contemporary Jewry made by his generation.

2. The typically condescending attitude toward Orthodoxy can be gleaned in this characteristic passage: "Orthodox adherents have succeeded in achieving the goal of institutional perpetuation to only a limited extent: the history of their movement in this country can be written in terms of a case study of institutional decay" (Sklare 1955:42).

3. "Ashkenazic" is the term used for Jews of Central and East European origin. It is derived from *Ashkenaz*, a biblical name applied by Jews to Germany in medieval times. The dominant language of these Jews for a long time was and is Yiddish, a Germanic language deriving a significant part of its vocabulary from Hebrew.

4. The tradition of psychological anthropological research established a pattern for anthropological participation in mental health studies. The research by Leichter and Mitchell on Jewish families vis-a-vis case workers in New York, for instance, was sponsored by a Jewish family agency (Leichter and Mitchell 1967; Mitchell 1978). The influence of cultural anthropology on several Jewish historians and others is noted below. One of the articles referred to is that of Abraham Duker (1950). The title of his veritable monograph is: Emerging Culture Patterns in American Jewish life: The Psycho-Cultural Approach to the Study of Jewish Life in America." Duker's footnotes show both a positive response to and criticism of this perspective.

5. The rise of the women's movement at this time was also the catalyst for many women's studies programs and research among groups of women.

6. See David Mandelbaum 1958 and Sol Tax 1981. Using his anthropological insight in surveying American Jewry, Tax pointed out that most American Indian tribes, if they were not exterminated completely, have survived, despite small numbers. The numbers of members of North American groups were and are much smaller than those of the Jews, many never having more than a few thousand. A. I. Epstein, who comes out of a British School of social anthropology has also addressed himself to such questions of ethnic persistence (Epstein 1978).

7. The modernization perspective has received its fair share of criticism. One of the more recent critiques is by Marcus and Fischer 1987.

8. The present discussion follows that of Claude Fischer 1975. Fischer's "subcultural theory of urbanism" is a "critical mass" approach. It is a synthesis and critique of Wirth's assumptions about the effect of numbers in urban areas leading to anomie and assimilation and later theories which deny the effects of urban concentration on behavior. Also see Wirth 1938 and Gmelch and Zenner 1980.

9. On these processes, see Kugelmass 1986, C. Weiner 1972, Y. Ginsberg 1985, Steven Cohen 1983. Ruth Fredman 1982 describes the relatively weak institutions of metropolitan areas built around beltways.

10. Several theories and generalizations have been offered to explain the economic success and political position of ethnic groups which, like the Jews,

have achieved a high degree of affluence and/or economic concentration through commerce. These are generally labeled middleman minority theories. Zenner 1978, 1980, 1980b, 1982; Light 1972, 1984; Bonacich 1973, 1980. Also Goldscheider 1985:135–150.

11. Exceptions to this trend are the studies of Zweigenhaft and Domhoff 1982.

12. Cf. Schumach 1980; Gross 1975:158–161; Gutwirth 1968; van der Laan 1975. The concept of enclave economy comes from Wilson and Portes 1980.

13. Some of this is derived from interviews and oral communications with Henry Kay and Bert Shapiro.

14. A good description of peddling in upstate New York for Syrian Christians can be found in McHenry 1979. Also see Karp 1976:28–84. For urban and resort-town peddling by Syrian Jews, see Herling 1929. Also see Pilling and Pilling 1970.

15. Cf. Birmingham 1967, 1971, 1984, Talese 1969; Harris 1979; Newman 1978; Auletta 1986. Also see Zweigenhaft and Domhoff 1982. As this book goes to press, books and articles are beginning to appear which deal with the recent spate of "insider trader" prosecutions, as well as the New York City scandals, in both of which Jews have been prominent, e.g. Frantz 1987. Future research into Jewish economic behavior should include these events.

16. On the treatment of consumer behavior, see Mary Douglas and Baron Isherwood 1976.

17. The Jewish role in community organization within New York City is prominent in descriptions of the New York City school strikes of the 1960s and 1970s, as well as in other studies of community organization in that city (see Rogers 1968). Lowenstein (below) touches on community organization in one neighborhood, Washington Heights. For a description of orthodox Jewish political organization on the Lower East Side, see Turner 1984.

18. For an analysis of the way in which such symbolism operated in other circumstances, see G. Landsman 1986.

19. Also see Zweigenhaft and Domhoff 1982; for the 1930s, Bayor 1978. Also see Warner and Low 1947:140–158 for the perception of Jewish manufacturers in Yankee City during the Depression.

20. See Herz and Rosen 1982 for social work and family therapy; see Cohen and Hyman 1986 for the social history of the Jewish family.

21. Although services and other rituals do take place at the center, it is not a synagogue but a place of fellowship.

References

Arzt, Donna
  1986   The People's Lawyers: The Predominance of Jews in Public In-
         terest Law. Judaism 35:47–62.

Auletta, Ken
  1986   Greed and Glory on Wall Street. New York: Random House.

Barth, F.
  1969   Ethnic Groups & Boundaries. Boston: Little, Brown.

Baum, Charlotte, Paula Hyman and Sonia Michel
  1976   The Jewish Woman in America. New York: Dial Press.

Bayor, Ronald
  1978   Neighbors in Conflict: Irish, Germans, Jews and Italians of New
         York City. Baltimore: Johns Hopkins University Press.

Becker, Howard P.
  1940   Constructive typology in the social sciences. *In* Contemporary
         Social Theory H. E. Barnes, H. P. Becker and F. B. Becker, ed.,
         New York: Appleton Century, pp. 17–46.

Belcove-Shalin, Janet
  forthcoming. Becoming More of an Eskimo: Fieldwork Among the Has-
         idim of Boro Park. *In:* Between Two Worlds: Essays on the Ethnography
         of American Jewry. Jack Kugelmass, editor, Ithaca: Cornell Press.

Bienenstock, T.
  1950   Social Life and Authority in the East European Jewish Shtetl.
         Southwestern Journal of Anthropology 6:238–254.
  1952   Anti-authoritarian Attitudes in the East European *Shtetl* Com-
         munity. American Journal of Sociology. 57:150–158.

Birmingham, Stephen
  1967   "Our Crowd": The Great Jewish Families of New York. New
         York: Harper and Row.
  1971   The Grandees: America's Sephardic Elite. New York: Harper &
         Row.
  1984   "The Rest of Us": The Rise of America's Eastern European Jews.
         Boston: Little Brown.

Bonacich, Edna
  1973   A Theory of Middleman Minorities. American Sociological Review
         38:583–594.
  1980   Middleman Minorities and Advanced Capitalism. Ethnic Groups
         2:211–219.

Broom, Leonard
  1942   The Jews of Buna. *In* Jews in a Gentile World, Isacque Graeber
         and Steward Henderson Britt, editors, New York: Macmillan.

Cohen, Steven M.
1983   American Modernity and Jewish Identity. New York and London:
       Tavistock.

Cohen, Steven M. and Paula Hyman, editors.
1986   The Changing Jewish Family. New York: Holmes & Meier.

Cohn, Werner
1958   Politics of American Jews. In The Jews: Social Patterns of an
       American Group M. Sklare, editor, Glencoe: The Free Press, pp.
       614–656.

Deshen, Shlomo
1979   The Kol Nidre Enigma: An Anthropological View of the Day of
       Atonement Liturgy. Ethnology 18:121–134.

Dolgin, Janet L.
1977   Jewish Identity and the JDL. Princeton: Princeton University Press.

Douglas, Mary and Baron Isherwood
1979   The World of Goods: Towards an Anthropology of Consumption.
       New York: Norton.

Dressler, C.
1971   Is It Fresh? An Examination of Jewish American Shopping Habits.
       New York Folklore Quarterly 27:153–160.

Duker, Abraham G.
1949   On Religious Trends in American Jewish Life. YIVO Jewish Social
       Science Annual IV:51–63.
1950   Emerging Cultural Patterns of American Jewish Life: The Psycho-
       Cultural Approach to the Study of Jewish Life in America. Pub-
       lications of the American Jewish Historical Society 40:351–389.
1960   Notes on the Culture of American Jewry. Jewish Journal of So-
       ciology 2:98–102.

Elazar, Daniel J.
1976   Community and Polity. Philadelphia: Jewish Publication Society
       of America.

Epstein, A. L.
1978   Ethos & Identity. Chicago: Aldine.

Epstein, Shifra
1977   The Celebration of a Contemporary Purim in the Bobover Hasidic
       Community. Ann Arbor: University Microfilms International.
1987   Drama on a Table: The Bobover Hasidim Piremshpiyl. In: Judaism
       From Within and From Without. Harvey E. Goldberg, editor.
       Albany: State University of New York Press, pp. 195–217.

Fauman, J. S.
1941   Jews in the Waste Industry of Detroit. Jewish Social Studies
       3:41–56.

Fischer, Claude
1975 The Subcultural Theory of Urbanism. American Journal of Sociology 80:1319–1341.

Frankel, Barbara
1980 Structures of the Seder; American Behavioral Scientist 23:575–632.

Frantz, Douglas
1987 Levine & Co.: Wall Street's Insider Trading Scandal. New York: Henry Holt.

Fredman, Ruth G.
1982 Cosmopolitans at Home: Sephardic Jews of Washington, D.C. Ph.D. dissertation. Temple University, Philadelphia. Ann Arbor University Microfilms International, Order No. DDJ:82–17744.

Freilich, Morris
1977 Marginal Natives. New York: Shenkman.

Friedlander, Judith
1983 The Jewish Feminist Question. Dialectical Anthropology 8:113–120.

Fuchs, Lawrence
1956 Political Behavior of American Jews. Glencoe: The Free Press.

Furman, Frida Kerner
1987 Beyond Yiddishkeit: The Struggle for Jewish Identity in a Reform Synagogue. Albany: State University of New York Press.

Ginsburg, Faye
1986 Review of "Religion in Suburbia." American Anthropologist 88:745–746.

Ginsberg, Yona
1975 Jews in a Changing Neighborhood: The Study of Mattapan. New York: The Free Press.

Gilman, Sandor
1986 Jewish Self-Hatred: Anti-Semitism and the Hidden Language of the Jews. Baltimore: Johns Hopkins University Press.

Glazer, Mark
1973 Psychological Intimacy among the Jews of North Metropolitan Chicago and the Sephardic Jews of Istanbul, Turkey. Ph.D. dissertation. Anthropology. Northwestern University. Ann Arbor: University Microfilms International, Order No. 73,30,591.

Glazer, Nathan
1950 What Sociology Knows about American Jews. Commentary 9(3):275–284.

Gmelch, George and Walter P. Zenner
1980 Urban Life: Readings in Urban Anthropology, First Edition. New York: St. Martins.

Gordon, Albert
1949   Jews in Transition. Minneapolis: University of Minnesota Press.

Gordon, Milton M.
1964   Assimilation in American Life. New York: Oxford University Press.

Glick, Leonard
1982   Types Distinct from our Own: Franz Boas on Jewish Identity and
        Assimilation. American Anthropologist 84:545–565.

Goldscheider, Calvin
1986   Jewish Continuity and Change. Bloomington: Indiana University
        Press.

Gross, Nahum, editor.
1975   Economic History of the Jews. New York: Schocken.

Gutwirth, Jacques
1968   Antwerp Jewry Today. Jewish Journal of Sociology X:121–138.

Harris, Leon
1979   The Merchant Princes: An Intimate History of Jewish Families
        Who Built Great Department Stores. New York: Harper and Row.

Heilman, Samuel C.
1976   Synagogue Life. Chicago: University of Chicago Press.
1980   "Jewish Sociologist: Native-As-Stranger." The American Sociol-
        ogist, Vol. 15, 2:100–108.
1982   The Sociology of American Jews. Annual Review of Sociology
        8:13–160.

Herling, Lilian
1929   Study in Retardation. Master's Thesis, Sociology. Columbia Uni-
        versity Press, New York City.

Herz, Fredda M. and Elliott J. Rosen
1982   Jewish Families. In Ethnicity and Family Therapy. Monica
        McGoldrick, John K. Pearce, and Joseph Giordano, editor, New
        York: Guilford Press, pp. 364–392.

Hsu, Francis L. K.
1971   Psycho-social Homeostasis and Jen: Conceptual Tools for Ad-
        vancing Psychological Anthropology. American Anthropologist
        73:23–44.

Howe, Irving
1976   The World of Our Fathers. New York: Harcourt Brace Jovanovich.

Isaacs, Stephen
1974   Jews in American Politics. New York: Doubleday.

Karp, Abraham J.
1976   Golden Door to America: The Jewish Immigrant Experience. Bal-
        timore: Penguin.

Kramer, Judith R. and Seymour Leventman
1961 Children of the Gilded Ghetto. New Haven: Yale University Press.

Kirshenblatt-Gimblett, Barbara
1975 A Parable in Context: A Social Interactional Analysis of Story-telling Performance. In Folklore Performance and Communication. D. Ben-Amos and K. Goldstein, editor, The Hague: Mouton 11:106–130.
(forthcoming) The Folk-Culture of Jewish Immigrant Communities. Research Paradigms and Directions. In Jews in North America: Immigration, Settlement and Ethnic Identity M. Rischin, editor, in press.

Kugelmass, Jack
1986 Miracle on Intervale Avenue. New York: Schocken Books.

Kuznets, Simon
1960 The Economic Life and Structure of the Jews. In The Jews: Their History, Culture and Religion. New York: Harper and Row, pp. 1597–1666.
1972 The Economic Structure of U.S. Jewry. Jerusalem: Hebrew University Institute for Contemporary Jewry.

Landes, Ruth and Mark Zborowski
1950 Hypotheses Concerning the Eastern European Jewish Family. Psychiatry 13:447–464.

Landsman, Gail
1985 Ganienkeh: Symbol and Politics in an Indian/White Conflict. American Anthropologist 87:826–839.

Landes, Ruth
1967 Negro Jews in Harlem. Jewish Journal of Sociology 9:175–190.

Landes, Ruth and Mark Zborowski
1950 Hypotheses Concerning the Eastern European Family. Psychiatry 13:447–464.

Lasry, Jean-Claude
1981 A Francophonel Diaspora in Quebec. In Canadian Jewish Mosaic. M. Weinfield, W. Shaffir, I. Cotler, editors, Toronto: John Wiley, pp. 221–240.

Leichter, Hope J. and William E. Mitchell
1967 Kinship and Casework. New York: Russell Sage Foundation.

Light, Ivan
1972 Ethnic Enterprise in America. Berkeley and Los Angeles: University of California Press.
1984 Immigrant and Ethnic Enterprise in North America. Ethnic and Racial Studies 7:195–216.

Lipset, Seymour
  1955   Jewish Sociologists and Sociologists of the Jews. Jewish Social
         Studies 17:177–178.
  1963   The Study of Jewish Communities in a Comparative Perspective.
         Jewish Journal of Sociology 5:157–166.

Liebman, Charles
  1973   The Ambivalent American Jew. Philadelphia: Jewish Publication
         Society of America.

Lowi, Theodore
  1961   Southern Jews: Two Communities. Jewish Journal of Sociology
         3:103–117.

Leyton, Elliott
  1970   Composite Descent Groups in Canada. In Readings in Kinship
         in Urban Society. C. G. Harris, editor, New York and Oxford:
         Pergamon, pp. 179–186.

Maibaum, Matthew
  1971   The Berkeley Hillel and the Union of Jewish Students: The History
         of a Conflict. Jewish Journal of Sociology 13:153–172.

Mandelbaum, David
  1958   Change and Continuity in Jewish Life. In The Jews: Social Patterns
         of an American Group. M. Sklare, editor, Glencoe: The Free Press,
         pp. 509–519.

McHenry, Steward
  1979   The Syrian Movement into Upstate New York. Ethnicity 6:327–345.

Mintz, Jerome
  1969   Legends of the Hasidim. Chicago: University of Chicago Press.

Mitchell, William
  1978   Mishpokhe: A Study of New York City Jewish Family Clubs. The
         Hague: Mouton.

Myerhoff, Barbara
  1978   Number Our Days. New York: E. P. Dutton.
  1984   The Passover Seder as a Failed Performance. Paper delivered at
         the Conference on Jewish Living Traditions. City University of
         New York Graduate Center, May 14.
  1987   Life, Not Death in Venice: It's Second Life. In: Judaism From
         Within and From Without. Harvey E. Goldberg, editor, Albany:
         State University of New York Press, pp. 143–169.

Newman, Peter C.
  1978   The Bronfman Dynasty: Toronto: McClelland & Steward.

Ortner, Sherry B.
  1984   Theory in Anthropology Since the Sixties. Comparative Studies
         in Society and History 26:126–166.

Pilling, Arnold and Priscilla Pilling
1971   Cloths, Clothes, Hose and Bows. *In* Migration and Anthropology R. Spencer, editor, Seattle: University of Washington Press for American Ethnological Society, pp. 97–119.

Plotnicov, Leonard
1968a First and Second Generation American Jewish Families: Sources of Conflicts and Tensions. Kroeber Anthropological Society Papers. No. 38:11–24.
1978b An American Jewish Vacation Pattern: The Accommodation of Conjugal Tension. Kroeber Anthropological Society Papers. No. 39:54–62.

Plotnicov, Leonard and Myrna Silverman
1978   Jewish Ethnic Signalling: Social Bonding in Contemporary American Society. Ethnology 17:407–423.

Poll, Solomon
1962   The Hasidic Community of Williamsburg. New York: The Free Press.

Prell, Riv-Ellen
1978   Coming of Age in Kelton: The Constraints on Gender Symbolism in Jewish Ritual. *In* Women in Ritual and Symbolic Roles. Anita Spring and Judith Hoch-Smith, editors, New York: Plenum Press.
1987   Sacred Categories and Social Relations: The Visibility and Invisibility of Gender in an American Jewish Community. *In:* Judaism Viewed From Within and From Without. Harvey E. Goldberg, editor, Albany: State University of New York Press, 171–193.

Prosterman, Leslie
1984   Food and Celebration: A Kosher Caterer as Mediator of Communal Traditions. *In* Ethnic and Regional Foodways in the United States: The Performance of Group Identity Linda Keller Brown and Kay Mussell, editors, Knoxville: University of Tennessee Press, pp. 127–142.

Regelson, Stanley
1976   The Bagel: Symbol and Ritual at the Breakfast Table. *In* The American Dimension: Cultural Myths and Social Realities.

Rogers, David
1968   110 Livingston Street, New York: Random House.

Rosenthal, Erich
1980   The Jews of Boro Park. Jewish Journal of Sociology 22:187–192.

Schumach, Murray
1980   The Diamond People. New York: Norton.

Seidler, Murray B. and Mel Jerome Ravitz
1955   A Jewish Peer Group. American Journal of Sociology 61:11–15.

Shaffir, William
1981   Hassidic Communities in Montreal. *In* Canadian Jewish Mosaic
       M. Weinfeld, W. Shaffir, I. Cotler, editors, Toronto: John Wiley,
       pp. 273–285.
1983   Hassidic Jews and Quebec Politics. Jewish Journal of Sociology
       25:105–118.
1985   Some Reflections on Approaches to Fieldwork in Hassidic Com-
       munities. Jewish Journal of Sociology 27(2):115–134.

Sharot, Stephen
1921   Judaism: A Sociology. Newton Abbey, David & Charles.

Shuldiner, David P.
1984   Of Moses and Marx: Folk Ideology within the Jewish Labor
       Movement within the United States. Ph.D. dissertation: Folklore
       and Mythology. University of California at Los Angeles.

Sklare, Marshall
1955   Conservative Judaism: An American Religious Movement. Glen-
       coe: The Free Press.

Snyder, Charles R.
1958   Alcohol and the Jews. Glencoe: Free Press.

Spicer, Edward H.
1971   Persistent Cultural Systems: A Comparative Study of Identity
       Systems that Can Adapt to Contrasting Environments. Science
       174:795–800.
1980   The Yaqui: A Cultural History. Tucson: University of Arizona
       Press, pp. 333–362.

Spiro, Melford E.
1955   The Acculturation of American Ethnic Groups. American An-
       thropologist 57:1240–1252.

Steinberg, Stephen
1982   The Ethnic Myth: Race, Ethnicity and Class in America. Boston:
       Beacon Press.

Stern, Stephen
1977   The Sephardic Jewish Community of Los Angeles: A Study in
       Folklore and Ethnic Identity. Ph.D. dissertation, Indiana University
       (Folklore). Ann Arbor: University Microfilms International Order
       No. 77–22, 676.

Sutton, Joseph A. D.
1979   Magic Carpet: Aleppo-in-Flatbush. Brooklyn: Thayer-Jacoby.

Tax, Sol
1981   Jewish Life in the United States: An Anthropological Perspective.
       In Jewish Life in the United States: Perspectives for the Social
       Sciences, J. Gittler, editor, New York: New York University Press.

Talese, Gay
1969 The Kingdom and the Power. New York: World.

Turner, Joan Alyne
1983 Building Boundaries: The Politics of Urban Renewal in Manhattan's Lower East Side. Ph.D. dissertation, Anthropology, City University of New York. Ann Arbor: University Microfilms International: Order No. 84–09424.

van der Laan, H. L.
1975 The Lebanese Traders in Sierra Leone. The Hague: Mouton.

Warner, W. Lloyd and J. O. Low
1947 The Social System of the Modern Factory—The Strike: A Social Analysis. New Haven: Yale University Press.

Warner, W. Lloyd and Leo Srole
1945 The Social Systems of American Ethnic Groups. New Haven: Yale University Press.

Weiner, Carolyn
1972 A Merger of Synagogues in San Francisco. Jewish Journal of Sociology 14:167–196.

Weinreich, Max
1967 "The Reality of Jewishness versus the Ghetto Myth: The Sociolinguistic Roots of Yiddish." To Honor Roman Jakobson: Essays on the Occasion of His Seventieth Birthday. The Hague: Mouton, pp. 2199–2211.
1980 History of the Yiddish Language. Chicago: University of Chicago Press.

Weissler, Chava (Lenore E.)
1983 Making Judaism Meaningful: Ambivalence and Tradition in a Havurah Community. Ph.D. dissertation, Folklore. University of Pennsylvania, University Microfilms International, Order No. 83–07376.
1986 Coming of Age in the Havurah Movement: Bar Mitzvah in the Havurah Family. In The Jewish Family: Myths and Reality. J. M. Cohen and P. E. Hyman, editors, New York: Holmes and Meier, pp. 200–217.

Whitfield, Stephen J.
1984 Voices of Jacob, Hands of Esau: Jews in American Life and Thought. Hamden, CT: Archon Books.

Wilson, Kenneth L. and Alejandro Portes
1980 Immigrant Enclaves: An Analysis of the Labor Experiences of Cubans in Miami. American Journal of Sociology 81:295–319.

Wirth, Louis
1928 The Ghetto. Chicago: University of Chicago Press.
1938 Urbanism as a Way of Life. American Journal of Sociology 54:1–24.

Wimberley, Howard and Joel Savishinsky
1978 Ancestor Memorialism: A Comparative of Jews and Japanese. *In* Community, Self and Identity B. Misra and J. Preston, editors, The Hague: Mouton, pp. 115–132.

Wolfenstein, Martha
1955 Two Types of Jewish Mothers. *In* Childhood in Contemporary Cultures (M. Mead and M. Wolfenstein, editors). Chicago: University of Chicago Press, pp. 424–440.

Yancey, W. L., Eugene P. Ericksen, and George H. Leon
1985 Structure of Pluralism: "We're all Italian around here, aren't we Mrs. O'Brien." Ethnic and Racial Studies 8:94–116.

Zborowski, Mark
1949 The Place of Book-Learning in Traditional Jewish Culture. Harvard Education Review, Vol. 19, pp. 97–109.
1969 People in Pain. San Francisco: Jossey-Bass.

Zborowski, Mark and Elizabeth Herzog
1952 Life is with People. New York: International University Publisher.

Zenner, Walter P.
1970 International Networks of a Migrant Ethnic Group. *In* Migration and Anthropology. R. Spencer, editor, Seattle: University of Washington Press for American Ethnological Society, pp. 36–48.
1978 Jewish State Employees in the Albany (New York) Area.
1980a American Jewry in the Light of Middleman Minority Theories. Contemporary Jewry 5:11–30.
1980b Middleman Minority Theories: A Critical Review. *In* Sourcebook on the New Immigration. R. J. Bryce-Laporte and D. Mortimer and S. Couch, editors, New Brunswick: Transaction Books, pp. 413–425.
1982 Arabic Speaking Immigrants in North America as Middleman Minorities. Ethnic and Racial Studies 5:457–477.
1983 Syrian Jews in New York City Twenty Years Ago. *In* Fields of Offerings: Studies in Honor of Raphael Patai V. Sanua, editor, New York: Herzl Press, pp. 173–196.
1985 Jewishness in America: Ascription and Choice. Ethnic and Racial Groups 8:117–133.
Common Ethnicity/Separate Identities. Intercultural and International Communications Annual, in press.

Zweigenhaft, Richard L. and G. William Domhoff
1982 Jews in the Protestant Establishment. New York: Praeger.

Part I

Identities and Identification

The rubric, ethnic group, implies a group which is self-identified and which is recognized as an entity by outsiders. In addition, the principle of real or fictional common descent and common destiny are added to this element of labeling to make a group "ethnic." The term, "identity," as used by psychologists suggests that ego sees herself or himself in a certain way because of the way she or he applies a label to her- or him-self. Hence, psychologists often use an open-ended test in which subjects label themselves, by filling in with as many labels as they have by completing the sentence, "I am . . ." Similarly psychologists have used word-association tests in the labels supplied to "other peoples" in their study of stereotypes. Ego identity and alter-identification are, however, considered subjective phenomena by psychologists.

Legal bodies, whether governmental or religious, utilize objective criteria in deciding "who is an American citizen" or "who is a Jew." These criteria apply regardless of how individuals regard themselves or are seen by laymen. This is true whether the legal intent is benevolent or malicious. An immigrant child, reared from childhood in the United States, may think of herself as an American, even if she is not a citizen. A child adopted by Jewish parents who attends religious school may think of himself as Jewish, even though he has undergone no formal conversion. Yet both would be seen as outside the group in a legal sense. The emotional intensity of such issues as "who is a Jew?" stem, in large measure, from a conflict between formal, objective, definitions and subjective identification.

The anthropological approach differs from both the legal and psychological perspectives by studying the context of self-identify and objective identification. Strict legal criteria may be written down in codes, but they are applied by human beings who must apply them in a particular environment. Kugelmass (1986:46–81) has shown how a South Bronx synagogue, needing to keep a prayer quorum, closes its eyes to the lack of evidence of clear Jewish ancestry or conversion and conformity to Jewish practice. On the other hand, actions by Israeli religious courts which deny full admission to various groups of Jews from India and Ethiopia act in response to political competition between different groups of Orthodox and ultra-Orthodox Jews.

The cases in this section utilize the contextual approach. Three studies deal with serious conflicts between the self-image of two Jewish groups and the way in which they are perceived by other North Americans, Jews and non-Jews alike. In North America, Jewishness is generally seen in its East European Ashkenazic/Yiddish form. Jews who come out of different traditions such as Arabic-speaking or Ladino-speaking Sephardim or Yemenites are not seen as Jews and must prove themselves.[1] The Yemenites, because of their skin color, are not seen as Jews, who in the contemporary New York City context are perceived as relatively fair-skinned (although they would be rather swarthy by Minnesota standards). The problems faced by the Yemenites, a fairly traditional community, resembles that of other small groups who stand between black and white in this racially dichotomous society. The problems faced by recent immigrants from the Soviet Union is that, while they are East European Ashkenazim, they have developed a radically different image of what Jewishness means after sixty or more years of Soviet rule. The criteria for validating Jewishness is quite different for Soviet Jews than it is for American Jews.

The ethnography of a Hebrew school deals with problems in ethnic socialization. Schoem discusses the lack of saliency of Jewish tradition for American seventh-graders, their parents, and their teachers. He touches here on one of the weakest points in American communal life and the softness of Jewish ethnic and religious identity. As he suggests the problem is shared by other ethnic groups as well as Jews. Indeed, the disdain for history and the humanities in general is like the ambivalence towards Jewish education, a product of the fact the humanities are not easily translated into a formula for success.

Jewish identity in North America, however, is not frozen at puberty. Some move away from the Jewish community entirely, others zig-zag in and out of it, while still others seek self-fulfillment within it. The richness of the Jewish tradition, both oral and literary, means that many can find themes to fit their own personal needs. The small groups, prayer and discussion known as Havurot among the religious non-Orthodox Jews, and the ba'alai teshuvah (penitents) among the Orthodox have affected small, but significant, numbers of American Jews.

Still, whether moving toward assimilation or a return to tradition, the concern with self-fulfillment as well as success is a product of an individualistic society in which collective concerns are secondary.[2]

Notes

1. For further elaboration of such relationships, see Zenner forthcoming.

2. See Zenner 1985.

References

Kugelmass, Jack 1986: Miracle on Intervale Avenue. New York: Schocken.

Zenner, Walter P. 1985: Jewishness in America: Ascription and Choice. *In* Ethnicity and Race in the U.S.A. R. Alba, editor, London: Routledge & Kegan Paul, pp. 117–133.

Zenner, Walter P. Common Ethnicity, Different Identities: Interaction among Jewish Immigrant Groups. *In* International and Intercultural Communications Annual. Y. Kim & W. Gudykunst, editors, in press.

Stigma, Identity, and Sephardic-Ashkenazic Relations in Indianapolis[1]

2

Jack Glazier

Jack Glazier places the relationship between East Mediterranean Sephardim with their East European Ashkenazic neighbors in the context of local Jewish-Gentile interaction in a Midwestern city. Added to the assumption that the Ashkenazic way defined Jewishness, the East European Jews of this middle-sized community were under great pressure to conform to a presumed American way of life. Glazier stresses the relationship of assimilation to social and economic forces in the environment. His study of stigma can be compared to the relationship of recent Soviet Jews to American Jews in Brooklyn by Markowitz and to the study of Yemenite Jewish identity by Dahbany-Miraglia, as well as to the development of the Lincoln community as described by Gradwohl and Gradwohl.

Introduction

The fate of Jewish identity in the United States has historically represented an important concern of both the American Jewish community itself and of social scientists who have closely observed American ethnic groups during this century. But regardless of popular or social scientific pronouncements about the state of Jewish religiosity and ethnicity, the American Jewish experience has been represented almost exclusively in terms of Ashkenazic Jewry. The Sephardim of America usually constitute little more than a passing remark or an occasional footnote in the array of books and articles documenting Jewish life in the United States. And then of the two major Sephardic migrations to the New World—the Jewish passage of the seventeenth and eighteenth centuries and the immigration of the twentieth century—it is the former, celebrated in such popular accounts as Birmingham's *The Grandees* (1971), which receives the greater emphasis. As a result, our collective understanding of Sephardic life in America during this century is severely limited. The much larger body of writings on the earlier wave of Sephardic migration during the formative years of the United States provides no insight into more recent events. Of course, the emphasis on Ashkenazic Jewry reflects their vastly greater numbers since only about 25,000 Sephardim emigrated to America from 1899–1925 (Angel 1974:87), and that number has not been substantially augmented in the ensuing years.

Still, the lives of four generations of Sephardim present some distinctive aspects of Jewish cultural life and the struggle for ethnic identity in America. The midwestern context of the present account also includes some unique features which would not be found in the larger ethnic centers of the United States. Moreover, in discussing the stigmatization of twentieth century Sephardic immigrants and their relationship to Ashkenazic Jews, the present article takes up an important but heretofore neglected aspect of Sephardic experience in America.

The problem at hand represents a paradox. Simply put, the unique qualities of openness and freedom in American society, which have enabled Jews to flourish and prosper, have profoundly transformed the very communities seeking to use this freedom to maintain themselves—to practice a way of life threatened and beleaguered in other times and places. Halpern phrases the problem as a question: "How can the Jewish people survive in the face of hostility which threatens to destroy it, and, on the other hand, in the face of a friendliness which threatens to dissolve group ties and submerge Jews, as a whole, by absorbing them individually?" (1974:71).

Both Ashkenazim and Sephardim confront the paradox, although the experience of Sephardim, particularly in Indianapolis, assumes an added dimension. Specifically, the immigrant generation of Sephardim and their children faced more than the challenge of adapting to the very alien parochial culture of midwestern America with its periodic expressions of anti-Semitic sentiment. They also confronted a broad spectrum of Ashkenazic opinion openly skeptical about the authenticity of Sephardic Judaism. These attitudes are an important aspect of Sephardic life and figure very prominently in the way the Sephardim think about themselves and the particular character of their community. Slow to give way to a rational understanding of Sephardic custom, Ashkenazic attitudes stigmatized Sephardic identity, thus limiting for more than two generations Sephardic participation in a broad range of Jewish communal activities. Many Sephardic narratives of the first decades in the city thus elaborate the theme, "They didn't believe we were Jews."

My use of the term "stigma" follows Goffman's reference to "the situation of the individual who is disqualified from full social acceptance" (1963:preface). This lack of social acceptance ranged from limited numbers of adult friendship networks in the years before World War II to active discouragement by Ashkenazim of marriage to Sephardim during the same period. Although the past forty years have witnessed a marked pattern of convergence between the two groups and collective participation in the activities of the wider Jewish community, the vivid memories of social exclusion collectively shared through personal narratives contribute importantly to the ways in which the Sephardim depict their community both to themselves and to Jewish society at large. At the same time, their shared representations can, at least expressively, firm up now greatly diminished ethnic boundaries.

In this account, I will examine Sephardic experience in Indianapolis against the background of the wider Jewish community. In so doing, I will discuss the distinctive context of Indianapolis which seriously constrained Jewish life and Sephardic-Ashkenazic relations in ways not found in larger Jewish and immigrant centers. I consider this latter point particularly important because too often, anthropologists and sociologists who have investigated city life do not give sufficient attention to the particular historical and demographic character of their research locales. As a consequence, cities assume a kind of collective identity defined in terms of their larger scale and accompanying social features which distinguish them from traditional anthropological research sites in tribal or other rural areas; but the particular profile of each urban center is too often neglected. Relatedly, the general portrait of American Jews, drawn mainly from their experience in Eastern cities, obscures distinctive features of Jewish life in towns, smaller urban centers, and regions beyond the East— differences which the present article points up.

As an anthropologist, I am also especially interested in the manner in which people represent and interpret their community and individual lives both to themselves and to each other. Anthropological perspectives thus enable us to get behind, so to speak, the aggregate trends and forces portrayed by sociologists in their characterization of ethnic populations. Valuable as they are, sociological views often fail to assess the impact on individuals of the large scale patterns they identify. Accordingly, as an anthropologist also interested in this human dimension, I have made use of personal documents—informants' narratives of community life, which I can only allude to in this brief account. Moreover, I have also been a participant-observer in the most important extant Sephardic institution, the synagogue.

But the nature of Sephardic community life has also taken form through its complex relationship to the larger Jewish community over the approximately eighty years since the first Sephardim settled in Indianapolis. By the very nature of American society, Sephardic life at the outset was not circumscribed within the confines of a closed community. The Sephardim often depended for their livelihoods on employment in a large Ashkenazic clothing firm lying well outside the area of immigrant settlement. Subsequent formations of Sephardic-owned businesses always occurred in the broader context of the commercial world beyond the immigrant neighborhood. Consequently, I have also made use of sources documenting the relationship between the Sephardim and the wider community of Jews and non-Jews. These sources include interviews with Ashkenazim actively involved in community organizations and with those who could recount the early stages of Sephardic-Ashkenazic contact. Additionally, I have also utilized historical documents, including the records of the Jewish Federation, the Jewish Welfare Fund, newspaper accounts of Indianapolis Jews, and synagogue records. Finally, in addition to this formal research, I draw upon my experience as a native, which provides intimate personal knowledge complementing the analytical interpretations I offer (Glazier 1985).

The Setting

In a 1905 commemoration of the arrival of Jews in America, Governor Hanly of Indiana spoke to a crowded gathering convened by a Reform Jew who was prominent in civic affairs. The celebration was also attended by three local rabbis. After remarking favorably about the way in which Jews had "preserved not only their racial but their moral integrity" despite their wanderings, the Governor continued in a wholly different vein: "As there should be no Irish-Americans, no German-Americans, no Swedish-Americans, so there should be no Jewish-Americans. I have little patience with the man who comes to this country and participates in its blessings and its government and continues even in thought to remain a foreigner." The newspaper account concludes by noting that the Governor's sentiments "evoked great applause and great patriotic fervor" (Indianapolis Star November 27, 1905).

In 1925, when he took up Governor Hanly's theme of twenty years before, another Indiana Governor, Ed Jackson, reiterated the condemnation of cultural hyphenations such as Jewish-American. What makes Jackson's remarks particularly noteworthy is the wholly improbable context in which they were uttered. Jackson, a well-known member of the Ku Klux Klan who had been exposed by the anti-Klan newspaper, *Tolerance* (April 15, 1923), spoke at the dedication of a Conservative synagogue! Improbable as it appears, his themes were "freedom and tolerance." He spoke of the flag as "the emblem of a nation which believes in freedom, liberty, and fairness and justice for all." He concluded by saying, "I do not like adjectives or hyphens to differentiate one person from another, but rather I like to refer to all [of] them as American citizens" (Indianapolis News, December 14, 1925).

Similar sentiments from other political leaders were by no means uncommon but the words of these Indiana governors are especially revealing of the strongly nativist feelings in the state. These attitudes greatly affected the adaptation of the Jews by reinforcing their desire to fit into a city and state generally uncongenial toward ethnic practice and cultural pluralism. Nativism in Indiana was traditionally very strong. With 95% of its population native-born and 97% of its population white in 1920 (Madison 1982:3) Indiana provided fertile ground for the growth of the Ku Klux Klan, culminating in the considerable political influence the Klan wielded in the 1920s (Madison 1982:44). Although heavy-handed, the governors' messages, which in various forms were regularly repeated over the years, were very clear. If Jews wished to gain all the benefits America had to offer, they would have to put aside the most overt symbols and behaviors of their old country origins.

Such pressures were very acute in Indianapolis. Unlike New York or even other larger midwestern cities, Indianapolis historically had a very high proportion of descendants of northern Europeans, particularly Germans and Irish, who arrived long before the massive migrations of Eastern and Southern Europeans. The latter never settled in Indianapolis in great numbers. In 1900, those born outside the United States constituted only 10.1% of the city's population (U.S. Census 1902:104). The distinctive nativist cast of Indianapolis history is more apparent when the percentage of immigrant residents of other midwestern cities is noted for the same year. In 1900, the foreign-born made up 31.2% of the population of Milwaukee, 32.6% in Cleveland, 33.8% in Detroit, and 34.6% in Chicago (U.S. Census 1902:103–105). Indianapolis Jewish immigrants thus were in no way insulated from strong pressures toward assimilation or in any way capable of maintaining closed enclaves within the city. In Indianapolis and throughout the state, moreover, the emphasis on "Americanism" promulgated by the American Legion (which was headquartered in Indianapolis beginning in 1919, Madison 1983:38) and grotesquely represented by the Klan, created a climate unfriendly to the maintenance of the most visible cultural and ethnic accoutrements of European life.

The Jews of Indianapolis were exposed, and they lacked the kind of self-assurance which might come from large numbers or from the presence of other communities of immigrants. Since the Jews were not embedded in a multiplicity of large, viable ethnic communities, they felt visible among a city population dominated by native-born Protestants. Further, the sense of Jewish vulnerability bred an extraordinary defensiveness, ever-vigilant to Jewish actions which the leadership believed would endanger the entire Jewish community. Underlying this caution was the optimistic view that prejudice and discrimination were at base subject to reason; that is, if Jews did not give their antagonists cause to hate them and to limit their life chances, then prejudice and discrimination would attenuate. Across the spectrum of American Jewish fears in the decades before World War II, the anxiety of Indianapolis Jews was by no means unique, but the efforts at self-policing and guardedness appear extreme. In 1934, for example, a meeting of the B'nai B'rith Lodge considered a Jewish Federation resolution to eliminate as far as possible from the city newspapers publicity about the activities of Jewish organizations (B'nai B'rith 1934:1). It did not matter that the items in question were in no respect negative, but only that they centered on Jewish life in the city. Such reporting in the public press was deemed somehow dangerous in calling excessive attention to the very existence of a Jewish community.

In this social climate where overtly expressed differences from the mainstream were actively discouraged, it is not surprising that Reform Judaism, with its historic emphasis on adaptation and assimilation, has flourished. The Reform congregation of Indianapolis has over the years maintained the largest membership of any Jewish house of worship.[2] Reform Jews, who provided the leadership for the organizations of the wider Jewish community, accordingly reinforced assimilationist values.

With a population of approximately 10,000 during the 1970s, (according to the Jewish Welfare Federation) the Jews of Indianapolis have historically constituted about 1% of the city's population (Endelman 1984:60), although this may well be an overly generous estimate. And within this minority, the Sephardic community numbering approximately 300 individuals in about 70 families has remained since its inception only a small fraction of the Jewish population.

The Emergence of the Sephardic Community

About two years after Governor Hanly both lauded the survival of Jewish culture and admonished those who would preserve its practices, the first Sephardim arrived in Indianapolis from Monastir, a town in the Ottoman territory of Macedonia. Now the Yugoslav town of Bitola, Monastir was the home of most of the Sephardim who ultimately settled in Indianapolis. Prompted to leave their homes by a combination of "push" and "pull" factors, the immigrants were drawn to employment opportunities in the United States at the same time that economic and political conditions were generally deteriorating in the Ottoman Empire. The extension of military conscription to the Jews also spurred much of the immigration, but this action and the worsening fortunes of the Sephardim in their native land was not a consequence of specifically anti-Jewish policy. My informants of the immigrant generation consistently rank anti-Jewish feeling as a negligible factor in accounting for their own migration. Instead, the prospect of job opportunities in the New World figured prominently in accounting for migration. An elderly informant put it simply when he said that as a youth he was determined not to be a *hamal* (Turkish for carrier or porter) or to work in the lowly jobs held by his kin.

Thus attracted to the United States for both political and economic reasons, the first Sephardic immigrants to Indianapolis—mostly single young men—represented the first links in a chain migration. A number of them came to Indianapolis after periods of employment in one or another American city—Detroit, Cincinnati, Chicago, or New York. Once employed and gaining some semblance of stability and regular income in their new home, they assisted parents, siblings, and other family members in reaching Indianapolis.

The small settlement of Monastir Sephardim which was developing over the years just before World War I was augmented by another, smaller migration of Sephardim, when the first young men from Salonika settled in Indianapolis in 1914. Like their predecessors from Monastir, the Salonika immigrants sought employment at the Kahn Tailoring Company, a German-Jewish firm which provided many immigrants with both skilled and unskilled jobs in the needle trade. For some, Kahn's would provide them lifelong employment, while for a number of others, it was a stepping stone to the founding of their own businesses which included tailoring shops or wholly new ventures in produce. By the 1920s, then, the diverse character of the larger Jewish community had taken shape, with the Sephardim representing a poor but extremely hard-working group who came to be greatly admired, if sometimes grudgingly, by the Ashkenazim.

Clustered on the city's Southside in an area already occupied by the Eastern European immigrants, these two segments of Indianapolis Jewry remained socially and culturally distinct from the established, affluent Reform Jews of the Northside—the uptown Jews of mostly German origin. The latter, moreover, were a class apart—prosperous, civic-minded denizens of the finest neighborhoods of the city and models of assimilation, who cultivated an image of Judaism far removed from the experience and values of Southside Sephardim and Ashkenazim so closely bound to immigrant beginnings. Although the Sephardim and the Eastern European Ashkenazim inhabited many of the same social worlds—neighborhood, school, community center—the immigrant generations remained culturally very distinct from each other. Augmenting cultural distinctions were differences of class and status marked in part by street of residence. The immediate area inhabited by the Sephardim and the poorer Ashkenazim was the least esteemed.

Stigma: Cultural and Social Dimensions of Exclusion

The conceptual distinction anthropologists have customarily drawn between cultural and social phenomena can shed considerable light on the nature of the problem at hand—the denial of full social acceptance. Simply put, cultural phenomena include the diverse customs, beliefs, and practices characterizing a particular group or community and setting it off from other groups or communities. By contrast, the group itself, with regular patterns of interaction and continuity over time, constitutes the realm of the social. In the real world, of course, social and cultural phenomena interpenetrate and are indistinguishable, but the anthropologist in attempting to understand the dynamics of community life finds it extremely useful to draw at least an analytical distinction.

The most crucial marker of cultural identity among the immigrant generation of Jews was language. The Indianapolis Sephardim spoke Ladino as their first language—the language of family life and Sephardic social activity, including some portions of the synagogue service. Immigrant Ashkenazim, on the other hand, whether from Russia, Hungary, Romania or some other area of Eastern Europe, spoke one or another of the mutually intelligible dialects of Yiddish. Vastly different languages, aside from rendering communication impossible except through a third common alternative such as English, represented powerful cultural symbols—primordial representations of different histories, experiences, tastes, and even values. Differing cuisines and other divergent practices, such as the Sephardic proclivity for naming children after the living and the Ashkenazic aversion to this custom, established additional diacritics of identity, both distinguishing the communities and providing a basis for their estrangement.

These various cultural distinctions—features of what the anthropologist Robert Redfield called the little tradition—pervade the most intimate domains of a community and are bound up with the mundane routines of family and collective life, thus fundamentally shaping a people's view of itself. But beyond the little tradition Redfield identified a great tradition (1956:41–42), which in the case at hand finds expression in Jewish law and liturgy, the Hebrew language, and other shared features of religion which have transcended the particular local experience of Jews in culturally diverse communities. Yet so strong were the little traditions—both in their own right and in their associations with class, status, and neighborhood—that they shrouded the common bonds of the Jewish great tradition. Ashkenazim, especially, seized on the symbols of their own experience, such as Yiddish, to represent the most essential markers of the common faith.

The Sephardim for at least two generations thus found the legitimacy of their Jewishness questioned. Not speaking "Jewish" (Yiddish), and lacking the associated qualities of the little tradition of "Yiddishkeit," they were cast into another category, "Turk," juxtaposed to "Jew." This designation attributed to the Sephardim a national identity they never embraced owing to the particular nature of their experience in the Ottoman territories. They had lived there in essentially self-governing communities defined by their Jewish faith and enjoying considerable autonomy and religious freedom. Given the orthodoxy of their religious practice and the manner in which Judaism determined much of their existence in Yugoslavia and Greece, the Sephardim found the designation "Turk" a particularly ironic ethnic slur. A pervasive conceptual opposition between "Jew" and "Turk," or, politely, "Jew" and "Sephardi" has been incorporated into the perspective of many Sephardim themselves and continues even now among first and second generation Sephardic and Ashkenazic Jews. An elderly Sephardic woman, for example, explained that at a party she had been very warmly greeted by many Sephardics and that "even Jewish people" whom she knew wished her well. In recounting her family history, she explained that as a young woman she had gone out with a "Jewish fellow," and then corrected herself by saying he was Ashkenazic.

Given the clearly defined cultural and linguistic differences between the Sephardim and their Ashkenazic neighbors, the basis for social differentiation and exclusiveness was palpable. During the first years of the Indianapolis Sephardic settlement, the Sephardim saw themselves as a distinct community and established institutions filling their spiritual, social, and economic needs. These institutions were largely transplanted versions of community organizations which had helped to maintain Sephardic life in Monastir and Salonika. Included here was the founding of a synagogue by the Monastir immigrants in 1913, which the Salonika families later joined, the establishment of a burial society, the formation of a Sephardic social club, and the organization of a secret fund to insure monetary assistance on a confidential basis.

A small group of Sephardim oversaw assessments to the secret fund—ten cents per adult per week in the early years. They controlled disbursements from it, which were intended as loans rather than as charity. The identity of recipients was said to be privileged information, but in view of the small, highly personal quality of the Sephardic community, it is likely that maintaining its confidentiality was difficult. Still, given the sacrifice of honor which receipt of charity was believed to entail, the collective value on the secrecy of the aid, although most probably an unacknowledged fiction, had much to recommend it. The pride of recipients was thereby preserved, despite the understanding that ultimate repayment into the fund was expected. The secret fund mostly provided small sums to tide families over particularly rough economic circumstances, but it sometimes in later years made sufficient funds available for recipients to start up small businesses.

The existence of distinctive Sephardic social institutions and a clearly delineated Sephardic culture unambiguously established the visible markers of separation and hence a basis for the Ashkenazim to stigmatize this wholly unfamiliar Jewish group. Yet the Ashkenazic response to Sephardic distinctiveness represents only a partial picture of this complex relationship, for the Sephardim themselves also chose exclusiveness through their support of Sephardic institutions and occasional resistance to incursions from the larger Jewish community. Opposition included the rejection by some families of unsolicited assistance from the Jewish Welfare Fund in the form of children's clothing, although others certainly accepted some help such as coal in winter. The first Sephardic college graduate in the early 1930s also incurred criticism from the immigrant generation when he informed them that he had sought financial assistance for his education from organizations of the wider Jewish community. The Sephardim maintained a keen sense of both personal and collective honor, which might be compromised by the receipt of assistance from the outside.

Since stigma derives from some degree of social exclusion, patterns of marriage and accompanying attitudes represent perhaps the most telling indicators of the degree of social distance between distinct groups. Endogamy, or marriage within a defined group, maintains social boundaries around the family itself. The dissolution of barriers to marriage between members of once estranged or hostile groups thus marks the last obstacle to mutual social acceptance, for it undermines the most essential personal and familial bulwarks of exclusiveness. Accordingly, marriage patterns prove particularly useful in charting the evolution of Sephardic and Ashkenazic relationships in Indianapolis. Up to the end of World War II, Sephardic-Ashkenazic marriages were notable for their rarity, numbering probably fewer than half a dozen. Some of these occurred only with the grudging approval of the respective families, but they succeeded in establishing a precedent which, by the 1950s, no longer seemed remarkable. But even in the post-World War II era some Ashkenazic families worked sedulously to terminate budding romances between their children and Sephardic partners.

Although the Ashkenazim manifested the more parochial attitudes in their narrow conceptions of what constituted Jewishness and hence discouraged intermarriage, Sephardic attitudes toward intermarriage were by no means either monolithic or entirely sympathetic. Although the Ashkenazim were defining status differences between themselves and the Sephardim, the latter did not consider a union with an Ashkenazic Jew as marrying up. What Sephardic resistance there was to intermarriage, however, is not attributable in any significant degree to skepticism about the authenticity of Ashkenazic Judaism. As a result, the Sephardim never attached the stigma of religious illegitimacy to their Eastern European co-religionists, who, by their sheer numbers, defined the terms of Jewish communal life. Rather, resistance to intermarriage lay in very practical considerations and varied in an intensity that depended upon whether a son or daughter was to marry. In one Sephardic family, for example, a son's marriage to an Ashkenazic woman in the early 1950s met with some resistance, particularly from the mother, an immigrant, who was especially worried about talking with her non-Ladino-speaking daughter-in-law. Her daughter's marriage to an Ashkenazic man a few years later met no resistance, in part because a woman's relationship to her son-in-law represented in itself a greater formality, even if they spoke a common language.

Although one Sephardic male informant claimed that, even from the Sephardic point of view, marriage to an Ashkenazic Jew would be tantamount among the Sephardic immigrants to marriage to a non-Jew, this assertion is only hyperbole. It should not, however, mask the common preference of immigrant parents for their children to marry Sephardim. In the Sephardic family just mentioned, one of the daughters in fact married a non-Jew in the 1930s, and this event was the virtual equivalent of death, replete with the ritual of mourning. Nothing approaching such lamentation ever characterized even the earliest Sephardic-Ashkenazic unions. In some instances, Sephardim expressed a reactive opposition to unions with Ashkenazim as a result of ubiquitous Ashkenazic prejudice. The elderly woman referred to earlier explained that because of diffuse Ashkenazic hostility, her mother asked her not to bring home any Ashkenazic young men.

In the years since World War II, when the decline of the Southside settlement and accompanying northward migration accelerated, Sephardic-Ashkenazic marriages no longer were noteworthy events. On the contrary, given the dramatic increase in Jewish-Gentile marriages, the intrafaith Sephardic-Ashkenazic unions were more often welcomed than condemned. Although Sephardim may have preferred to wed Sephardic partners, the small size of the community, its internal cross-cutting kinship bonds, and the breakdown of ethnic barriers insured that marriage outside the Sephardic community to Ashkenazim and non-Jews would occur with greater frequency.

Sephardim and the Wider Community

Were the two segments of Indianapolis Jewry wholly separate socially, stigmatized identity would likely not have figured as prominently as it has in Indianapolis Jewish experience. Exclusion is particularly telling when it is partial, occurring in the midst of other social connections between two otherwise distinctive groups. Or, to recall Goffman's simple definition, stigma represents a barrier to *full* social acceptance. Thus, although cultural differences set the stage for separate social institutions among Sephardim and Ashkenazim, other forces were at work from the very beginning to overturn tendencies toward complete social separatism.

Before the first Sephardim settled in Indianapolis, the seeds of community integration had been planted by established Jewish organizations. Dominated by the leading lights of Reformism, these organizations, such as the Jewish Federation, eased the process of settlement for newly arrived immigrants—especially the Ashkenazim. The Indianapolis Jewish community centralized and amalgamated its various social welfare organizations which, as in other cities, marked the onset of a modern "urban Jewish community life . . . to replace the family, *Landsmanschaft* (sic), and synagogal forms of Jewish life of the nineteenth century" (Morris and Freund 1966:3). Although this effort to formalize social welfare was adapted to the problems created by large scale immigration, particularly to the larger urban centers of this country, the more informal welfare groups centered in synagogues continued for some time in Indianapolis to co-exist with the newer community-wide organizations.

Through the institutional control and leadership exercised by very prominent Reform Jews, the immigrants from the outset had before them Jewish models, however distant from their own religious and social experience, of highly successful adaptation to the New World. Many members of the Reform community were exemplars of what Jews in America might become—prosperous, assimilated participants in the civic life of the city and before whom class and residential mobility lay virtually unobstructed for cultural or religious reasons. The social and economic achievements of the Reform Jews pointed the way for subsequent Jewish immigrant groups, and such success depended on a willingness—even eagerness among the second generation—to conform to the mainstream. Lacking even the rudiments of economic self-sufficiency, the Southside communities of immigrant Eastern European Ashkenazim and Sephardim continually looked outward for ways to climb the economic ladder as the Reform Jews had done before them.

Established Jewish organizations promoted the adaptation of both the immigrant Sephardim and Ashkenazim. Under the sponsorship of Jewish agencies, citizenship and English classes were available to all immigrants. Their children were actively encouraged to participate in the Southside community center, which, with the public school, was an important meeting ground for the American-born Sephardim, Ashkenazim, and their non-Jewish neighbors. Thus was created a Jewish community which, if highly diverse in its constituent elements, nonetheless forged the first tenuous social bonds between essentially different Jewish cultures struggling to become Americanized.

Organizations encompassing the entire community of Indianapolis Jews were spawned by the imperatives of Jewish immigration and resettlement in the United States, and the staffs and planning of these institutions, including the Jewish Federation, Welfare Fund, and the Industrial Removal Office, were oriented to the needs of the much larger population of Eastern European Ashkenazim. They took little account of the relatively small number of non-Yiddish speaking immigrants. The Sephardim were thus estranged not only from the Ashkenazim in their early years but also from Jewish institutions ostensibly established to mediate between immigrants and the wider society. The Sephardim were torn between contradictory forces—on the one hand, a strong tendency, abetted by Ashkenazic prejudice, to grow involuted as a small, unique community and, on the other, the pressures for integration.

Yet amid the efforts to integrate Sephardim, community-wide institutions emphasized Sephardic differences from the mainstream of Jews. Initially, the designation "Turk" was probably applied very innocently by the Jewish agencies assisting the Sephardic immigrants. In a short time, the term assumed its derogatory connotation. Barriers of communication and cultural differences between Sephardim and the rest of the Jewish community, including its formal institutions, were taken by these latter groups as an index of Sephardic exclusiveness. Jewish organizations did not fully appreciate that the Ashkenazim and the agencies primarily oriented toward their needs were also casting the Sephardic Jews into a marginal position, or at least underscoring and negatively evaluating their uniqueness. The following portion of a 1928 unpublished report to the Jewish Federation, written by a trained social worker and highly respected leader of that organization, represents a typical "official" view of the Sephardic community:

> This group of about sixty five families, most of them coming from Monastir, Jugoslavia, (sic) are a very distinct entity and present a series of definite community problems. Most of the men are employed at the Kahn Tailoring Company and there are a small number of commission merchants, fruit peddlars and keepers of second hand clothing stores. They are a thrifty people, very separatist, speak a Spanish dialect instead of the Yiddish common to other Jews, and they have organized for themselves the various activities necessary to community life. They have their own resources to take care of internal disputes and similar matters, a congregation with a building, a Ladies Auxiliary and a Social Club. Their standards of living are different, their family life is almost patriarchal, in the domination of the male and women have suffered from the further disadvantage of illiteracy. Superstition is common, as is inbreeding, and there has been a mutual antipathy between the Sephardic group and their Ashkenazic neighbors. (Jewish Federation Archives 1928).

A highly visible minority is especially vulnerable to stereotyping, and descriptions of "superstition" and "inbreeding" have at times been applied to many other minorities, including Ashkenazic Jews. I have no indication that the proportion of marriages between cousins was any higher among the Sephardim than among the Ashkenazim. But the popular view of "inbreeding" persisted owing to the small size of the Sephardic community and the many bonds of kinship spawned by the chain of migration. The Eastern European Ashkenazic pattern, to the extent it can be generalized, was similar, but much less visible within the larger Ashkenazic population. Nonetheless, any suggestion that "all the Sephardic Jews are somehow related," because it plays on an old stereotype, still rankles many Sephardim.

For the Ashkenazim, economic gains were quickly translated into improved housing and other overt representations of heightened living standards. From the 1920s through the 1950s, a steady movement proceeded from the original Southside settlement to the more valued neighborhoods on the Northside of the city. Northward residential shifts were the most visible indication of the continuum of achievement and prosperity. As families moved further north, they advanced their status while distancing themselves, both literally and symbolically, from immigrant beginnings and their unhappy associations with poverty. Even the Southside itself was internally divided, although not rigidly, along lines of residential prestige with Sephardim and poorer Ashkenazim living in the least valued area. Although the Sephardim eventually joined the northward migration, they remained in the original neighborhood much longer than did the vast majority of Ashkenazim, choosing as they did to continue to separate themselves long after they were economically able to relocate.

A 1943 unpublished report on the Southside Jewish neighborhood clearly documents this pattern. It found that a disproportionate number of residents were Sephardic. The Southside Sephardic community of 264 individuals, nearly the entire Sephardic population of the city, constituted 25% of the total population of 1041 Jewish residents on the Southside. The study also reported that 80% of Sephardic homes, compared to an overall rate of 56% among all Southside Jews, were tenant-owned (Jewish Community Center Association and Jewish Federation of Indianapolis 1943:5).

The Indianapolis Sephardim saw themselves as more tightly bound to the old neighborhood and their stronger and more prolonged connection to the immigrant settlement reiterated their differences from the Ashkenazim. Their residential attachments diminished their social status in the eyes of the Ashkenazim, but the Sephardim were not caught up as quickly in the prevailing Jewish pattern of status attainment through residential shifts. Spurning the most obvious symbols of assimilation assured the continuation of stigmatized identity. In a strongly nativist setting where the most economically successful people among the minority set an assimilationist tone for community life, those least willing to set aside the obvious markers of immigrant life are likely to be the most denigrated.

The larger question here is why the Jews and other European immigrant groups felt compelled to choose between maintaining ethnic and religious traditions and improving their economic condition. Since ethnic settlements were not economically self-sufficient, the immigrants had to accommodate themselves to the rhythms and demands of an economy governed by commercial imperatives lying outside the areas of immigrant settlement. Stories thus abound of immigrant Sephardim and Ashkenazim unhappily going to their jobs on Saturday, sometimes at German-Jewish concerns, in contravention of all their accustomed routines in Europe. Yet they had to make a living, even if it required compromising cultural and religious observance.

In his excellent study of ethnic groups in America, Steinberg incisively addresses this issue by analyzing the way class and status were articulated to culture:

> Their immediate economic survival . . . required that they become Americanized. The fact that immigrant status was virtually equated with poverty and disadvantage inevitably played havoc with ethnic self-conceptions. All immigrant groups developed a disdain for the "green-horn" . . . But the word also carried with it a powerful message from the larger society, which was that the "greener" was destined to remain on the periphery of the society and its systems of rewards. (1981:53)

If the stigma attaching to the Sephardim was in part an indication of their slower adoption of the overt symbols of economic achievement, it is also points up a more persistent effort to succeed on their own cultural terms.

The immigrants themselves were of course well aware of the conflicts between tradition and mobility. Angel, in his study of the Sephardic press, notes the dimensions of the internal struggle people waged as they considered how best to meet the demands of American life and what place Sephardic custom and Ladino might have in their new country (1982:49–52). Moise Gadol, the editor of *La America*, optimistically believed that the Sephardim could learn English, assume American citizenship, and enter the mainstream of American life, while still adhering to Sephardic tradition (1982:51).

Indianapolis Sephardim pondering the "decline of tradition" explain it as a failure of community will and leadership. Agreeing with Gadol, they argue that the best of both worlds could have been maintained. Yet such a position is overly self-critical, for it neglects the extraordinarily compelling economic and social forces impinging on the Indianapolis immigrant settlement from the very first days, when the Sephardim were stigmatized by culture, status, and class. Quite simply, it was not possible to steer a middle course between full participation in American life and the preservation of old world language and culture. What results is a pervasive nostalgia, especially among the second generation. Now mostly in their fifties and sixties and enjoying success after a protracted economic struggle, that group can now afford to embrace what they once regarded with considerable ambivalence. They thus paradoxically lament the loss of cohesive neighborhoods, old country institutions, and a flourishing ethnicity of language and culture—yet none would return to it (Glazier 1987:81–83).

Conclusion

The contemporary Sephardic community of Indianapolis constituted of four generations represents what is now a familiar Jewish success story in America—a success measured by economic achievement, distance traveled, culturally speaking, from immigrant beginnings, and acceptance by other Jews. The Sephardim and the Ashkenazim have culturally converged, bound together by many common features of Jewish life in America. They have witnessed the same precipitous decline in Ladino and Yiddish, respectively, among the American-born generations. Both groups face high rates of intermarriage with gentiles, and the fatal friendliness of an open society which diminishes the boundaries historically separating the Jews from all others. Other boundaries, which once also stigmatized the Sephardim while separating them from the Ashkenazim, have also diminished nearly to the point of extinction. American Jewish culture has tended not only to homogenize the two groups but also to accelerate the decline of the unique social institutions of each segment—welfare agencies, burial societies, and the like—in favor of overarching organizations serving the entire Jewish community.

Nevertheless the Sephardim still maintain the synagogue founded by the immigrant generation. All other ethnic congregations—Russian, Polish, Hungarian—have either dissolved or merged. For practical purposes, virtually all of the Sephardim maintain dual synagogue membership, choosing as they do to take advantage of the facilities and programs that the larger synagogues offer but which could not be maintained by the small Sephardic congregation. The synagogue is very much a symbol of Sephardic determination, especially by the second generation, to maintain at least a semblance of distinctiveness. Yet, like the many personal stories narrated by the Sephardim, it is more an honorific glimpse backward to the world of their European parents and an acknowledgment of their own past than it is a hopeful look forward to the unbounded world of their children and grandchildren. These expressions represent what Bernard Lewis calls "corporate historical memory"—a key factor, intangible as it is, shaping Jewish identity and a sense of collectivity (cited in Feingold 1981:283–284). For the Monastir and Salonika Jews and their descendants, corporate historical memory preserves the ironic story of a stigmatized and excluded American Sephardic community—and its costly vindication.

Notes

1. I acknowledge with thanks the research support of the National Endowment for the Humanities, the Wenner-Gren Foundation for Anthropological Research, and Oberlin College.

2. The Reform leader, Rabbi Feuerlicht, is remembered with particular fondness by the older generation of Sephardim for his efforts to persuade the Jewish community at large of the authenticity of Sephardic practice. He also presided over the Reform congregation when it lent financial assistance to the Sephardim for the purchase of an old Southside church, which they converted into a synagogue. Despite these connections, the social networks of the Sephardim and the Reform Jews remained very distinct up to the late 1950s. At least one major community leader suggested in recent years that a likely motive for Reform Jewish assistance to the Sephardim was to keep the latter on the Southside, well away from the residential areas and social worlds of the Reform Jews. While this view appears cynical, it accords with the stigmatization of the Sephardim and more general efforts by the wealthy to distance themselves socially from their less prosperous co-religionists lacking the accompanying symbols of social status and economic success. This pattern has been documented by a few observers of the relationship between established Reform Jews and the growing numbers of immigrant Eastern Europeans, particularly in New York (e.g. Manners 1972; Rischin 1962).

References

Angel, Marc D.
1974   The Sephardim of the United States: An Exploratory Study. New York: Union of Sephardic Congregations.
1982   La America. The Sephardic Experience in the United States. Philadelphia: The Jewish Publication Society of America.

Birmingham, Stephen
1971   The Grandees. New York: Harper and Row.

B'nai B'rith
1934   Minutes of May 4th Meeting. Indianapolis Lodge No. 58.

Endelman, Judith
1984   The Jewish Community of Indianapolis. Bloomington: Indiana University Press.

Feingold, Henry L.
1981   Jewish Life in the United States: Perspectives from History. *In* Jewish Life in the United States: Perspectives from the Social Sciences. Joseph B. Gittler, editor, New York: New York University Press.

Glazier, Jack
1985   The Indianapolis Sephardim. Shofar 3(3):27–34.
1987   Nicknames and the Transformation of An American Jewish Community: Notes on the Anthropology of Emotion in the Urban Midwest. Ethnology XXVI(2):73–85.

Goffman, Erving
1963   Stigma. Notes on the Management of Spoiled Identity. Englewood Cliffs: Prentice-Hall.

Halpern, Ben
1974   America is Different. *In* The Jew in American Society. Marshall Sklare, editor, New York: Behrman House.

Indianapolis News
1925   Religious Tolerance Stressed by Jackson. December 14.

Indianapolis Star
1905   Grand Celebration of Jewish People. November 27.

Jewish Community Center and Jewish Federation of Indianapolis
1943   Indianapolis Southside Communal Building Survey. Unpublished Report.

Madison, James H.
1982   Indiana Through Tradition and Change. Indianapolis: Indiana Historical Society.

Manners, Ande
1972 Poor Cousins. Greenwich, CT: Fawcett Publications.

Morris, Robert and Freund, Michael, editors.
1966 Trends and Issues in Jewish Social Welfare in the United States, 1899–1952. Philadelphia: The Jewish Publication Society of America.

Redfield, Robert
1956 Peasant Society and Culture. Chicago: University of Chicago Press.

Rischin, Moses
1962 The Promised City: New York's Jews 1870–1914. Cambridge: Harvard University Press.

Steinberg, Stephen
1981 The Ethnic Myth. New York: Atheneum.

Tolerance
1923 Indiana Secretary of State: We Have With Us Today Exalted Politician on Roll of Ku Klux Klan. April 23.

U.S. Census Bureau
1902 Abstract of the Twelfth Census: 1900. Washington, D.C. Government Printing Office.

3 American Yemenite Jews: Interethnic Strategies

Dina Dahbany-Miraglia

The great chasm dividing American society is that between blacks and whites. People of color who are not historically identified with Afro-Americans have been caught between these two identities. Since most Jews are considered white, Jews who can be perceived as black are anomalous. Yemenite Jews in New York City are among those caught in this position. Among other problems, Yemenite Jews in the United States must validate their Jewishness. Using sociolinguistics, Dahbany-Miraglia presents and analyzes some verbal strategies used by the Yemenis in coping with this situation.

Introduction

Ethnic identity is, as Bram (1965) and Nagata (1974) point out, like plastic: easily bent and shaped by societal and group ideologies, expectations, and practices. Societies may sortpopulations according to cultural, physiognomic, religious, national, and other criteria, and groups may differentiate themselves from each other by using one or more of these parameters of distinction. It is, however, individuals in situations who act out and therefore, reify these distinctions. To American Yemenite Jews ethnic identity is primarily instrumental, a series of strategies they exercise to implement personal goals. One of the more important of these goals is the establishment of their basic identity: that of Jews. In the United States Yemenite Jews are often obliged to "prove" their Jewishness, something they did not have to do in the Middle East.

Ethnic identity is often viewed in the professional literature as emanating from either a "cultural heritage shared by a group" or "as a form of social organization that functions to achieve certain common ends (Keyes 1981:4)." The first is often labeled "primordial" as it is seen to be based on genetic, culture content, and other heritable commonalities. In the second, called "circumstantial," ethnic identity is a "dependent variable, created and controlled by a broad combination of external interests and strategies, which invest it with a potential for action and mobilization (Nagata 1981:89)."

63

For American Yemenite Jews ethnic identity comes from a primordial base in which religion and genetics are two major components. Both components are part of the core from which instrumental expressions of ethnic identity radiate, expressions that are not always Yemenite Jewish. One reason is their second-class status in everyhost country in which they have lived: as Jews in Yemen and Turkish (Ottoman) Palestine, as Middle Eastern Jews in British Mandate Palestine, and as anomalous individuals in the United States where their physiognomy contradicts American ethnic categorizations. A people who are non-elite must exercise flexibility in "the presentation of self (Goffman 1959)." Adaptation to a host country's peculiarities is the first order of business. Inventing, developing, and manipulating a variety of ethnic-derived interactional strategies are especially necessary for populations that do not neatly fit into a host country's categories.

This paper deals with "circumstantial" elements of ethnic identity. The focus here is on why specific identities are selected and verbalized, and on a not very often examined aspect: how individuals verbalize ethnic identities in situations. Analyses of verbal expressions of ethnic identity are few. They are scattered in the sociolinguistic literature and can be found in only a small number of the vast number of publications on ethnicity and ethnic identity.

Joshua A. Fishman, a sociolinguist, is noted for his in-depth longterm investigations into the relationships of speech and ethnic identity (1965, 1968). Other linguists, such as Gumperz (1971, 1982), Fox (1974), and Sankoff (1974) have dealt with language in situations, concentrating on codeswitching, but not necessarily as it relates to ethnic identity. The few anthropological publications include Karen Blu's 1980 book on the Lumbee, my dissertation (Dahbany-Miraglia 1983), and a handful of articles, such as Plotnicov's and Silverman's on Ashkenazic Jewish (Yiddish-speaking European Jews) ethnic signalling (1978). Blu's data are mostly anecdotal examples of boundary maintainance and her approach is entirely ethnographic. My dissertation examines American Yemenite Jewish verbal expressions of ethnic identity from a sociolinguistic perspective. Plotnicov's and Silverman's article exemplifies Ashkenazic intra-ethnic behavior with Yiddishism and Yiddish-based verbalizations that are tied to Judaism and Ashkenazic Jewish culture.

My work with Yemenite Jews in the Greater New York area has shown that although the criterion of their basic identity is immutable, they will verbally claim or silently acquiesce to other identifications in response to situational conditions and to various host country perceptions of their identities.[1] In every society populations are sorted according to cultural, racial, religious, national, and other criteria, and groups differentiate themselves from each other using one or combinations of these parameters of distinctiveness. Nevertheless, individuals in situations are the ones who must deal with these criteria and express them as they see fit (Barth 1959; Gumperz 1982; Fox 1974; Sankoff 1974).

American Yemenite Jews have been employing an ethnic identity strategically long before they began emigrating in small numbers from Yemen more than 100 years ago (Dahbany-Miraglia forthcoming a; 1983). For them, then and now, ethnic identity is a tool and is rarely ever aimed at the simple raising and erasing of boundaries. For Yemenite Jews ethnic identities are categories which are based primarily on cultural distinctions. These distinctions are tied to, and are sometimes seen as, synonymous with one or more of the following: religion, language, country of origin, regional origin and race, cultural practices, or foods. In their simplest forms these categories are symbolized linguistically by means of labels which are mnemonics for one or more stereotypes that are, so to speak, in the public domain. That is to say, Yemenite Jews and the people among whom they live recognize the combinations of traits that refer to or are associated with various populations. This does not mean, however, that Yemenite Jews accept the stereotypes that are current in a society, especially when some of those stereotypes are applied to them.

As Jews, in Yemen and in Turkish (Ottoman) Palestine, Yemenite Jews were obliged to labor under the onus of negative stereotypes and second-class citizenship. When the British officially supplanted the Turks in 1923 and encouraged the Ashkenazim to run the Yishuv, the Jewish community, Yemenites and the other non-European Jews retained their second-class status as Middle Eastern Jews. This situation has remained unchanged since the state of Israel was created. Yemenite Jews' second-class status in the United States was complicated by American conceptions of color.

Nevertheless, in all the societies in which they lived Yemen's Jews pressed against the limitations imposed on them, often through the judicious manipulation of ethnic identities. For Yemenite Jews ethnic identity was and remains one means of effecting social, personal, and economic goals. In the Middle East Yemenite Jews enhanced personal status, negotiated advantageous business transactions, married their children, bought homes, made and kept friends, and once in a long while lowered and raised boundaries between themselves and other populations, by dint of effective manipulation of Yemenite, Jewish, Middle Eastern and other identities. They were able to do so because their basic identity as Jews was recognized and accepted without demur. Only in the United States are Yemenite Jews obliged to reassess their earlier strategies and to develop defensive ones to fit the new criteria they have encountered.

Middle Eastern and American Perceptions

Throughout the Middle East religion is the most important ethnic criterion. On the other hand, the most significant socio-political marker in the United States is skin color. This contrast between Middle Eastern and American criteria is further complicated by the American equation of "Jew" with European Jews who are, despite the stereotypes, physically indistinguishable from European Christians. Another difficulty is the association of white skin color with Jews. For the first time Yemenite Jews were put in the position of having their basic identity challenged, denied, and disbelieved. Their original strategies of ethnic expression needed to be revised and adapted to American perceptions.

In contrast to the Middle East which has been pluralistic for thousands of years, the United States is essentially mono-cultural. In this respect it is a proper offshoot of the northwestern European states whose majority populations fed these shores with their dissatisfied and disadvantaged. In those countries only one culture and one language dominates. Variations such as subcultures have very little effect on the society as a whole.[2] That means that cultural diversity is not only unacceptable, it is disdained. Outsiders must acculturate and if possible, assimilate. A side effect of this attitude is widespread ignorance of human cultural variety that is too often internalized as a virtue. Today, despite the pressures of large Spanish-speaking populations in the Greater New York area and in the American West and Southwest, despite the enormous imprint American black culture has been making on the arts, and the recent influx of non-European immigrants, America remains a white Anglo-Saxon Protestant country. Even now throughout most of the United States bi- and multi-linguals are viewed with suspicion.

Yemenite Jews could not and still do not, in the United States, depend on the widespread knowledge and acceptance of their basic identity that was and remains a comfortable reality throughout the Middle East. The lack of convergence between their Jewishness and the identities with which other Americans ascribed to them forced them to shift their interactional strategies from offense to defense, from emphasis on social, economic, political and personal goal satisfaction to spending a great deal of time on justifying their basic identity. In fact, the darkest-skinned individuals, particularly those with curly or kinky hair, are continually obliged to prove they are Jews (i.e. white). When looking for apartments in Jewish neighborhoods they must resort to the strategy that many blacks and Hispanics use: sending the lightest-skinned family member or a friend to do the necessaries. Similarly, job hunting, especially before the late 1960s, usually required the mediation of a friend or a relative. But Yemenite Jews, in common with everyone else, live in the real world where they encounter people every day and so must deal with ethnic identity and ascription during face-to-face interactions.

The Data: Encounters with Non-middle Easterners

A characteristic face-to-face situation which is rare in the Middle East but common in the United States occurs in public places between Yemenite Jews and a non-Middle Easterners. The participants in one interaction are a native-born American Yemenite Jew in her early twenties and a Chicano male a few years older. They are seated side by side on a bus moving across Los Angeles' downtown area in the summer of 1960. The male initiates verbal contact, no doubt because the Yemenite is wearing a Jewish star clearly visible against her blouse.

"What are you?" "A Yemenite." "A Monomite?" "A Yemenite. A Middle Eastern Jew." "A what?" "From the Middle East." "Where?" "Yemen." "Where?" "Arabia." "You're an Arab?" "No, a Jew!" "I thought you said you were a Men . . ." "A Yemenite. Yeh, that's a Jew." "Yeh?" "Yeh." Response: a glazed look of incomprehension.

In order to cope with such situations American Yemenite Jews often identify as other than Yemenite: they "pass," a strategy they hardly ever had to use in the Middle East. Before 1948 a common label Yemenite Jews employed to pass as Jews and simultaneously as white, and to explain their distinctiveness, was "Palestinian;" after 1948 the label became "Israeli." Other much-used alternatives included "Sephardic" (Judeo-Spanish and Judeo-Portuguese-speaking Jews) and "Syrian." A frequently heard response to all of these labels was "Oh, that explains why you are so dark."[3]

Many Yemenite Jews easily pass as Italians, especially Sicilians, for several reasons: (1) a number of last names end in *uzi, essi, ani, azi, ufi* and *elli;* (2) nearly all the Oldtimers' children grew up in working class neighborhoods where a large number of their neighbors and public schoolmates were Sicilian Italians; and (3) thanks to the film and television media's love affair with the Mafia practically all American Yemenites can mimic Sicilian Italian body language and accented English.

An often resorted-to form of passing is to accept ascription as black, Hispanic, Italian, American Indian, and East Indian. Here, too, the majority of these ascriptions occurred and still occur in public places: a gas station, a clothing shop, an unemployment line, supermarket checkout counters, on airplanes, at bus stops, in a New York city subway train or on an MTA platform. The encounters are brief, usually between thirty seconds and two minutes. During such encounters the most common strategy is to accept the ascription assigned and sometimes verbally reinforce the inaccurate assumption. This is usually done through articulating dialect variants associated with non-white American culture groups. The following anecdote characterizes such encounters. The informant is a light-skinned Israeli-born Yemenite Jew sporting a shock of kinky hair cut in a modified Afro. He was in his twenties in 1972 when this encounter occurred:

> I was standing on Sixth Avenue and 47th Street in Manhattan waiting for the light to trurn green. These two Black guys came from behind. One of the them said

```
                                               t ?
                                          gh
                                       li
                 er:           u              a
     e  y        o th          yo      gott
 H             br
            ,
```

I answered:

```
                        a
               er;    t   ke
     u         o th              i
 S    re    br                   t
        ,                      .
```

> I gave him the book of matches. Then the light changed and I crossed the street.

It is reasonable to assume that the informant's appearance encouraged the black man to assume that he was talking to another black American. This does not, of course, mean that the initiator would have modified his speech pattern had he thought the Yemenite was white. That the Yemenite was able to reply as one black man to another without being thought of as mocking him or as embarrasingly pro-black is because this informant is seen, as are most other Yemenite Jews, as non-white and, by extension, non-Jewish.

Many Yemenite Jews, especially the Oldtimers, their children, and some Newcomers, can mimic varieties of Southern black dialect and "Spanglish," combinations of Spanish and English.[4] A substantial minority can speak Judezmo (Judeo-Spanish) and many of the Oltimers' children and grandchildren are moderately fluent in high school Spanish. They will often reply in Spanish to a query in Spanish for directions, thereby reinforcing the non-Yemenite protagonist's perception of their Hispanic identity. In public places one informant habitually responds smilingly to requests for directions from Spanish speakers with *yo no hable espanol* (I do not speak Spanish). The reactions of the questioners can only be surmised.

With few exceptions every informant has reported at least one incident where s/he was approached in a public place, usually by a Hispanic, who asked directions and who invariably initiated her/his request in Spanish. When the Yemenite disclaims Hispanic identity the Hispanic often continues the conversation and asks the Yemenite "Aren't you Spanish?" Sometimes the Yemenite will reply with a simple "No, I'm not." and walk off or turn away. At other times s/he will say "No, I'm Jewish."

In situations of this sort the Hispanic invariably glances at the Yemenite with an expression of disbelief, that informants describe as a nonverbal substitute for "Oh, yeh, sure!" The American association of "white" with "Jew" is so widespread that to some Hispanics it must seem that the Yemenite who, to the Hispanic looks Hispanic, is trying to pass as white by claiming to be Jewish. There is little doubt that the white/Jew association exists throughout the Hispanic world as well. It certainly is viable among my immigrant Haitian and Asian students who express surprise and disbelief when I tell them that I am taking time off for the Jewish holidays.

Other identification as a black is so widespread that it is common for a Yemenite Jew to receive or exchange a smile accompanied by a " 'Mornin' " or a "Nice day." with a black woman or man. At other times, particularly when the Yemenite is a female, a black man's smile becomes a leer and the neighborly greeting changes to a:

```
        A
      B
   y,           by!
He                        PO                    YE
                     pp       WANTS        W !
             Yoh           a
```

Hispanic males will call out *linda,* (beautiful) or *mira! mira! que linda!* (Look how beautiful she is!). White male construction workers have called out variations of the following:

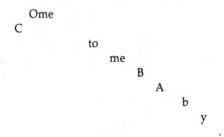

It is often difficult to sort out the sexual from the ethnic as these comments are often verbal attacks against young, sometimes sexually attractive females. A few of my female informants claim that some of these aggressive attacks are racial. One related an incident that occurred during the 1960s when she and an Ashkenazic girlfriend were walking past a construction site in Boro Park late one chilly weekday afternoon on their way home from high school. Both were bundled in winter coats as they hurried past the men. Black and white workers alike whistled and catcalled, clearly pleased with their own wit. Furious, the girls increased their pace, intent on moving out of earshot. They did not walk fast enough. One worker yelled "I'll take the nigger; she's cuter." The rest roared their appreciative laughter.

To counteract this frustrating, ever present necessity, that of disavowing the black and therefore Christian status that contradicts their basic identity, and to claim and then too often be required to defend their basic identity, individual Yemenite Jews will frequently select outrageously inappropriate ethnic identities precisely because, to mix a metaphor, the fit is so far from the mark.

A common trigger is "What are you?" This question is a catchall mnemonic for a complex of questions which include "Where do you come from?", "Where do your parents come from?", "Where were you born?", "Where were your parents born?", and "What is your religion?". Every Yemenite Jew has had to respond to or else ignore this question, particularly in the United States.

The following anecdote is characteristic of situations in which Yemenite Jews are challenged to identify themselves, usually with a "What are you?". The contexts are most often private homes, rented halls in which personal and business events, such as weddings and award dinners, are held, and other locations where the protagonists are friends of the host/ess and are likely to be, but are not necessarily, known to each other. Dances, large cocktail and company Christmas parties, charity dinners as well as more public places, such as suburban shopping mall parking lots and department store aisles and elevators are other physical locales.

In this situation the Yemenite is American-born and approximately thirty years old. She attended a large party at the home of an acquaintance during the 1970s and knew only one or two of the other guests. After staring at her for several minutes from across the room, a young man approached her and introduced himself. She reciprocated (her surname is Levy) and they proceeded to exchange pleasantries. After a few minutes he asked her: "What are you?" to which she replied with some asperity: "Chinese, of course!"

Most American Yemenite Jews take these confrontations more or less seriously. Some reply as one twelve-year-old did in the 1970s to the "What are you?" query. Widening his eyes, hunching his shoulders, and clawing his fingers, he rasped: "I'm a Martian. Can't you tell?"

Encounters with Ashkenazim

There is a form of passing in which the lighter-skinned Yemenites find themselves involved, especially those who are fluent in Yiddish. Ashkenazim often assume that these Yemenites are, like them, European Jews and behave towards them accordingly. They initiate conversations, usually in Yiddish, sometimes in English, and treat them as "insiders." One Oldtimer was fair-skinned and has been repeatedly told that she looks Polish (Jewish). A polite, soft-spoken woman, she rarely disabused the Ashkenazim she met when she thought that she would never see them again. Her reluctance to let them know she was Yemenite was abetted by her fluent Yiddish which she learned in Turkish Palestine, just after she was married, from her next door neighbor, an old woman from Eastern Europe who spoke only Yiddish.

Using Yiddish, Yiddishisms, and Yiddish intonation in English has always been problematic for Yemenite Jews because of the associations many Ashkenazim make between Yiddish and intracultural closeness (see Plotnicov and Silverman). Yiddish is, for many Ashkenazim, more than an ingroup language; it is the language of intimacy, the *mame loshn*, the language they learned at their mothers' knees. To these Ashkenazim, Yemenites who speak Yiddish are trying to pass as Ashkenazim.

In the 1970s there were three *kanāyīs*, Yemenite synagogues. One of them was run by a Newcomer couple who turned their home into a *kanīs* (synagogue). On a late spring afternoon in 1979 the couple were sitting around their kitchen table when a plump Orthodox Ashkenazi who may have been in his late twenties and who dressed like a Hasid, walked in through the open front door. He tried to sell them Ashkenazic *siddurīm*, prayer books. To persuade them to buy from him he said in a Yiddish-accented Hebrew, "*Kol hateymanim koru bey haseyfur hazeh.*" (All the Yemenites use (read) this (prayer)book.) Husband and wife shook their heads no. As he was leaving the wife warned him in Yiddish, "*gib akhtik af des shtikl wid fin di telefon.*" (Watch out for the telephone wire.) The salesman waved and then replied in Hebrew, "*Ken, todah.*" (Yes, thank you.)

There are several explanations of this dialogue and it is more than likely that all are correct. One has nothing to do with ethnic identity. It concerns good salesmanship. Leave the customer with a good impression; you never know when s/he might buy from you. Another is clearly ethnic in that it sets up boundaries between kinds of Jews. The salesman chose to speak in Hebrew rather than Yiddish, correctly assuming that this couple were Israelis. When the woman switched into Yiddish the salesman replied in Hebrew. He might have wished to maintain the character of his interchange with them. He could have been more interested in leaving and so did not choose to pick up on the language switching. He might have rejected speaking Yiddish to them because he could not be sure that both spoke the language. Or else he stayed with Hebrew because they were not Ashkenazim. Even though they may have been fluent Yiddish speakers, Yiddish is the language he speaks almost exclusively to his own "kind," other Hasidim.

To Middle Easterners speaking another group's language is not deemed intrusive. Rather, it is recognized as a most effective means of communicating with members of that group. It is also understood to be the most useful means of effecting social, economic, political, and personal as well as ethnic goals. In fact, in the Middle East, the ethnic element is often the least important reason for speaking another group's language.

Yemenite Jews do not want an Ashkenazic identity; they simply want to be recognized as Jews. For too many American Jews "Jew" and "Ashkenazi" are synonymous, and to speak Yiddish is to claim group membership. The dialogues below are one more example of the wide variety of responses to which most Yemenite Jews must resort when their Jewish identity is challenged by Ashkenazim. Oddly enough, white Christian Americans rarely challenge Yemenite Jews' assertions of their identity. Perhaps they believe that with Jews anything is possible.

Dialogue No. 1

Ashkenazi:

You're   ish?
        JEW

Yemenite:

    Yeh.

Ashkenazi:

                    OK   ish.
            LO   J
    You don't   EW

Yemenite:

        MY   YOU   JEW   EI
    To   group   don't look   ish   ther.

        LOOK   CHRIS
    You   like a   tian.

Dialogue No. 2

Ashkenazi:

    You're   ish?
            JEW

Yemenite:

        eh.
    Y

Ashkenazi:

                    w   sh ?
    Then ho   come you don't speak   i
                            JEW
                            (Yiddish)[5]

Since Ashkenazim are the most numerous Jewish population in the United States, it behooves Yemenites to learn some Yiddish. A substantial minority are fluent speakers and almost every Yemenite in the United States is expert in manipulating Yiddish phrases and American Yiddish intonation patterns. Sometimes, however, playing with Yiddish and its variants in order to validate Yemenite Jews' Jewish identity, backfires. Some Ashkenazim deduce that the Yemenite speaking Yiddish was once a servant (here read black and therefore, Christian) in an Ashkenazic home and learned the *mame loshn* from her/his employers.

That many if not the majority of Ashkenazim in America categorize Yemenites as black is evident in much of the data that I have collected and as exemplified by those depicted and analyzed above. Many Ashkenazim with whom I have talked about the Yemenite dilemma generally agree with my findings. Some have contributed to the data pool as well. One colleague offered the following:

In 1958 when he was a graduate student and had made it known that he was interested in working with a Middle Eastern population, he was approached by another graduate student with a serious suggestion. It seemed that some Ashkenazic women were having sexual relations with blacks and were giving birth to "mixed race" children who were notoriously hard to place in adoptive homes. He offered what was, to him, a viable solution: place such children in Yemenite homes.

Many of the Ashkenazim who have married Yemenites, especially the darker-skinned ones, report that it was fairly common for their marriages to be seen by most Americans as racially mixed ones. They were and still are obliged to assert their Jewishness and, by extension, their joint membership as whites.[6] During the early 1960s when my ex-spouse and I, newly married, were at a party in Greenwich Village a middle-aged woman smilingly commented on our association with "Oh, how nice! A mixed marriage!" to which I replied "Yes, male and female."

With few exceptions the Oldtimers' children who married Ashkenazim in the 1940s and 1950s had to deal with the issue of color from their spouses-to-be's families. Many of the prospective Ashkenazi in-laws rejected the Yemenites their children wanted to marry because they considered them too dark. Even in the 1970s there were a few Newcomers who were objected to by their intendeds' parents because of their skin color. (An equal number were delighted at the prospect of having Yemenite in-laws). Regardless of time period, the verbalized objections were remarkably similar and ranged from the overt "S/he's too dark!" and "What are you doing(,) marrying a nigger?" to the more polite "What a lovely color you have. Were you in Florida/California/the sun recently?" and "You must spend a lot of time in the sun."

Clearly, American Yemenite Jews are caught on the horns of a dilemma. Because Ashkenazic Jewish culture is viewed as the prototypical American Jewish culture, in order to be accepted as Jews most Yemenites have had to adopt speech, customs, food, and practices that are culturally very different from their own. A few, mostly those who have married Hasidim and other Orthodox Ashkenazim, have adopted their dress codes in addition to other Ashkenazic cultural particulars. The women wear wigs and longsleeved dresses. Men don the black uniform that distinguishes those Ashkenazic men who are, according to Ashkenazic definitions, strictly observant of Jewish laws. Hardly any of those Yemenites who keep kosher homes eat many of the foods, especially the meats, that they enjoyed in Yemen. Ashkenazim control the kosher food business and the certifying of slaughterers.[7] For this small group it is easier to follow than to reinterpret. Some express their Yemeniteness by preparing and eating certain *shabboth* or Sabbath foods, such as *maraq, kubaneh, hilbeh* and *zahuq*.[8]

In common with most other Yemenites, those who follow the Orthodox Ashkenazic pattern do not care to pass as Ashkenazim. According to a number with whom I have spoken and have observed, they rarely seem to be challenged with respect to their identity. It must be that the small world of the Ashkenazic Orthodox in America is more aware of the variety of Jews in the world than the much more numerous assimilated. Too, a very small number of Hasidim and other Orthodox Ashkenazim are as dark and as kinky/curly haired as Yemenites.

It is only when the protagonists are other Middle Easterners or the few Americans who are familiar with Middle Eastern cultural diversity that the American Yemenite Jewish defensive posture relaxes and passing becomes irrelevant. Otherwise, American Yemenite Jews are "damned if they do and damned if they don't." Ignorance of the enormous cultural variety among Jews was, before the 1970s, as widespread among Ashkenazim as it was among non-Jewish Americans. Defensive strategies, especially verbal ones, have replaced the offensive ones that Yemenite Jews have been accustomed to using in the Middle East. Employed rarely in the Middle East, passing has become, next to asserting Jewishness, the single most important and oft-used ethnic strategy. Given the character of American society it is not likely that this general situation will be very different twenty five years from now. The Middle East has been pluralistic for more than 5,000 years. The United States is, because of changes enacted in immigration laws during the early 1970s, just beginning to feel the stirrings of pluralism. Such things take time.

This brief explication of some verbal circumstantial aspects of Yemenite Jewish ethnic identity has demonstrated the importance of host country perceptions and their effects on how an immigrant population expresses ethnic identity. Aggressive and assertive manipulation of ethnic identities in the Middle East were modified in the United States to adopt more defensive strategies. Yet, basic identity has not changed. For Yemenite Jews being Jewish was and remains the base line of their existence as a group.

Notes

1. As one of the Oldtimer's children born and raised in the Boro Park section of the community, I have been doing fieldwork with Yemenite Jews in the Greater New York area since January 1970 and in Israel during the summers of 1984 and 1985. I have witnessed or else have experienced a substantial amount of the data included in this paper.

2. Northwest Europe is strongly monocultural with state-imposed national languages and effective educational systems. Only Belgium is bicultural (the Flemish and the Francophone Walloons). Although many Belgians are bilingual in Flemish and French, French has been the dominant language and relatively few Walloons speak Flemish.

3. In the summer of 1986 two of my sons, their blood brother, and a female friend traveled to California and back in six weeks. Coming and going my children were subjected to "You sure have/got some tan." at least once a day. The contexts included motels, diners, gas stations, rest stops, tourist traps and shops.

4. The Oldtimers are those 100 or so emigrants who migrated from Turkish and British Mandate Palestine to the United States between 1905 and 1931. Their primary languages are Judeo-Yemeni Arabic, Palestinian Arabic, Israeli Hebrew and American English. Most of their children were born in America (Dahbany-Miraglia 1983). Their main language is English. The Newcomers are Hebrew-speaking Israelis who began immigrating to the United States beginning in 1959. Their migration continues until now.

5. See Weinreich 1956 for an excellent analysis of the Yiddish rise/fall intonation contour, especially p. 642.

6. This is no doubt one of the most important reasons why the majority of the Oldtimers' children married Ashkenazim and other whites and why many of the younger Newcomers also seek and marry Ashkenazim. For numbers see Chapter 5 of my dissertation.

7. In Europe the Jews shared slaughtered animals with their Christian neighbors. Jews kept the portions above the midsection and gave the lower parts to the non-Jews. On the other hand, the complex of laws governing *kashruth* or ritually acceptable food, was thoroughly learned by the Yemenite slaughterers. The nether parts of animals were carefully cleaned so that the stomach, the testicles, and the rear haunches could be consumed. I do not know of one Yemenite butcher who will go through the Ashkenazic certi-

fication process, here or in Israel. They consider the Ashkenazim to be ignorant of the complexities of traditional slaughtering techniques and reject their competency to evaluate Yemenite skills.

8. *Maráq* is a meat soup; *kubâneh* is a raised bread that is baked overnight; *ḥilbeh* is a condiment made of crushed fenugreek seeds that is spiced with *zaḥûq*, a combination of crushed hot peppers.

References

Barth, Fredrik. Introduction. *Ethnic Groups and Boundaries*. Boston: Little, Brown and Company, 1969:9–38.

Bauman, Richard and Joel Sherzer, editors. *The Ethnography of Speaking*. New York: Cambridge University Press, 1974.

Blu, Karen. *The Lumbee Problem: The Making of an American Indian People*. New York: Cambridge University Press, 1980.

Bram, Joseph. "Change and Choice in Ethnic Identification." *Transactions of the New York Academy of Sciences*. Ser.II.28, 1965:242–248.

Dahbany-Miraglia, Dina. "An Analysis of Ethnic Identity Among Yemenite Jews in the Greater New York Area." Ph.D. dissertation, Columbia University, Department of Anthropology, 1983.

Dahbany-Miraglia, Dina. "The Jews of Yemen." In *The Jewish Peoples, An Ethnographic Survey*. Jane S. Gerber, editor. Westport, CT: Greenwood Press, in press a.

Dahbany-Miraglia, Dina. "Yemenite Jewish Immigration to the United States: 1905–1941." In *Crossing the Waters*. Eric Hoogland, editor. Washington, D.C., The Smithsonian Press, in press b.

Fishman, Joshua A., Robert L. Cooper, Roxana Ma, et al. *Bilingualism in the Barrio. The Measurement and Description and Language Dominance in Bilinguals*. Washington, D.C.: United States Department of Health, Education and Welfare. August, 1968.

Fishman, Joshua A. "Varieties of Ethnicity and Varieties of Language Consciousness." In *Report of the Sixteenth Annual Round Table Meeting on Linguistics and Language Studies*. Charles A. Kreidler, editor. Washington, D.C.: Georgetown University Press, 1965:69–79.

Fox, James. "Our Ancestors Spoke in Pairs:' Rotinese Views of Language, Dialect and Code." In Bauman and Sherzer, editors. 1974:65–85.

Goffman, Erving. *The Presentation of Self in Everyday Life*. Garden City, NY: Doubleday & Company, Inc. 1959.

Gumperz, John J. *Discourse Strategies*. New York: Cambridge University Press, 1982.

Gumperz, John J. *Language in Social Groups. Essays by John J. Gumperz.* Selected and introduced by Anwar S. Dil. Stanford, California: Stanford University Press, 1971.

Keyes, C. F. "The Dialectics of Ethnic Change." *In Ethnic Change.* Charles F. Keyes, editor. Seattle: University of Washington Press, 1981:4–30.

Nagata, Judith. "In Defence of Ethnic Boundaries: The Changing Myths and Charters of Malay Identity." In Charles F. Keyes, editor. 1981:87–116.

Nagata, Judith. "What is a Malay? Situational selection of ethnic identity in a plural society." *American Ethnologist* 1#2 (May) 1974:331–350.

Plotinicov, Leonard and Myrna Silverman. "Jewish Ethnic Signalling: Social Bonding in Contemporary American Society." *Ethnology* 18#4 (October) 1978:407–424.

Sankoff, Gillian. A Quantitative Paradigm for the Study of Communicative Competence. In Bauman and Sherzer, editors. 1974:18–49.

Weinreich, Uriel. Notes on the Yiddish Rise-Fall Intonation Contour. In *For Roman Jacobson. Essays on the Occasion of his Sixtieth Birthday,* 11 October 1956. Compiled by Morris Halle, Horace G. Lunt, Hugh McLean and Cornelius H. Van Schooneveld. The Hague: Moutont Co., 633–643.

4 Jewish in the USSR, Russian in the USA: Social Context and Ethnic Identity[1]

Fran Markowitz

Like the Yemenis and the Sephardim, the recent groups of Soviet Jews who have immigrated to the United States were simply Jews in their country of origin, but they have found themselves *dubbed* with other labels in the United States. In fact, their Jewishness has been questioned by the receiving population of American Jews. Fran Markowitz discusses how these Soviet emigres in Brooklyn react to the gap between their self-identity as Jews, which was enhanced as they challenged the Soviet system while applying to emigrate, and the American Jewish perception of them as "dejudaized" Russians. During her 20 months of fieldwork among Soviet immigrants in New York City, Fran Markowitz discovered the strategies these immigrants develop in order to cope with a new situation in which their formerly evident Jewish identity is challenged because it now requires open demonstration.

Introduction

Several recent examinations into the persistence of ethnic identity have focused on utilitarian, instrumental aspects of maintaining a sense of belonging to ethnic groups (See, *inter alia*, Bell 1975; Duran 1974; Glazer and Moynihan 1970; Patterson 1975; Shibutani and Kwan 1965). These studies point out that in complex societies, where each person has a range of identities at one's disposal, individuals assess the situations in which they find themselves and pull out the identity they deem most appropriate and beneficial for the moment. They demonstrate their ethnic group belonging to facilitate getting a good price at the market (Berreman 1975), finding employment in certain professions (Light 1972; Kim 1981), gaining access to scarce resources (Cohen 1969) and inclusion in friendship networks (Plotnicov 1967).

Studies of situational ethnicity assume that all participants in the situation automatically understand which symbols demonstrate ethnic group belonging; the sender and the recipient of information agree on the ethnic code. There is a seemingly natural, commonsense understanding that a green sash means one is a Slavic Moslem (Lockwood 1975:49), long hair and footwear made of poorly cured hides means one is a Kohistani (Barth 1969b:130), speaking Choctaw means one is a Choctaw from a particular community (Thompson and Peterson 1975:187–189), and appending the title *Syed/Sharifah* to one's name indicates being an Arab among Malays (Nagata 1974:336).

These unspoken understandings, this ethnic code, is so deeply embedded in and so basic to the interactions of situational ethnic display that it of itself is hardly worthy of note. To Barth (1969a:15) and his followers, the "cultural stuff" of an interaction is a given that allows two people to play the same ethnic game—to include themselves into one group and draw a boundary that excludes others. Since these symbols by which people demonstrate common origin (and through this affective ties) are variable, changing over time, the "cultural stuff" in itself is considered unimportant to the analysis of boundary maintenance and ethnic group persistence.

Such felicitous meetings of the minds, however, do not always occur. Interactions will be thwarted when two people ascribe to themselves the same ethnic label but fail to agree on the cultural content, because of the different social contexts in which each developed the same identity, that makes the label applicable to them both. If time after time ethnic displays are unsuccessful due to disagreement about symbolic content and result in reluctance or outright refusal to bestow one's identity to others also claiming it as theirs, what should happen? Without question, at least initially, identity confusion and intra-group conflict will develop. What time will tell is whether this cleavage deepens, resulting in the development of two distinct identities, or if the groups move together, resolving their conflicts by each learning and incorporating some of the other's symbols into one wider meaning system (see Keyes 1981).

This paper examines the development of such a disconnection between self-ascribed identity and ethnic labels bestowed by others resulting from cultural content misunderstandings. It analyzes the case of Jewish immigrants from the Soviet Union who identify as Jews and are ironically called "Russians" after arrival in America. Specifically, the paper looks at the symbols these immigrants use in their daily lives, how they understand the meaning and display of their Jewish identity and how these symbols and meanings came to be read and interpreted by American Jews as "Russian." Finally, a discussion will be made of the inapplicability of circumstantialist theories of ethnicity to this case and its implications for understanding the dynamics of ethnicity among other dispersed ethnic groups.

Soviet Jews' Jewishness

Soviet Jews do not question or challenge their Jewishness. "We are Jews by our blood, our genes, our historical experience. While one can change religion, it is very difficult, if not impossible, to change genes and blood," is the prevalent understanding of Jewish identity. Being a Jew is an immutable biological and social fact, ascribed at birth like sex and eye color. It may or may not include belief in the Jewish religion, but being a Jewish atheist is not considered a contradiction in terms.

Being a Jew is self-evident; many informants tell of being called *zhid* (kike) in childhood and adulthood and of having no difficulty giving bribes since Jews are less suspect than others of being KGB. To the question, "How did they know you were Jewish?" the response is invariably given with an air of condescension—isn't it obvious? "From my face, they just knew." When pressed further: "In Russia we don't have so many Mediterranean peoples, Italians and so on. Maybe here and there a Georgian, an Armenian, but even so—they always knew I was Jewish." And in cases where being a Jew may not have been so self-evident, at school, during university admission exams, on the job, when applying for a driver's license, voting, obtaining an official apartment, entering a hospital or hotel, and at death, note is taken of one's Jewish "nationality," written as it is in all identification documents.

Thus, all a Soviet Jew has to do is present oneself—face, last name, and in the final instance, passport—to demonstrate Jewish identity. Like it or not, a Jew is a Jew and always will be.

Jews in the Soviet Union consider themselves members of a Jewish nationality, not only in terms consistent with Soviet nationalities policy but, more importantly, as one large descent group. Birth into the Jewish people in the Soviet Union guarantees that, as individuals, they will have to be smarter and wilier and work harder to get ahead. The other side of the coin is that it gives to them the rights and obligations of family toward other Jews. It becomes obligatory to treat a fellow Jew as someone special, to protect him and take care of him as one would do for a family member. All the cunning, street-smarts, and sheer intellect that are requisite to making it in the Soviet system should be used to better the lot of one's family, and by extension, the Jewish people:

Solomon Israilevich walked into a store in which there was a long line for milk. He got on the back of the line and waited 30 minutes. When he got to the front he was sent to the back again. After this happened three times, Solomon Israilevich, in a soft angry voice, asked, "What's wrong with you? Are you an anti-Semite?" "No," replied Rabinovich from behind the counter, "the milk is sour."

In short, when Soviet Jews think about what makes them Jewish, they arrive at one certain criterion—being born a Jew. Birth of Jewish parents is necessary and sufficient to claiming membership; having a specific physiognomy, last name, Yiddish-tinged accent or religious beliefs makes one no more and no less Jewish. Being a Jew implies responsibilities—to oneself, to one's family—to be smarter and better than everyone else. It also includes expectations that other Jews will do the same. Soviet Jews arrived in America with these very expectations; remembering how much they endured throughout their lives as Jews in the USSR, they thought that American Jews would welcome them as heroes and greet them as long-lost relatives:

> When I got to New York and was treated as just another body in the bureaucracy I was appalled. I thought—this is a Jewish organization, and they will treat me as one of the family *(kak rodnoi)*.

> When I got to New York, I took the Brooklyn and Manhattan phone books and called everyone with my father's last name and everyone with my mother's last name. No matter that I couldn't speak English, I was just so happy to be here that I thought everyone else in New York who could possibly be my relative would be just as glad as I was!

Thus, being a Jew in the Soviet Union means that outside the Jewish group life is harder, but among Jews one has a family—an assortment of people with whom one can relax, show one's true personality and develop a set of connections through which food, medicine, clothes, and shoes which are everywhere but in stores can be obtained. This family has the responsibility to support those in need, to offer a feeling of belonging, and those who can help must. There is no moral question about deserving support; each Jew is entitled to it simply because of being Jewish.

Being an American Jew

Being a Jew in America[2] is quite a different matter; it is based more on voluntary affiliation than on ascription. Not only can one change name and appearance, but those born of Jewish parents can pass unnoticed into the American mainstream. In fact, the responsibility is placed on the individual to prove one's Jewishness—to join Jewish organizations, to go to synagogue, to close businesses on Jewish holidays, to donate money to Jewish causes. In American society where one's Jewishness is not self-evident, it is necessary to demonstrate, both to the Gentile world and to the Jewish community, that one is a Jew by doing specifically Jewish things.

Being born of Jewish parents[3] is a fundamental component of Jewish identity. Whereas in the Soviet Union, no one's claims to being Jewish are challenged—after all, Jewish "nationality" is a liability there—in America such claims may be carefully examined before Jewish identity is freely conferred:

> We go through their *yikhes* (pedigree; genealogy) very carefully to be sure that not one of their maternal grandmothers or great-grandmothers was a non-Jew. We have even stopped circumcisions on the hospital table,

said an Orthodox rabbi who has worked with Soviet Jewish immigrants. But Jewish ancestry is not *sufficient* for being a "real" Jew. Jews by birth who do not participate in Jewish organizations, do not attend synagogue at least on the most important holidays are chided, "You can't be a Jew just out of a book or just by buying bagels and lox."[4]

Finally, identification with and belief in the Jewish religion is considered requisite to many in determining Jewish status. While certainly New York has its share of secular Jews, they are less numerous and far less outspoken than their religious counterparts. Moreover, for their own ideological reasons, they tend to avoid contact with Soviet Jewish immigrants (Howells 1985:9). On the other hand, the views of Orthodox and Conservative denominations are most often represented in Jewish communal affairs and emphasize the importance of the religious aspect of Jewish identity. "How can they respond to questions about being Jewish?" an influential *rebbetzin* (rabbi's wife) asked about a survey of Soviet Jewish immigrants, "when they haven't any idea of what being Jewish is. Imagine—atheists who say they are Jews! It's like asking a sick man to prescribe his own medicine!"

In short, ways of demonstrating Jewish identity differ in the broader social contexts of the Soviet Union and the United States. In the first case, being Jewish is a self-evident, unquestioned fact which results in discrimination within the wider society and extended kinship rights and obligations within the group. In the second case, being Jewish is highly dependent on knowledge of Judaism, display of this knowledge and participation in Jewish organizations. It is a voluntary social identity for which the accident of birth is necessary but not sufficient (see Herman 1976; Dashevsky and Shapiro 1974; Sklare 1971).

The Ethnic Game Thwarted

The meaning of one's Jewish identity is shaped within a broader sociopolitical context and is manifested by a certain behavioral pattern learned in that context. It was only with contact that American Jews began to doubt the Jewishness of the new immigrants. Prior to their arrival in the United States, American Jews pressed for the right of their Jewish brethren in the Soviet Union to emigrate. Then they activated a network of Jewish social service agencies to assist the resettlement of those who were choosing the United States over Israel as their place of destination.[5] As American Jews found some of the ways Soviet Jews act to be alien, they came to label these behaviors and the individuals associated with them not "Jewish" but "Russian."

First is the matter of how Soviet Jews request assistance at Jewish organizations, from initial contacts at resettlement agencies to local community centers: they tell their social worker or rabbi precisely what they want. They tell them what kinds of apartments, what kinds of jobs and salaries, what kind of schooling for their children they require. They are insistent, and they present their requests as demands that are their due.

"Typical Russian behavior! In order to get through the Russian bureaucracy they had to act like that—pushy, arrogant, aggressive," said staff members at NYANA (New York Association for New Americans), HIAS (Hebrew Immigrant Aid Society) and Federation of Jewish Philanthropies-affiliated agencies. Certainly there is a ring of truth to this explanation, but the immigrants themselves may have believed they were acting "Jewishly," not as "Russians." Certain that America is the land of plenty where anything is possible, especially for an educated, professionally-trained urbanite from a modern country, all they did was relate their needs to their "Jewish family." How else could their American cousins fulfill familial obligations if they weren't told exactly what was wanted?

The expectation on the part of the immigrants was that the Jewish agency would take upon itself the kinship obligation of resettling fellow Jews into the conditions that the immigrants themselves deemed necessary for their future—the very same conditions in which, by and large, American Jews live. Therefore, they very clearly stated their living requirements to let their fellow Jews know how they might fulfill their obligations. The American Jews didn't quite see it that way; they expected these refugees to be oppressed Jews, grateful for the opportunity to come to America and thankful for every piece of advice and for every dollar. Instead they found pushy, aggressive, obnoxious "Russians" wheeling, dealing, and demanding assistance way beyond the wildest dreams of their own parents and grandparents.

Second is the matter of religion and religious expression. Jews in the Soviet Union do not attend synagogue to express their Jewishness; not only were most houses of worship shut in the two decades following World War II, but those that remain open are either showplaces where the officials are monitored by the police (Moscow, Leningrad) or small run-down halls on the edge of town where old men are the only congregants (Odessa, Kiev).

Although public declarations of Jewishness are not made—either by synagogue attendance or by not workong on Jewish holidays—many informants speak about Jewish New Year dinners, Passover meals, and baking *hamentaschen* (a special pastry) for Purim. Jewish holidays are celebrated within the confines of one's home, in private with family, by eating certain foods which are prepared only at those times of year. Some informants tell of going to the synagogues in Moscow and Leningrad when the 1967 Arab-Israeli war broke out and of attending yearly Simchat Torah demonstrations. These were specific, mass demonstrations of Jewish youth, linked to assertions of Jewish pride and the gathering momentum of the emigration movement, not ordinary expressions of Judaism. Quite a few people tell of having stood in line outside synagogues to get matzoh for Passover. This too was recounted as a rather brave act because note was taken of those who showed up at the synagogues and became an item for discussion at work committee meetings as part of *kritika i samokritika* (criticism and self-criticism).

In sum, Soviet Jews, with few exceptions,[6] have, at least for the past forty years, no tradition of regular synagogue attendance. They do, however, mark important Jewish holidays in their homes. Going to synagogue is a political statement, associated with something special and out of the ordinary. It is a rebellious act, a flaunting of one's Jewishness in a society that says the more quiet one is about being a Jew, the better.

In America, synagogue membership, or at least attendance during the most important holidays, is a critical dimension of Jewish life.

From the very first days of arrival in New York, Soviet Jews are brought into synagogues, given holiday workshops, presented with books about Judaism in Russian and entreated to have their sons circumcized. New immigrants are given scholarships so that their children can attend Jewish day schools, and many synagogues offer free one-year memberships.

"Our rabbis and congregations just got fed up," a representative from the Reform movement said, "They invited them to come to a service and then a *kiddush* (reception) afterward—and they came, rushing at the food table like crazy. The second time they sent out invitations again—and again they came. So we figured, now they see what our temples are like, and they can come on their own. And no one came—no food, no invitations, no 'Russians'." An Orthodox woman involved in Jewish acculturation phrased the same sentiment somewhat differently, "We learned that when we put on Jewish activities for the 'Russians' we need to have food and music or else they just won't come. And that we have to get on the phone and call."

American Jews were very disappointed: First, that Soviet Jews decided against going to Israel, and second, that once in America they did not flock to the synagogues to take advantage of the opportunity denied to them in the USSR—expression of their religious beliefs. During the first few years after arrival many immigrants not only did not attend synagogue, but several immigrant businessmen kept their shops open on Jewish holidays. This further infuriated their American neighbors who decided that the "Russians" are really not "Jews" after all.

Thus, although Soviet Jewish immigrants do celebrate Jewish holidays in their homes (Federation of Jewish Philanthropies 1985:27–29), they have not consistently made a public display of their holiday observances. Seeing shops open and seeing immigrants go to and from work on the most holy of days was read by American Jews as non-Jewish behavior, making the immigrants in their minds "Russian atheists."

Third, and most obvious, is language. According to a recent survey of New York's Soviet Jewish immigrants, 85 percent claim Russian as their mother tongue (Federation of Jewish Philanthropies 1985:11). Although almost 40 percent state that they can speak Yiddish, the language immigrants use among themselves is Russian. Most American Jews are native speakers of English, but many were surprised to find that these Russian Jews, unlike those who immigrated at the turn of the century, speak Russian and not Yiddish. Use of the Russian language, added to the unexpectedly demanding

behavior at Jewish agencies and a surprisingly low amount of synagogue attendance on the part of the immigrants[7] combined to shape
American Jews' perception of these Jewish immigrants as "Russians."
For former Soviet citizens who have been Jews since birth and were
in the USSR denied inclusion into the Russian majority, this identity
confusion is the supreme irony of their immigration experience.

Intra-Group Cleavage or Identity Resolution?

As most immigrants from the Soviet Union reject the label
"Russian" (Simon & Simon 1982:75–76; Federation of Jewish Phi-
lanthropies 1985:20) and think of themselves instead as "Jew," they
have two choices: either operate as a separate sub-group (apart from
American Jews) as the Jews that they have learned to be in the
Soviet context, or to incorporate symbols and behaviors defined as
Jewish by American Jews into their repertoires, to "earn" the label
"Jew." Both strategies are now being employed, and a nesting phenomenon (see Moerman 1965) in which a "Russian" identity is
enmeshed within the Jewish one[8] may in fact be the end result of
the immigrants' identity confusion.

Soviet Jewish immigrants have already begun to show movement
toward Americans' understanding of Jewishness. First, jewelry displaying Jewish emblems—stars of David, a *chai* (the Hebrew word
for life), and facsimilies of the Ten Commandants—are often worn
as necklaces by men and women, young and old alike. This is a
visible sign that the immigrants recognize that their Jewishness is in
question, and they proclaim the contrary by prominently displaying
their identity around their necks.

Second, during the 1984 and 1985 high holidays, most immi-
grant-owned shops in Brighton Beach, New York's largest Soviet
Jewish immigrant neighborhood, were closed. On Rosh Hashonah
all of the large shops, the biggest Russian grocery-delicatessens,
beauty salons, bakeries and clothing shops were shut; only some of
the smaller grocery stores remained open. Restaurants, however, were
open in the evening because many immigrant families were celebrating the Jewish New Year there. On Yom Kippur, with one or
two exceptions, all Russian-Jewish businesses were closed.

Third, synagogues in Brighton Beach had modest but noticeable
immigrant attendance during Rosh Hashonah, the Jewish New Year.
On Yom Kippur (Day of Atonement), during *yizker* (remembrance of
the dead) service, however, the synagogues were filled beyond capacity with Russian-speakers. They did not simply listen to the prayer;

they broke out into tears and sobs. Immediately prior to the service, many pledged money for the synagogue.[9]
Finally, more than 35 percent of those immigrants surveyed in New York City stated that they belonged to a YM-YWHA or Jewish Community Center. Over half the members of the Shorefront Y in Brighton Beach are Soviet Jewish immigrants.

There is a fine line, however, between incorporation of some symbols of Jewishness which is acceptable to the immigrant sub-group and a complete makeover which, if crossed, can lead to rejection by the immigrant group. Displaying the makings of a religious Jew overnight is considered unethical, analogous to Soviet Jews spouting the party line louder than their Russian neighbors, embracing hypocrisy to curry favor:

> When this dentist Alex, after a few weeks of not receiving ample assistance to enable him to take necessary dental courses and provide for his wife and children came to our English class wearing a great big yarmulke and announcing that he found an apartment in Boro Park (an Orthodox Jewish neighborhood), we were all in shock. During our break we asked him, "What's going on?" and he just smiled at us. He figured out the system—there it's being a big Communist; here it's being a big Jew. He got his stipend, put his children in Jewish schools at no charge, and got his wife, who has no bigger psychological problems than you or I, SSI.

Parents have told of sending their children to Jewish schools and having terrible inter-generational fights because the children wanted their homes to be kept kosher and for their parents to observe the Sabbath. "Oh, we had big problems with that for a while, and I almost pulled my son out of that school. But then he understood that there are some things we can do and some things we cannot, and I am glad that he is learning about the history and traditions of our Jewish people and that he got those crazy ideas out of his head."

Most immigrants take a middle line in their adoption of American Jewish customs, incorporating symbols and behaviors that do not challenge headlong their own conceptions of being Jewish. Most consider full-fledged makeovers into religious Jews to be hypocritical and/or against their very natures.

At the same time as they are incorporating (American) Jewish symbols into their lives, Soviet Jewish immigrants have been developing parallel institutions in which they have very little contact with American Jewry. About twenty five Brooklyn-based immigrants gather together for discussions and socializing on an informal basis about once a month. They consider themselves "cosmopolitans, Russian intelligentsia"; several of them have non-Jewish spouses, and most have experienced a considerable drop in social status after emigration. Their evenings together usually consist of a presentation, a slide show of someone's recent trip to Europe, a poetry reading, an artist's exhibition or an evening devoted to a singer. These evenings rarely revolve around Jewish themes and are more consciously directed at "maintaining our Russian culture and our Russian circle." But, when hosts or performers call for attention, the neutral *reb'ata* (kids, guys) is often substituted with *evrei* (Jews). In deciding on a monument to an immigrant singer who continued to write in Russian and who this group has linked with a long line of Russian poets and bards, they decided to collect money for an arbor of trees in Israel.

Maintaining an active interest in Russian culture and a Russian-speaking circle of fellow "intelligentsia" requires effort. Being Jewish is an integral part of the identity of most of the members of this network. This identity is understood by all of them, and within the circle it remains precisely what it was in the Soviet Union, passive. This informal group has consciously chosen not to affiliate with any of the "Russian programs" at local Jewish Centers for this, among other reasons.

Another example of parallel institutions is found in Russian restaurants. In the Brighton Beach area there are already eleven. During regular weekend evenings, orchestras play a variety of songs which always includes at least two or three Jewish tunes. In the assortment of appetizers served in the *prix fixe* dinner, Jewish specialties such as gefilte fish, are always included.

Many immigrants opt to have wedding ceremonies and bar/bat mitzvahs in these restaurants. These rituals are vivid examples of syncretism between passive Jewish identity and more active demonstrations of Jewish religion. They also attest to the incorporation of some American symbols of Jewishness into the Russian-Jewish immigrant context.

A small number of Reform rabbis ignore the shrimp and pork served and come to the Russian restaurants to perform these rituals. While the ceremonies usually maintain traditional forms, their contents are greatly altered. The rabbi takes a very active role, announcing and explaining each segment of the rite and encouraging and cajoling the participants at every step of the way. The ritual is a learning experience for the actors and the audience rather than a time-worn presentation that is done simply because it has always been done that way. The rabbi's performance is very much like that of a game show host[10]—enthusiastic, excited, constantly holding the interest of all by calling attention to the participants' beauty, youth, goodness and talents and by explaining precisely what is being done and why. These joyful ceremonies, carried out in shiny, luxurious settings by a clean-shaven, modern-looking rabbi, are very appealing to the immigrants because they allow them to be modern cosmopolitans and Jews at one and the same time—exactly how they see themselves. By explaining the ritual and extolling the virtues of the actors, the immigrants do not feel alienated from the "Judaism" they lost long ago. Instead, they receive a two-fold message from the ritual, first, that they are part of the Jewish people in America; after all, the rabbi himself is an American Jew, and second, that it is fun to be a Jew, a welcome change from the ever-present reminder that "It's hard to be a Jew," one of the compelling reasons they cite for having left the Soviet Union.

In sum, Soviet Jewish immigrants have indeed built some "Russian" institutions of social life that parallel American ones—their restaurants, informal social circles, particular ways of celebrating Jewish holidays and key rites of passage. On the other hand, they have begun to adopt some American symbols of "voluntary Jewishness" such as wearing Jewish emblems as jewelry, shutting businesses on Jewish holidays, joining Jewish communal organizations, having Jewish ceremonies for their children, attending synagogue on important holidays and making contributions to specifically Jewish charities. While Soviet Jewish immigrants by and large have not changed their basic cognitive premise that Jews are a people and not a religion, they are incorporating some religious signs and symbols, as defined by American Jews, into their Jewish repertoires. Although their primary social networks still consist mainly of other immigrants, with these changes in cultural content of Jewishness, the gap between self-ascribed and other-ascribed ethnic identities should diminish.

Conclusions and Implications

In the instrumental sense, the "ethnic game" did in fact work for Soviet Jewish immigrants. Being Jewish by birth, having Jewish nationality, made it possible for them to leave the Soviet Union. American Jews, who strongly lobbied for the right of Jews to emigrate from the USSR (Orbach 1979), provided immediate assistance to the refugees from their first stop in Vienna to several months after arrival in the United States. By virtue of being a stateless refugee fleeing from Communism, each Soviet Jew came to America entitled to an array of social services. Jewish resettlement agencies administered their applications for assistance, provided free English language classes, assisted with job re-training and placement, and helped recent arrivals find apartments. In the beginning, the immigrants' Jewish status was unquestioned, how else could they have left the Soviet Union?

Only with contact did challenges to the immigrants' Jewish identity begin. The behaviors and attitudes described above began to rankle American Jews, not only case workers and rabbis but also the immigrants' neighbors. Jewish Community Councils of many changing neighborhoods throughout New York called NYANA requesting that Soviet Jewish immigrants be sent to them to revitalize their Jewish neighborhoods. The elderly Jews who had been left behind in these neighborhoods were at first happy to see other Jews move in. They quickly developed resentments as they saw "the Russians" amass gold jewelry, decorate their apartments in Italian velour, not go to synagogue and receive government assistance. "You should hear them on the first of the month when their social security checks come in," said a postman in Brighton Beach, "I never thought these sweet old people could be so angry." Although most of the elderly American and Russian Jews are able to communicate with each other in Yiddish, to a large extent they choose not to, and they maintain two distinct linguistic and social circles.

Being Jewish by birth enabled recent immigrants to get a good deal of the instrumental help they required for resettlement. But by fulfilling these needs they were denied the affective side of ethnicity, a feeling of warmth and belonging.

With the passage of several years since Soviet Jews immigrated in large numbers to America (1976–1980) changes have occurred in the cultural content of their Jewish identities to bring them closer to Americans' notions of what is Jewish. They want to belong to the Jewish people, and they resent the imposition of the label "Russian." In many cases, whether it means wearing a Jewish star on a chain around one's neck or having a bar mitzvah for one's son, the immigrants are incorporating many signs and behaviors of American Jewishness into their cultural repertoires. At the same time, their basic cognitive premise of who they are and their ties to the Soviet-Russian context in which they grew up are still strong.

Ethnic change occurs when people undergo radical shifts in sociopolitical contexts which undermine their commonsense, epistemological bases of everyday life. "People often respond to these changes in terms of their established ethnic identities, but find these identities, either in their cultural content or because of the assumptions of who shares the same identities, are not appropriate in the new situation" (Keyes 1981:28). For Soviet Jewish immigrants, the disconnection between their own ethnic identity and that foisted upon them in the American environment is still unresolved. In looking for an attachment to a group in a primary, primordial way, they are discovering avenues of Jewish expression that can lead to the affective ties and sense of belongingness that they have wanted with American Jews.

Ethnic identities require signs and symbols to give them salience. While the media may have brought all peoples throughout the world closer together, geographic mobility and ethnic dispersal have had the opposite effect, resulting in symbolic breakdowns between people claiming the same identity. The case of Jews from the Soviet Union being denied the label "Jew" in the United States is just one of many. In our examinations of ethnicity it is necessary to analyze how "cultural stuff," shaped in specific contexts, gives salience and meaning to these labels and in large part determines the outcome of ethnic interactions. Change in content is not haphazard and must be carefully considered in developing theories of ethnic group persistence, boundary maintenance, and ethnic change.

Notes

1. This paper is a revision of a paper with the same title first presented at the session on Contemporary Jewry during the Annual Meetings of the American Anthropological Association, Washington, D.C., on December 5, 1985 under the name of Fran Markowitz Baskin.

Funding for the research reported herein was generously provided by a FLAS fellowship from the Center for Russian and East European Studies, University of Michigan, a grant-in-aid from the Wenner-Gren Foundation for Anthropological Research and by NIMH's National Research Service Award # 3 F31 MH09168–01S1.

I am very grateful to the many people who patiently answered my questions and included me in their friendship circles and family life. I am especially indebted to Misha, Sasha, Zhenya, and Lina. Thanks too go to William G. Lockwood, Mark Baskin and Eva Huseby-Darvas who read an earlier draft of this paper and offered valuable comments.

2. In this paper, Jewish America is confined to New York where Jews constitute a large plurality of the population and have succeeded in making major Jewish holidays school holidays as well. Further, it focuses primarily on the affiliated Jewish community because these are the American Jews with whom Soviet Jewish immigrants have the most contact.

3. Traditionally Jewish status is conferred matrilineally. In the USSR the child can choose the "nationality" of either parent. Some Reform rabbis in the USA recognize patrilineally-based claims to Jewish status.

4. Quoting Samuel Breidner, headmaster of the new Liberal Jewish Day School, in *The Jewish Week*, August 23, 1985, p. 16. Certainly many New York Jews are precisely that—"bagels and lox Jews"—but the affiliated Jewish community urges them to add deeper dimensions to their Jewishness.

5. Since 1976, when 49 percent of emigrating Soviet Jews opted for destinations other than Israel, more than one half have been coming to the United States (Gitelman 1982:4).

6. The exceptions are some Georgian and Central Asian (Tat or Mountain) Jews whose relative isolation among more tolerant non-Russian national groups allowed their religious and cultural traditions to continue with a minimal amount of disturbance.

7. Interestingly enough, Soviet Jewish immigrants' rate of synagogue attendance is not dissimilar from that of Americans' overall (Federation of Jewish Philanthropies 1985:31). The expectation, however, that they would rush to participate in the religious life denied them in the USSR, coupled with the fact that many immigrants live in older, more traditional Jewish neighborhoods where synagogue attendance rates are high, have contributed to an impression that Soviet Jewish immigrants do not go to synagogue at all.

8. Or, to a lesser extent, as in the case of the group described (p. 14–15) and others like them, Jewish may be enmeshed in the broader "Russian" identity. In both cases, Jewish identity remains strong.

9. The *kaddish* (prayer for the dead) here is one which is chanted at the Yom Kippur memorial (Yizkor) service. It remains salient for Soviet Jews; many have told of hiring old men for 1–5 rubles to intone this prayer over their parents' graves. At Yom Kippur, memories of dead loved ones buried in the USSR are called forth and all the other associations of having been a Soviet Jew. It is a powerful symbol, evoking very strong emotions.

10. Among many immigrants' favorite television programs is "Family Feud," hosted by the ebullient Richard Dawson.

References

Barth, Fredrik
    1969a   Introduction. In *Ethnic Groups and Boundaries*, edited by Fredrik Barth. Boston: Little, Brown: 9–38.
    1969b   Pathan Identity and Its Maintenance. In *Ethnic Groups and Boundaries*, edited by Fredrik Barth. Boston: Little, Brown: 117–134.

Bell, Daniel
1975   Ethnicity and Social Change. In *Ethnicity, Theory and Experience*, edited by Nathan Glazer and Daniel Patrick Moynihan. Cambridge: Harvard University Press: 141–174.

Berreman, Gerald D.
1975   Bazer Behavior: Social Identity and Social Interaction in Urban India. In *Ethnic Identity*, edited by George De Vos and Lola Romanucci-Ross. Palo Alto: Mayfield: 71–105.

Cohen, Abner
1969   *Customs and Politics in Urban Africa: A Study of Hausa Migrants in Yoruba Towns*. London: Routledge & Kegan Paul.

Dashevsky, Arnold and Howard M. Shapiro
1974   *Ethnic Identity Among American Jews*. Lexington, Mass.: Lexington Books.

Duran, James J.
1974   The Ecology of Ethnic Groups from a Kenyan Perspective. *Ethnicity* 1: 43–64.

Federation of Jewish Philanthropies of New York
1984   *The Jewish Population of Greater New York: A Profile*. New York: Federation of Jewish Philanthropies.

Federation of Jewish Philanthropies of New York/Fran Markowitz Baskin
1985   *Jewish Identification and Affiliation of Soviet Jewish Immigrants in New York City—A Needs Assessment and Planning Study*. New York: Federation of Jewish Philanthropies of New York.

Gitelman, Zvi
1982   Soviet Resettlement in the United States. *Soviet Jewish Affairs* 12, 2: 3–18.

Glazer, Nathan and Daniel Patrick Moynihan
1963/70   *Beyond the Melting Pot*. Cambridge: MIT Press.

Herman, Simon N.
1976   *Jewish Identity: A Social Psychological Perspective*. Beverly Hills: Sage.

Howells, Polly
1985   Bad Jews, Good Jews: A Story of Soviet Jewish Immigrants in the Promised Land. *In These Times* (Sept. 11–15): 8–9.

Keyes, Charles F.
1981   The Dialectics of Ethnic Change. In *Ethnic Change*, edited by Charles F. Keyes. Seattle: University of Washington Press: 4–52.

Kim, Illsoo
1981   *New Urban Immigrants: The Korean Community in New York*. Princeton: Princeton University Press.

Light, Ivan
1972   *Ethnic Enterprise in America.* Berkeley & Los Angeles: University of California Press.

Lockwood, William G.
1975   *European Moslems: Economy and Ethnicity in Western Bosnia.* New York: Academic Press.

Moerman, Michael
1965   Ethnic Identity in a Complex Society: Who Are the Lue? *American Anthropologist* 67: 1215–1230.

Nagata, Judith A.
1974   What is a Malay? Situational Selection of Ethnic Identity in a Plural Society. *American Ethnologist* 1: 331–350.

Orbach, William W.
1979   *The American Movement to Aid Soviet Jews.* Amherst: University of Massachusetts Press.

Patterson, Orlando
1975   Context and Choice in Ethnic Allegiance: A Theoretical Framework and Caribbean Case Study. In *Ethnicity, Theory and Experience,* edited by Nathan Glazer and Daniel Patrick Moynihan. Cambridge: Harvard University Press: 305–349.

Plotnicov, Leonard
1967   *Strangers to the City: Urban Man in Jos, Nigeria.* Pittsburgh: University of Pittsburgh Press.

Shibutani, Tamotsu and Kian M. Kwan.
1965   *Ethnic Stratification: A Comparative Approach.* New York: Macmillan.

Simon, Rita J. and Julian J. Simon
1982   *The Soviet Jews' Adjustment to the U.S.: Report of A Study.* New York: Council of Jewish Federations.

Sklare, Marshall
1971   *America's Jews.* New York: Random House.

Thompson, Bobby and John H. Peterson, Jr.
1975   Mississippi Choctaw Identity: Genesis and Change. In *The New Ethnicity, Perspectives from Ethnology,* edited by John W. Bennett. St. Paul, MN: West: 179–196.

5 Learning to Be a Part-Time Jew

David Schoem

Nowhere is the ambivalence which North American Jews feel towards their heritage better illustrated than in the way in which Jewish educational institutions are supported. Hebrew schools can constitute a large part of congregational budgets. Yet Jewish schools, both day and afternoon, are underfunded and the teachers are underpaid. Jewish children are forced to attend while the parents subvert the lessons of the schools. Schoem's ethnography of a West Coast Hebrew school shows how such equivocality is communicated to children preparing for bar and bat mitzvah. He also compares this Hebrew school to other such ethnic educational institutions and finds that the contradictory pattern of seeking to impart the ancestral heritage while striving to conform to the American way of life is shared. Sociological studies suggest that what Schoem has found on the West Coast exists throughout North America.

"What is a *Shofar?*"[1] asked the Jewish afternoon school teacher at the start of the new school year. The seventh grade class sat without emotion, no one attempting to identify this symbol of the Jewish New Year season. "I know," one student finally called out." A *Chauffeur*[2] (sic) is the person who drives your car around."

Caught in the pull of two cultural worlds, the teacher and the student speak in two different languages. Although the student's answer is inappropriate for this lesson at the Jewish afternoon school (or Hebrew School), it is the more meaningful term to both the teacher and the student once they leave class at the end of the day. For them, what occurs each day as they enter the complementary Jewish afternoon school is an uncomfortable "stepping in and out" of cultures. Although as Jews they share a history and tradition spanning thousands of years, it is not the teacher's "shofar" but the student's "chauffeur" that plays a more significant role in their lives in America.

This paper examines the conflicts and dilemmas that the Jewish people in America face as an ethnic minority group[3] in their attempt to survive in their struggle to balance ethnic authenticity with societal

96

integration. Employing the assumption that schooling serves as an agent of cultural transmission (Spindler 1976) and that it reflects the society in which it exists, the study focuses on a Jewish school and its community. The Jewish afternoon school is an example of the complementary ethnic and/or religious school. Berkson (1920) has explained the functioning of the complementary school, saying, "Each system of schools would insure the integrity of the community which supports it; the public schools would further the society of the state; the religious and ethnic schools, the society of minority communities."

Research Methodology

Choosing a school raises difficult though important conceptual and methodological questions. In thinking about studying a school, one obviously does not wish to study the school per se but rather the school within a much broader socio-cultural context. To begin to correctly define the school, one needs to go beyond its physical and written attributes to the people themselves, their thoughts, and their actions. The principal, the teachers, and most important, the students were all part of what constituted the school. In addition, the interaction of these individuals and groups with one another and with the material units of the school added the substantive "living" element of what this school was and what it was about (Blumer 1969).

Nevertheless, these official, or perhaps, contractual partners of the school still represented only a partial picture of even the immediate social fabric. It was necessary to study each of these segments of the school or what one might refer to as the "community of the school" in order to develop a holistic view. Not to be forgotten were the school board, who acted as overseers of the principal; the synagogue and its board of directors, which ultimately operated and funded the school; the rabbi, who had substantial formal and informal influence on the school; the parents, who chose to send their children to the school; and the regional and national educational networks and organizations with which this school was associated.

Finally, the many components of the school and its community were influenced by elements of an even broader social-cultural context essential to the study of the Jewish people. It was important to understand the religious and ethnic traditions and the history of the Jewish people as well as the origins of this particular community of Jews. It was essential to understand the place of Jews as a minority within history, their historical place as a minority within American society, and their place and socio-economic standing within the community they now lived. It was necessary to know what role Jewish education had played in the history of the Jewish people and to ask what kind of life the Jews of this community led when they were not concerned with Jewish schooling or synagogue issues and events.[4] Education has always been a central part of Jewish life, and the Jewish afternoon school, which was created in the 1920s, was developed by Jewish cultural pluralists as an example of the supplementary ethnic school. While the reference "school" could at its most minimalist definition mean no more than the internal and external attributes of the physical plant, such a working definition would severely curtail any hope of understanding Jewish life in a deeper, more comprehensive fashion. Goodlad (1977) has pointed out that even in regard to a study of curriculum, one would depart with a very limited picture if the written curriculum were studied alone without the study of the curriculum as it is perceived, operationalized, and experienced. For this study to be thorough, it needed to be both micro (Burnett 1976) and macro (Ogbu 1981) in purpose. What needed to be studied was not only the internal operation of the school, but also the community of the school and the school community in society.

The specific school chosen for this study was known as a "very good" elementary afternoon school and one which was attached to a "conservative" Jewish synagogue in a suburb of a large metropolitan area on the west coast of the United States. It was important to study a positive example of these schools and one that was statistically typical of a very high percentage of Jewish schools in America. Further, it became clear that the research would best be served by conducting an ethnographic study. An ethnographic approach was chosen because it is best for gathering data on incidents and histories and on norms and statuses (Zelditch 1962), and would allow for "face-to-face" knowing (Lofland 1971), in depth and detailed analysis, and a holistic view.

Data was collected over a period of one school year using participant observation and in-depth interviews. The researcher was present at all school sessions as well as at other school and community-related events in the role of participant-as-observer (Gold 1958). Eighty interviews, ranging from twenty minutes to two hours were conducted with students, school staff, school board members, and parents. Theoretical sampling was used to determine who would be interviewed, employing the techniques of quota sampling, snowball sampling, and deviant sampling. Informal interviewing was also used frequently as part of the researcher's role as participant observer.

Although the school included classes for students from ages five to sixteen, this study focused on students in the school aged nine to thirteen. Classroom observations were focused on grades four through seven. For the purpose of comparison, observations for approximately one week were made at two reform and one orthodox afternoon schools, and at one Japanese and one Native-American afternoon school. In addition, the researcher collected various school and synagogue documents that were made available to him, such as curricular materials, budget reports, and memos. Finally, the researcher himself is a Jewish male. The school met two afternoons (1½ hr. each) and one Sunday morning (2½ hr.) each week although one of the afternoon sessions was optional. Approximately two hundred fifty students were enrolled in this school. The curriculum in general conformed with the standard curriculum of the Conservative movement.

One Day at School

After a full day of work and study, Steven, Suzanne, Marcy and Moshe, four of the teachers at the school, gather to drive together to Hebrew School. In their carpool, these four tired souls talk about and analyze their experiences at the school and also prepare themselves for the upcoming session. Their mood is one of frustration and anger and the tone of their comments ranges from caustic humor to thoughtful resignation. One teacher, Steven, reflects on his experience at the school, saying:

> I had some faith in it in September, but I didn't realize how futile and frustrating it would be until I was here for awhile. Within two weeks I realized I had made a mistake. If I made the commitment, though, I wasn't going to break it . . . I have never worked with a more difficult group of kids in any setting. They are a very wild, very rowdy, very hyperactive bunch of kids.

As is usually the case, the topic of the parents immediately follows talk about the students themselves. In the same bitter tone, Suzanne continues:

> They have no respect for us whatsoever . . . In a community such as this where status values are firmly connected with financial success, this is a job for schmucks. And the kids know it, too. I mean, it's absolutely beyond them that we could be anything besides Hebrew School teachers.

For the students, their day at public school blends into their afternoon at Hebrew School. They feel tired from sitting in class all day only to have to rush to get to Hebrew School on time. If they are lucky, they are able to get home for a very quick snack before their mothers drive them to school. Some students try not to think about what lies ahead for them in the afternoon school; others, who do, think about being with their Jewish friends, but being bored by both the content and instruction of the classroom. Anticipating the approaching session that afternoon, one girl, Hannah, says:

> And no one listens. We just draw pictures and stuff and the teacher talks to himself. He knows what he's talking about, but we don't.

Most students arrive at school between 3:55 and 4:05. School officially begins at 4:00. They talk and play among themselves, fantasizing about futuristic aircraft, remembering sports events, whispering and giggling about boys, girls, doing public school homework, or just wandering around the building. The teachers arrive in a rush by 4:10, apologizing to the principal and running to their classes. By this time of the year some students feel they can accurately describe what will occur in school on any given day. A cynical seventh grader, Andy, relates the following:

> You go in and you find no one is in the classroom. This is at four o'clock. So you decide to walk around, find another kid or something. And then you get back and it's ten minutes late. And the teacher says, 'Why are you late?' But you were already there on time. And then you sit down and have a discussion about how if you are ever late again they will have to call your parents. But they never call the parents. And then usually the teacher reads something from a book. About twenty minutes into it, the recess questions begin. Then you go out for recess and come back a little late, same as before class. Class continues; people listen to what's worth listening to—either the teacher or a friend. I fool around with a pencil. And that goes on the rest of the day.

When Steven, the teacher, actually arrives in his classroom on this day, he finds his students relaxing in their chairs, most already bored in anticipation of the lesson to follow, a few feeling feisty and antagonistic, and a few ready to listen. Since Steven has prepared for only half of the lesson time, he decides to use his other time to discuss a recent PLO raid in Israel. Shortly after he begins, about 4:15, the principal walks in, looking very harassed after once again having had a rather tense discussion with her administrative assistant. She gives Steven flyers for the students announcing an event at the synagogue. The students begin to talk while the principal is there and their talk grows louder when she leaves.

Steven attempts to begin his discussion again but is upset at the noise and lack of interest. He warns the students that he takes this subject very seriously and that he will get very angry with them if they continue to make jokes. At 4:20, the school board chairperson opens the door, smiles at the teacher, looks around the classroom, and then leaves. The students all turn around to watch her.

Steven decides to change the focus of his discussion and asks the students what the word "Tzedakah" means to them. No one answers. He then begins lecturing on a related subject when Judy, one of his students, finally raises her hand to answer the original question. "Oh yeah," she says, "You mean Neil Sedaka."

At 4:25 Steven decides to begin the lesson that he has prepared on Siddur, the prayer book. Although he thinks the subject is important, he is critical of the way the administration wants him to teach it. He also is aware that the students do not find it interesting. He thinks to himself:

> They expect you to teach the kids the prayers by heart. But the minute you bring the prayerbooks out, the kids turn off their interest.

Indeed, the class responds as expected. As he takes out the book, one boy appears to be sleeping, another is playing with his eraser, a third is stuck in a contorted position having tangled and twisted himself in his chair.

At 4:35 another teacher walks in looking for books for her class. The two teachers talk for a moment and she leaves empty-handed. At 4:38, a sixth grade student comes in looking for his class. He is sent away. By 4:40, through insult, intimidation, and persistence, Steven has finally quieted down his class. The students read the same prayer aloud, one by one. The teacher helps them with their many mistakes in reading the Hebrew. By 4:45 several questions regarding recess and "what time is it" have already been asked and, after threatening to withhold recess, Steven excuses his students at 4:50.

Recess gives students and teachers alike time to socialize and recuperate. Two teachers, Marcy and Rivka, come by the classroom of the one being described. The teachers alternately speak (and complain) in Hebrew and English, using Hebrew exclusively when students walk by. Marcy describes an unpleasant incident that occurred in her class that day. She is not happy with the support she has received from the principal and remarks:

> We've been trying to throw this person out for five weeks without any success. Laurie [the principal] couldn't even get the student to leave the room. If the principal doesn't get respect, then the teachers can't get respect.

Rivka, nodding her head in agreement and support, adds a comment reflecting her own experience. She says: "I don't want to do this; why am I here?"

At the same time, the rabbi, school board chairperson, and administrative assistant have gathered in a room where the principal is making a phone call. Discipline is on their minds, too, and one says to the other:

> I think it is disturbing that a Hebrew School has discipline problems. It makes me sad. You would hope that we would be a different caliber of people. I think there's something basically wrong in the world. There's uncertainty. Expenses are very high. People may have to move because of their jobs. The rabbi is doing more and more counseling.

After recess, at 5 p.m., the students return to class and Steven begins to talk about a period of Jewish history. During the next half hour some students play with their wristwatches, others doodle, some make paper airplanes and a few busy themselves by making weird noises. Still other students spend their time passing notes, whispering, kicking one another, or just staring off into space. After 5:15 students become very anxious about knowing the exact time, ("What time is it?"), and questions about dismissal ("When do we leave?") begin. By 5:25 many students have already closed their books and packed their school belongings. They then begin putting on their overcoats and at 5:30 are finally dismissed.

The School Setting

There were some identifiable benefits that were attributable to the Jewish afternoon school. The very fact of the school's existence and the fact that parents required their children to attend the school, even if their concern was not with the substance or quality of the program, called attention to the parents' and children's identification as Jews (Schoem, 1983). Even if they learned an ambiguous message about the meaning of being Jewish for their lives, the children did learn very clearly that they were, in fact, apart, different, and not Christian, but Jewish. Although Himmelfarb (1974), and Dashefsky and Shapiro (1974) have worried whether there are indeed any long term effects of the Jewish afternoon school, this observer was aware of positive, immediate effects, such as an often positive identification of oneself as part of the Jewish people and Israel, and an ability to assert that identification and defend oneself more assuredly against negative comments and difficult situations at secular school and in other predominantly non-Jewish settings.

Parents, too, indicated that they "benefited" to some extent from their children's attendance at the Jewish school despite their less-than-passionate interest in school activities, curriculum, and financial support. The act of sending their children to the school not only fulfilled for them the parental mitzvah of "teach it to your children" but also forced them to face their own identification as Jews at unexpected moments as when arguing with their children that they could not skip class or "chauffering" their children to the school, or paying the school fees. For some parents, their children's attendance at the Jewish school even gave them an excuse or a stimulus to actually renew their own learning and involvement in Jewish life.

Nevertheless, despite the school's value in helping Jews identify as Jews, in time, money, attitude, and commitment, the Hebrew School was a part-time endeavor. The few hours that the school met represented that time when Jews of this community "stepped out" of their daily lives to be and to act Jewish. Being Jewish, except for their survival fears, was indeed a part-time concern. So, too, were most people only concerned about the school in terms of maintenance and survival, while putting it out of their minds most other times. One school board member described the degree of their concern:

> Parents are not very interested in religious school unless there is a crisis. For instance, they did come for the seventh grade meeting [an emergency meeting]. They stopped their tennis games and came. But I don't think there has been much communication beyond that.

When students talk about "school" among themselves, the reference was always to their public school, never the Hebrew School. One student who no longer attended Hebrew School explained that "when I went, Hebrew school didn't really count—oh, it's just Hebrew School." A seventh grader also spoke of the limited value attached to Hebrew School:

> It doesn't really matter to me. If we learned something really interesting, then, maybe, I would want to go more. But the way it is now, I'd rather go bowling.

A third student commented that she was "not even sure all the teachers want to be there."

Because it was an experience that was not integrated into their daily lives, the school was described by both students and parents as being inconvenient in that it interfered with their daily routine. The Sunday morning hours deprived students of their free time and the weekday after-school hours prevented them from participating in public school sports and clubs or from doing as their non-Jewish friends did at that time. Describing the problem of weekday classes, one student said:

> It's too long. You get home from school and then right away you have to go to Hebrew School. And then you eat dinner, and sometimes there's no time for homework.

Living in the business world of capitalist America, the congregational board saw to it that the synagogue's finances were organized according to business principles. It was permissible for the rabbi and principal, etc. to talk about Jewish values, but only after the financial structure was secured according to business values.

Using this business sense, the members of the congregation board viewed the school as a costly drain of dollars, particularly for a part-time program whose financial return, at best, was only the bar/bat mitzvah. Their monetary investment, therefore, was aimed at school maintenance rather than educational excellence. By refusing to equate in any sense, educational quality with monetary expense, the school went along with underemployed teachers, inadequate facilities, and limited numbers of employees until the very survival of the school came into question. At that point, small adjustments were made to insure its survival, yet the board's primary consideration continued to be one of: "We can fill the market cheap."

Given a part-time staff, the school was led by people who necessarily had other full-time concerns. One teacher, who had two other part-time teaching jobs, a weekend youth group position, and attended college full-time, remarked, "I sleep in my spare time." Another teacher, who was resentful that she had "no time for myself," ranked her teaching position after her half-time sales and her full-time studies. Another teacher worked part-time as a construction worker; a fourth was a full-time doughnut shop clerk; a fifth bought and opened a restaurant during the course of the school year. One teacher explained that she took the teaching position at this Hebrew School only "because I don't have another job. I like to teach but I would prefer an all-day school or public school," she said. As a result of their busy schedules and the demands of their more full-

time concerns, adequate classroom preparation, even any at all, was
an infrequent occurrence for many. Often the day's lesson plan was
created in the carpool while driving to work. The principal, too, was
bound by another half-time position. After working for four years
in a full-time capacity but at half-time pay, she had finally decided
to work where she would be paid for her extra time. However,
limiting her time at Hebrew School more closely to the agreements
of her contract left many things undone that she felt were essential.
Envisioning herself as a full-time person, she said, "if we could have
family weekend retreats, take the kids to Israel, have weekend retreats,
field trips—but as a part-time person I can't do it."

Finally, the limited meeting hours of school—two or three times
per week for a total of four to five and one-half hours—created
additional difficulties. For one thing, there was a rushed sense about
the school. The lack of time made it difficult for deep relationships
to develop between student and teacher, teacher and teachers, principal and teacher, etc. Directions, instructions, even casual conversation were conducted in a hurried manner. Class projects that initially
drew interest from students became boring to them as it took weeks
and weeks to accomplish tasks that demanded only a few hours.
Teachers found themselves almost immediately falling behind in
material that they already realized could be taught in only the most
superficial manner. Considerable time was spent every class session
reviewing that which the students did not learn in their previous
lessons. The limited time also inhibited the possibility of intensity
or deep involvement in any class session, as did the hungry and
tired feeling students had on weekdays coming after a full day of
studying in public school. One fifth grade student remarked:

> At public school we do things all day: I really get into it. Hebrew
> School is too short to get into it. It's hard to go to Hebrew School
> after public school.

In a never ending cycle, these part-time temporal and material
constraints fed and reinforced the part-time attitudes and assumptions
that in turn refueled the temporal and material constraints ad infin-
itum. The limited emotional investment in the school led to a limited
monetary investment which led to a "looseness" in administrative
policies and standards. That was reinforced by inadequate facilities
and part-time employment which led to inadequate and unprepared
teachers and students who came without interest and left bored.
Although the school did play a positive role in the children's and
parents' identification as Jews, there was an implicit understanding

that a full-time commitment could not or would not be made to a part-time program, particularly one that was only a part-time concern.

Surprisingly, this school compared quite favorably with the other Jewish and other ethnic schools that the researcher observed. Although the other observations were for a considerably shorter period of time, this Jewish school appeared to the observer to be at least as well organized as the other Jewish schools and, in most cases, much better organized. In the area of student behavior, this school, despite the many problems described in this paper, compared favorably to the others. In the areas of curriculum, materials, supervision, and parental involvement, this Jewish school was better organized, better supplied, more attentive, and more involved than the others.

At the suburban Japanese American school, the researcher was told that the primary goal for the handful of students present was to re-educate them so that they would be aware that they were Japanese, i.e. not to fully explore their culture, but to explain to and convince the young children that they were not from a white Anglo-Saxon Protestant heritage like all the children around them in their suburban neighborhoods and schools. This school's curriculum was comprised solely of language instruction. The Native American school received funding from the State and was held at a public school after school hours. However, the researcher was informed by the school director that this school was in jeopardy of closing because so few of the many Native American families in the suburban county were willing to publicly identify themselves as Native-Americans.

The Larger Socio-Cultural Context

Underlying much of what took place at the Jewish afternoon school was the assumption that an authentic and all-embracing Jewish "Way of Life" was a viable, actual, and desirable lifestyle for Jews in America. The rabbi and principal developed the curriculum, the teachers conducted their classes, and many of the parents sent their children to the school with the implicit understanding that underlying what was learned in the classroom was a Jewish culture and "Way of Life" to which that learning could be used, experienced, developed, and enriched. Furthermore, the staff and many parents of the school approached this classroom instruction and their children's education with the full belief that they, in their own lives, embodied this Jewish "Way of Life."

The Jewish "Way of Life," although never explicitly defined, implied some practice beyond the mere ability to identify and acknowledge one's historical roots. It suggested a continuity of the historical into the present so that one acted and thought in an ongoing and encompassing cultural present. It stated that one formed feelings, beliefs, values, and thoughts according to a framework of Jewish knowledge and understanding. The staff and many parents of the school assumed, therefore, that what was taught was actual, not historical, and that it was representative of many Jews in their communities and throughout America.

Despite the transcending presence of the Jewish "Way of Life" assumption with the school, the Jews of this community were unable to be more explicit in defining a Jewish "Way of Life" because they had only the vaguest notion of the content of a "Jewish Code" or of a "framework of Jewish knowledge and understanding." Furthermore, not all the adults of this school community shared that Jewish Way of Life assumption and, among those who did, there was often sharp disagreement.[5]

The daily lives of both the staff and the parents did not correspond to either the teachings of the classroom or the assumption of the Jewish Way of Life. In the classroom, the staff members acted as models for what were not their true lives. They did not strictly observe holidays—some even forgot them; they did not go to religious services except infrequently—some had altogether rejected prayer; with few exceptions they did not study or plan to study the classic Jewish texts in their adult lives; some did not even wish to live in or near a so-called "Jewish neighborhood." What did take priority in their lives were things more typical of Americans living in an upper middle class suburban community and of college graduates beginning their pursuit of professional careers. In fact, many of the teachers were even struggling with the practicality or relevance of Judaism for their modern American lifestyles. One teacher said,

> The question is, can you live as a Jew in this world: It's antithetical to urbanism, modernism . . . Judaism doesn't go with the political, social, economic values of American life. It's not the way we grow up here. It's antithetical to our whole existence in this country.

Yet this questioning attitude did not enter the classroom. The same questioning teacher, who reported that she did not use "Torah,[8] Bible or prayer" in her personal life, told the researcher that this was precisely what she taught at the school, "Torah, Bible, prayer— I wouldn't know how else to teach Hebrew School."

This inconsistency was not unusual among the staff. It seemed that they were unable to either integrate their Jewish "self" with their American "self" or to appreciate the inconsistency. Another teacher reported that her goal in the school was to "teach them enough Hebrew and prayer so that they can take part in prayers, holidays, and synagogue activities." However, this same teacher had the following to say about her own observances: "I feel uncomfortable in the synagogue and my husband is not interested—so we go very rarely." A third teacher, who in the classroom stressed the importance of adherence to ritual observance of Jewish holidays, said of her personal life, "My Jewishness is not that important to me. I won't close myself off to it, but I'm just not into it now."

The parents' behavior resembled the teachers'. Their expectations for the school and assumptions about their own lives as Jews were quite different from the lives they actually led. The contrast is evident in the following comments of a parent regarding a) the school and her children, and b) Jewish observance at home.

a) I wanted them to begin to sound Jewish. I wanted to hear Jewish songs being sung. I wanted to hear as part of their vocabulary words that are part of their religion.

b) I try to remember to light the Shabbos (Jewish Sabbath) candles, but with working and subbing (substitute teaching), sometimes we forget. And sometimes we eat out on Friday night because the whole week has been exhausting.

Few parents active in the school led lives that were any different from this parent. Most of these people had left family behind (strong family ties was often stated as being a Jewish value strongly held by these parents) in other cities and states to come to this community so they could earn more money at a job and have a higher standard of living. They did not regularly observe the Sabbath, or come to synagogue to pray, or study Jewish texts, speak Hebrew, or sing Hebrew songs. During one interview, a father and his son had the following exchange just as the father had been describing his active involvement in Jewish life:

Father: It's (Judaism) just in us. It's a tradition that's in us. For instance, we observe the holidays.
Son: You just watch football on TV.
Father: What do you mean?
Son: On Saturdays (the Jewish Sabbath) you just watch TV.
Father: Son, you don't know what you're talking about—that's not a holiday.

Here, in truth, it was the father who didn't know what he was talking about.

The students, most of whom were forced by parents to attend this non-compulsory (by state law) school, found that the classroom instruction was foreign to their lives. Certainly, the presumed behavior of the Jewish Way of Life was not something they themselves did or were accustomed to seeing done in their own community. Classes in which they learned prayers or about the Sabbath had little meaning for these students who only infrequently went to the synagogue to pray or never observed the Sabbath. One student expressed deep-felt confusion with the purpose and relevance for her own life of what she was learning at the afternoon school. It was with resentment that she said:

> Like even if our class learned Hebrew, where are we ever gonna speak it—y'know, you're not around enough—2½ hours—to learn a language anyway. Public school is important because that could do with getting a job or something. But with Hebrew School that's not gonna have anything to do with . . . well, if you learn—but what's it gonna have to do with when you get older. What do you care if Moses crossed the sea or something. I don't care.

The students, like this one, knew very clearly in their own minds that their own lives and their parents' lives were just like those of the non-Jewish families in the neighborhood. In addition, the students did not share the Jewish Way of Life assumption of the school, and many of them found their parents' inconsistency hypocritical. Furthermore, they were angry that they should have to be the ones to bear the burden of their parents' Way of Life assumption by having to go to the afternoon school. Many of the students, particularly the older ones, became disruptive in the school as a result. A well-behaved but sympathetic student explained,

> 'Cause people just don't want to go. If they had something good to look forward to maybe they would want to come. But they just know it's gonna be bad; so they start out bad and they just stay bad the whole time.

The students' disruptive behavior often reached proportions that made it difficult for teachers to teach as they would have liked. The parents at the same time grew tired of listening to their children's complaints about the school. There was a general consensus that all was not right in the school. However, the staff and the parents did not consider their common cultural conflicts in assigning blame for the problems at the school. The parents insisted that the problems of the school could be solved with a more dedicated and better trained staff; the staff lay the root of the problem with the home environment of the parent, arguing that it did not reinforce what was being taught at school.

Over the course of the school year, classroom problems only increased and the conflict, too, grew more intense. The staff became increasingly frustrated—some resigned; the parents became angrier and demanded that some staff not be rehired. Ugly gossip and rumors were whispered about. Throughout these arguments, however, the pressing dilemma of these Jews, an ethnic minority in America trying desperately to live with integrity in two cultural worlds and trying to transmit that cultural integrity to their children, never surfaced. Rather, the issue at hand was considered a school problem, and from their experience in the public schools, these people felt they knew how to handle school problems.

Without any apparent connection between the two, the staff and parents lived their "suburban American" lives one way, but, in the afternoon school, they spoke, acted, and seemingly believed in quite a different way. Both staff and parents cherished and admired the Way of Life assumed in the afternoon school, but they were unwilling and/or unable in their own "suburban American" lives to integrate that living model. Furthermore, even in the face of these serious conflicts in the school, neither group was willing to confront the obvious discrepancies that they perpetuated at home and in the classroom. To the student and to the outside observer, these inconsistencies were readily apparent, but to the parents and staff of the school the mask of deception was inpenetrable.

Dilemmas of Cultural Pluralism

The work, the routines, the goals, the values, and the emotions of both the staff and parents seemed tied to a system that appeared little different from that of the non-Jews residing around them. Although these Jews did identify with a Jewish people, history, culture, and religion, they did so largely out of a survivalistic concern and they did not in their own "suburban American" lives maintain a Jewish identity of any substance or live according to any Jewish Way of Life. It wasn't that these Jews didn't want to be living a Jewish Way of Life, but, rather, they seemed to find the demands of modern life uncompromising. The Jewish Way of Life, as they understood or misunderstood it for their own lives, could not serve as a standard for living that suited the modern circumstances of life in America. The Jewish things they did were set apart from their routine of life. Being Jewish meant "stepping out" of one's life some few hours every week or month to maintain an identification with one's heritage. For these Jews, Judaism was positive and important and, at the same time, historical.

Many of the parents and staff explained their reasons for not partaking in the Jewish Way of Life as being based on individual problems. Different people spoke of being lazy, of being too busy, of going through a phase of being uninterested or of feeling uncomfortable because they were not properly educated in Judaica. However, there were not enough "individual" excuses to account for an entire community's rejection of the Jewish Way of Life. One teacher had the following explanation:

> For anyone to move out there, (to this suburban community) they can't take their Judaism very seriously. The people who move there are pretty well on their way to assimilation. These people have taken on the middle class culture of America.

Furthermore, there was no sense that either within their own Jewish community or within some greater Jewish community there existed someone or something that had any more meaningful a grasp of the Jewish Way of Life for modern suburban living. As one parent stated:

> I guess if there weren't so many pressures and directions—what with work and bills and taxes and weeds—we might sit down with books and read about Judaism. But hell, we'd rather watch the Super Bowl.

For some of the students, too, their growing awareness of the extent of assimilation in their own lives and within their community, as well as the feeling that Judaism was unable to penetrate the present style of suburban life in America, was an indication to them that for themselves Jewish life was becoming outdated. One high school student stated her concern for this matter in the following way:

> I think Judaism is kind of dead . . . All of the stories were written in the past, all the prophets. It's just like a story book, but the history isn't continuing. No one is saying, y'know, they're not writing about the Inquisition or World War II. It's not part of the Bible, so it's not continuing history. So, in that respect, it died, and the only thing continuing now are the traditions and rituals that we derived a long

time ago from the Talmud; and that's why I think it's dying—it's just the traditions. I'm not sure you can be really Jewish outside of Israel. Because we're losing the traditions, and everyone is assimilating; and if we're not moving toward Israel we're going to lose all the old and be left with nothing.

Summary

Recognizing, as Berkson did in 1920, "the desire of the Jews to maintain their identity and to live the life of Jews in the midst of the social conditions of a divergent environment" the Jews established a network of complementary schools to satisfy this desire. Nevertheless, at least in the community described here they were not faring well in their attempt to live meaningfully within two cultural systems. Although they were still clinging to their Jewish heritage, to the extent of maintaining an association with the Jewish school and in that way helping their children to identify as Jews, they were drawn in their daily lives to what has been described as the lifestyle of the suburban upper middle class American. They were unable to interpret their Jewish heritage so that it made sense in their "American" life and, as a result, they increasingly turned to their Jewish background as a historical tradition. Yet, philosophically, these Jews were not truly comfortable with this fit and insisted that the school teach about Jewish life according to an imagined context that was in fact neither true to their own lives nor to their children's. Their self-deception about the inconsistency of their school assumptions and their own lifestyles further exacerbated problems in the school as hostilities and conflicts emerged during the school year due to a sense of failure about the school. Thus, as the school year ended, the school staff and the community were dissatisfied but not defeated, yet their unresolved cultural dilemma loomed ever larger about them.

Notes

1. *Shofar*—A ram's horn that is blown during the Jewish New Year season and High Holy Days.

2. *Chauffeur*—As used here refers to the practice of being driven about by another person to various places in the sense of "carpooling" and not in the sense of a paid driver. For these suburban youth who were several years younger than the legal age for driving, being chauffeured from school to

extracurricular activities or friends' homes was a daily event. Parents, usually meaning mothers, served as the children's chauffeurs.

3. *Ethnic minority group*—The changing characteristics of one ethnic group relative to other ethnic groups and cultures in the society make it difficult to develop a definition that is precise, explicit, and without qualification. The definition of the ethnic group used in this study, derived in part from the definitions proposed by DeVos (1975), Parsons (1975), Kallen (1956), Gordon (1964), and Isajiw (1974), is as follows: An ethnic group is a self-perceived group of people who are transgenerational, who share a common sense of peoplehood, and who hold common historical roots, a common sense of historical continuity, and a common culture that includes a common set of traditions. This common culture may include in whole or in part aspects such as religion, language, and geography. In addition, the group may have shared genetic characteristics. Inclusion in the group is most commonly involuntary. As a qualification of this definition, it should be understood that at any given time various aspects of the common culture and traditions, and the common sense of historical continuity may neither be shared nor practiced in all respects by all members of the group.

The Jewish people fit this definition along with the accompanying statement of qualification. The Jews are both a self-perceived group and perceived by others as a group, are transgenerational, and hold common historical roots, a common sense of historical continuity and a common culture that includes common traditions. They have a religion which is Judaism, a language which is Hebrew, and a geographical center which is Israel. Inclusion in the Jewish group is usually by circumstance of birth although conversion is also possible. There are also certain genetic disorders that are generally limited to Jewish people. Finally, some Jews neither accept nor practice much of the above in their personal identities as Jews but still remain Jews. In this study, the Jews in America are considered to be not just an ethnic group, but an ethnic minority group. As with the term "ethnic group," there is some disagreement and imprecision in the definitions scholars (Newman 1973; Schermerhorn 1970; Lavender 1975) have given to the term "minority." Defined here within the context of American society, however, the Jewish people are considered a minority group in this study because they are: 1) culturally subordinate while not necessarily being socio-economically subordinate and, less importantly, because they are: 2) numerically subordinate. Given Ogbu's typology (1978), the Jews living in America today could thus be accurately defined as an autonomous minority group, i.e., one which is not totally subordinate, but is numerically smaller.

4. For further reading on this topic, see Ackerman (1969), Bock (1976), Dashefsky and Shapiro (1974), Himmelfarb, (1975), Schoem (1982), and Silberman (1985).

5. Discussion of this issue is adapted from an article (Schoem, 1984) previously published by Magnes Press, Hebrew University.

References

Ackerman, Walter
    1969   Jewish Education—For what. American Jewish Yearbook, Vol. 70.
           New York: American Jewish Committee, pp. 3–36.

Berkson, Isaac
    1926   Theories of Americanization. New York: Teacher's College, Co-
           lumbia University.

Blumer, Herbert
    1969   Symbolic Interactionism. New Jersey: Prentice-Hall.

Bock, Geoffrey
    1976   The Social Context of Jewish Education. Jewish Education and
           Jewish Identity. New York: American Jewish Committee.

Burnett, Jacquetta Hill
    1976   Event Description and Analysis in the Microethnography of Urban
           Classrooms. In Educational Patterns and Cultural Configurations.
           Joan Roberts and Sherrie Akinsanya, editors, New York: David
           McKay Company.

Dashefsky, Arnold, and Howard Shapiro
    1974   Ethnic Identification Among American Jews. Lexington, Mass:
           D.C. Heath.

DeVos, George
    1975   Ethnic Pluralism: Conflict and Accommodation. In Ethnic Identity.
           George DeVos and Lola Romanucci-Ross, editors, Palo Alto: May-
           field Publishers.

Dushkin, Alexander and Uriah Z. Engleman
    1959   Jewish Education in the United States. New York: American
           Association for Jewish Education.

Gartner, Lloyd, editor
    1969   Jewish Education in the United States. New York: Teachers Col-
           lege Press.

Gold, Raymond
    1958   Roles in Sociological Field Observations. Social Forces 36

Goodlad, John
    1977   What Goes on in Our Schools. Educational Researcher Vol. 6 (3)

Gordon, Milton
    1975   Towards a General Theory of Racial and Ethnic Group Relations.
           In Ethnicity. Nathan Glazer and Daniel Patrick Moynihan, editors,
           Cambridge, Mass: Harvard University Press.

Heilman, Samuel
    1983   Inside the Jewish School. New York: American Jewish Committee

Himmelfarb, Harold
    1975   Jewish Education for Naught—Educating the Culturally Deprived
           Child. Analysis 51.
    1974   The Impact of Religious Schooling: The Effects of Jewish Education
           upon Adult Religious Involvement. Unpublished Ph.D. disserta-
           tion: University of Chicago.

Isajiw, Wsevolod W.
    1974   Definitions of Ethnicity. In Ethnicity. Vol. 1 (2).

Kallen, Horace
    1956   Cultural Pluralism and the American Idea. Philadelphia: Univer-
           sity of Pennsylvania Press.

Lavender, Abraham
    1975   Disadvantages of Minority Group Membership: The Perspective
           of a "Non-Deprived" Minority. Ethnicity Vol. 2 (1)

Lofland, John
    1971   Analyzing Social Settings. Belmont, Ca.: Wadsworth Publishing.

Newman, William M.
    1973   American Pluralism. New York: Harper and Row.

Ogbu, John
    1982   Societal Forces as a Context of Ghetto Children's School Failure.
           In The Language of Children Reared in Poverty. Lynn Feagans
           and Dale Clark Farran, editors, New York: Academic Press.
    1978   Minority Education and Caste. New York: Academic Press.

Parsons, Talcott
    1975   Some Theoretical Considerations on the Nature and Trends of
           Change of Ethnicity. In Ethnicity. Nathan Glazer and Daniel
           Patrick Moynihan, editors, Cambridge, Mass: Harvard University
           Press.

Schermerhorn, R.A.
    1970   Comparative Ethnic Relations. New York: Random House.

Schoem, David
    1984   Jewish Schooling and Jewish Survival in the Suburban American
           Community. In Studies in Jewish Education. Vol 2, Michael
           Rosenak, editor, Jerusalem: Magnes Press, Hebrew University.
    1983   What the Afternoon School Does Best. Jewish Education. Vol. 51
           (4)
    1982   Explaining Jewish Student Failure. Anthropology and Education
           Quarterly. Vol. 13 (4).

Silverman, Charles
    1985   A Certain People. New York: Summit Books.

Spindler, George
  1976   From Omnibus to Linkages: Cultural Transmission Models. *In* Educational Patterns and Cultural Configurations. Joan Roberts and Sherrie Akinsanya, editors, New York: Holt, Rinehart & Winston.

Zelditch, Morris, Jr.
  1962   Some Methodological Problems of Field Studies. American Journal of Sociology. pp. 566–576.

6 Integration into the Group and Sacred Uniqueness: An Analysis of Adult Bat Mitzvah

Stuart Schoenfeld

While David Schoem points to the crumbling of Jewish culture, Schoenfeld gives us an example of regenerative processes. The young woman who has chosen to create her Bat Mitzvah as an adult is representative of those who have rediscovered their Jewish roots and seek to use them in expressing their individuality. The *Havurah* movement among Conservative and Reform Jews and, in a different way, the orthodox Baalei Teshuvah (penitents) express this direction. Schoenfeld, who is engaged in a comprehensive study of the Bar and Bat Mitzvah ceremonies, uses a symbolic approach in his study. He relates this adult Bat Mitzvah to the individualism which pervades modern North American society.

Numerous writers who have examined the relationship of Judaism to the lives of twentieth century Jews have noted the decline in ritual observance and have advanced theories about why some rituals are likely to be retained or emphasized and others neglected.[1] Less attention has been paid to ritual revision or innovation, although even a cursory examination of practices in the Reform, Conservative, and Reconstructionist branches of Judaism indicates that new or radically amended rituals have become a major part of twentieth century Judaism.

One innovation is described and interpreted in this study. Anthropological fieldwork techniques of observation and interview were used to produce a description of an innovative ritual as it actually occurred and to place it in context. The interpretation is guided by a particular sociological perspective on how the process of modernization transforms religion, although no claim is made that this perspective is the only one which can enhance our understanding of ritual revision and innovation in Judaism.

The perspective used in this study emphasizes that in the past few hundred years, humanity has crossed a threshold into an era of complexity and role specialization. In modern society, the social environment of each individual is transformed, individual self-awareness is increased, and individual choice becomes a central cultural value.[2] The individualism of modern society challenges traditional understandings of what religious belief and ritual are about. It has been argued, however, that belief and ritual do not disappear with modernity, but that they are transformed to express individualism.

The phrase "the invisible religion," taken from Thomas Luckmann (1967) expresses the individualistic transformation of belief systems. Luckmann argues that people have a need to confront questions of ultimate values. Traditional religions give their adherents standard, authoritative meaning systems. In modern society, the individual becomes a consumer, selecting from a variety of meaning systems in a marketplace of ideas. Modern meaning systems are often personal products, synthesized from the wide variety of available ideas, and they need not be and often are not theistic. Such systems of ideas, however, may still be legitimately called "religions" because they meet the human need to place behavior in a meaningful context. This shift to personal, "invisible" (meaning systems because de-institutionalized) need not, however, mean the end of organized religion. Luckmann suggests that conventional religious groups may be transformed as they become the settings in which individuals voluntarily join together to search for personal meaning (1967:100).[3]

Just as modern individualism undermines the passive acceptance of traditional beliefs, it undermines passive acceptance of traditional rituals. Traditional Jewish rituals, like the rituals of other religions, may be interpreted, following Durkheim (1933), as expressions of group solidarity and acceptance of group authority, as powerful social devices for integrating the individual into the social role assigned by the group. Whether a traditional ritual is perpetuated by a self-conscious religious elite[4] or a traditionally religious family, maintaining forms in conformity with authority and past practice signifies the legitimacy of group standards over personal preferences.

Ritual, however, may remain an important social activity, with its content changed by individualism. Durkheim himself predicted this, speculating on the emergence of a "religion of humanity" (1975:63) which would have its distinctive assemblies, feasts, and ceremonies (1976:427; 1933; 1975). This religion, in which "the individual is considered as sacred" (1975: 61–62) was described by Durkheim as uncompromising in its individualism, energetic in its affirmation of the rights of man, and jealously protecting the individual "from external encroachments, whatever their source" (ibid.). The "first dogma" of this "cult of man" is "the autonomy of reason" and its "first rite . . . freedom of thought." (ibid.:65). While its rituals were still unclear, Durkheim had no doubt of their necessity. "There can be no society," he wrote,

> which does not feel the need of upholding and reaffirming at regular intervals the collective sentiments and the collective ideas which make its unity and personality. . . . this moral remaking cannot be achieved except by the means of reunions, assemblies and meetings where the individuals, being closely united to one another, reaffirm in common their common sentiments. . . . If we find a little difficulty today in imagining what these feasts and ceremonies of the future could consist in, it is because we are going through a stage of transition and moral mediocrity. (1976:427)

This perspective on the modern transformation of religion implies that the institutional structures of traditional religions could continue, and perhaps even flourish, in modern society with modifications in their content and style which reconcile integration into the group and the autonomous personality as the ultimate source of authority over meaning. This reconciliation would be collectively acknowledged by ritual scripts which either allow modification to accommodate individual preferences or even require a unique personal statement as part of the ritual.

The description which follows of an innovative Jewish ritual— an adult bat mitzvah—covers the decision to have one, the preparations and the celebration itself. The analysis explores the impact of modern individualism on Judaism by identifying how this bat mitzvah combined the traditional ritual theme of integration into the group with the modern sacredness of individual autonomy. Because the innovative ritual is an adaptation of a well-established conventional pattern of bar and bat mitzvah at the age of thirteen, the conventional pattern is described first in order that the differences between it and the innovative ritual described will be clear.

A Common Pattern of Bar/Bat Mitzvah Observance

In the *Mishnah*, the authoritative second century code of rabbinic law, the age of thirteen years and a day for boys and twelve years and a day for girls marks a major legal transition from minor to adult. The ritual celebration of a boy attaining this age—becoming a "bar mitzvah," a son of the commandments—with a combined religious and social event has been known for at least 500 years (Rivkind, 1942). Bat mitzvah is a twentieth century innovation. In some congregations it was introduced as a group ceremony and reception, having neither the liturgical sanctity, nor the difficulty of preparation, nor the expense of bar mitzvah. In most non-Orthodox settings, however, bat mitzvah is now celebrated as the equivalent of bar mitzvah. The social side of bar/bat mitzvah has become elaborate in the past 100 years. In North America, bar mitzvah celebration is close to universal, and bat mitzvah almost as common.

Although there are many variations in the arrangements and performance of bar and bat mitzvah, the following scenario, based on observations and interviews, is a composite of frequently found features:

Each year an administrator in a synagogue or synagogue school examines the birthdays of the ten-year-olds enrolled in the synagogue-affiliated school and allocates to each a date for bar or bat mitzvah in three years time. Parents may contact a caterer as soon as a date is set, but this is usually delayed until about a year before. Beginning six months to a year before the date of the ceremony, the child receives individual tutoring in chanting the sections from the Torah and the prophets to be read on the day of the bar or bat mitzvah. At the same time, the family is busy with the social side—guest lists, locations of the social events, menus, color scheme, etc.

The ceremony, on Friday night or Saturday morning, takes place within the context of a regularly scheduled service. Jewish worship includes numerous honorific roles in the service. These honors are almost always given to family of the bar or bat mitzvah. The bar or bat mitzvah is given the honor of being called for the first time to the reading of the Torah. This is followed by the bar or bat mitzvah's recitation of the weekly reading from the haftorah. The rabbi's sermon always includes congratulatory remarks to the bar or bat mitzvah and family, and there are usually personal face-to-face remarks made by the rabbi to the bar or bat mitzvah while both stand before the Ark, the sacred center of the sanctuary.

The many guests who are invited to witness and participate in this service include friends of the bar or bat mitzvah, friends of the parents, and, most of all, extended family. The social events surrounding the ceremony often include a Friday night dinner for close family, light refreshments for all those attending after services, and a dinner-dance for invited guests. The dinner-dance may include speeches by the bar/bat mitzvah, parents, grandparents and siblings. There are, of course, many presents given and a permanent record made in the form of a photo album or a videotape. And, for most b'nai mitzvot, the year of the bar or bat mitzvah is also the last year of formal Jewish education. The strongest themes in this composite are the mutually reinforcing ones of Jewish identification and extended family. The child has had at least several years of continuous enrollment in a Jewish school. Despite the difficulty of developing Hebrew language competence and an understanding of a sophisticated tradition in a few hours after school and on weekends, children who attend Hebrew school in preparation for bar or bat mitzvah learn an important lesson. They learn that it is important to their parents that they identify themselves as Jews, that they know "something" about what it means and that they acquire a minimal ability to participate in communal worship. This lesson is connected to the dramatization of the family as a group extending laterally and through generations. The ceremony honors the bar or bat mitzvah, but it also honors the extended family, which periodically regroups as the cohort in each generation "comes of age."

In this interpretation ritual performs an integrating function. The group gathers together to renew its moral bonds, to symbolically assert its cohesiveness. Participation in ritual integrates the individuals into the group, affirming and strengthening solidarity.

It could be argued that there is also an invisible religion theme in this composite. The emergence of the modern individual as an "autonomous" consumer and do-it-yourself assembler of meaning systems places the intergenerational continuity of group identity in some doubt. Among Jews, bar and bat mitzvah celebrate each early adolescent as a uniquely important member of the community of Israel. While the first impression of these rituals may be that they are initiation rites (La Fontaine, 1985), they actually express a more complex social reality. Bar mitzvah has become an important ritual occasion only in the modern period; bat mitzvah, which has quickly become an important ritual occasion, has an even shorter history. They use the formal structure of the integration of new members into the group to address the modern transition of Jewish identity from "fate" to "choice" (Dawidowicz, 1977). They are modern rituals of identification more than they are traditional rituals of initiation.

An Adult Bat Mitzvah

Descriptions of adult bar and bat mitzvahs began appearing in the mid-1970s. While they are structured around the adult doing something special in the context of being called to the reading of the Torah, other features are highly variable. Because they have not become institutionally routinized like bar and bat mitzvahs of thirteen-year-olds it is not possible to describe a typical composite. This difference has methodological and substantive implications. Methodologically, the above composite of common features of thirteen-year-old bar and bat mitzvahs will be contrasted with one adult bat mitzvah. This adult bat mitzvah has features in common with adult bat mitzvahs elsewhere and illustrates the adaptation of bar and bat mitzvah to include invisible religion themes, but no claim is made that all the details will be typical of adult bat mitzvah in general. The sample is simply insufficient. The bat mitzvah described below, however, is not idiosyncratic. Another adult bat mitzvah in the same congregation in the same year shared many features. Moreover, as will be discussed below, the choices made about the celebration of the bat mitzvah were socially structured by a loosely organized but self-conscious network of religious individuals and organizations. Substantively, the lack of institutionalized routine is itself indicative of the individualist character of these rituals and celebrations, a preliminary indication of the value placed on the unique individual.

Deciding to Have a Bat Mitzvah

Miriam grew up in a very Jewish social environment. Her family lived in a Jewish suburb and was affiliated with a Conservative congregation, which they normally attended, as is common in many households, only on the High Holidays. She attended a Jewish day school which emphasized culture rather than religion and a summer camp sponsored by the Conservative movement (one of the numerous Camp Ramah's). She recalled that all the boys in school had bar mitzvahs at thirteen, but that it was not an issue for the girls.

> I remember feeling completely relieved when I was thirteen that I didn't have to have a bar mitzvah, that I didn't have to learn all that stuff and get up in front of everybody and take on that responsibility. I even remember saying "Thank God I was born a woman" that I didn't have to do that. . . . I didn't have to go through the agony of learning for the bar mitzvah.

When asked whether she missed not having the associated party, she pointed out that girls got "sweet sixteen" parties instead, and added:

> It was only in retrospect that I felt very betrayed. (While at university, close friends who were not Jewish but who were involved with personal,

non-establishment spirituality) began to question me very deeply about my religious identity, something my Jewish friends and I never discussed . . . I couldn't answer their questions, and that really bothered me because I was known by many of my Jewish and non-Jewish friends as being very strongly Jewish.

She consequently began looking for a way of combining the spirituality of these friends and Judaism.

When she returned from the university, she found a group in which to do this. Non-Jewish friends from the university were instrumental. They called to give Miriam the name and phone number of a woman in Miriam's city that they had found out about. This woman, an employee of the Jewish community who had studied at Yeshiva in Israel, was known as having an interest in women, spirituality, and Judaism. Miriam called and was immediately invited to a Friday night dinner of women who met monthly before Rosh Chodesh (the new moon—traditionally marked as a "minor" holy day, now emphasized by a number of contemporary Jewish women's groups).

Miriam talked about a ritual from her first Friday night dinner with the women's group. The Friday night meal conventionally begins with someone reciting the blessing over the wine, everyone drinking a sip of wine after the blessing, someone reciting the blessing over the challah (the ceremonial twisted eggloaf bread made for the Sabbath), slicing the challah and everyone taking a bite. At the women's group dinner, when it was time for the blessing over the challah, everyone at the table put their hands on the challah, said the blessing in unison, and then pulled off a piece. When she had first arrived, Miriam had felt like an outsider; after this ritual she felt part of the group.

Through the women's group Miriam found out about a center for Jewish spiritual development in another city. Miriam went to the center for a four day retreat during the High Holy Days about half a year after entering the women's group. One of the sessions examined naming, the option of renaming oneself and the meanings associated with the participants' Hebrew names. Like many Jewish women, Miriam's parents gave her both a Hebrew name and an "English" name (i.e., one generally popular when she was born) which begins with the same letter as her Hebrew name. Role playing of biblical situations and relationships brought out the qualities associated with various Hebrew names. In discussion, one of the participants pressed Miriam[5] about the biblical character whose Hebrew name she has. What he told her about her Hebrew name "all fit what I was going through." She decided then that for her twenty-fourth birthday—

which was the next one coming and was coincidentally exactly double the traditional age of bat mitzvah—she was going to have a bat mitzvah and speak about her Hebrew name whether or not the biblical reading from the week involved the woman whose name she shared.

The decision was confirmed by a further coincidence. "It wasn't serendipity," she said when telling about it,

> it was supposed to happen. . . . Not only was [the biblical woman whose name she has central to the Torah reading] on the weekend of my birthday, it was a complete women's weekend. All these women's characters . . . It was magical. You had to see my face when I checked the weekend and found it was [her name], and then I knew I had to have my bat mitzvah then.

Planning

Miriam called a "family council meeting" with her parents to tell them of her plans. Although they had questions about the bat mitzvah, throughout the planning they were "completely supportive." Miriam arranged for the ceremony to be held at a small synagogue (both the sanctuary and social hall accommodate comfortably slightly more than 100 people) which she had found through the women's group. This congregation, whose services are led by members, does not make gender distinctions in ritual privileges. Its liturgy has been amended to include references to the matriarchs in prayers where the patriarchs are mentioned but otherwise follows the traditional prayer book. One of the caterers who is permitted in the synagogue's kitchen was hired for the reception. Miriam asked a Jewish community worker who works in the same building as she to tutor her on the reading of the Torah and haftorah.

> . . . His personality, his values represent something very important to me. There's a story about the Baal Shem Tov [founder of Hasidism], that he was a very simple, modest man who did his own thing, but was really very powerful and affected people. This is how I see [tutor's name], very unassuming, very modest, a kind human being. . . . Almost every day during my one hour [lunch] I would go into his office and we'd study together, discussing its [her Torah and haftorah portions] meaning. . . .

In addition to preparing for her Torah and haftorah readings, much time and thought went into Miriam's *d'var torah* (commentary on the weekly Torah reading delivered during the service). Her preparations were shared with a close friend, a "strictly orthodox" woman who "helped me along the whole way, coached me, gave insights to me." This close friend also prepared a brief commentary for presentation during the reception following the service.

Miriam invited about forty five people—friends, family, and friends of her parents whom she thought of as family.

> Making up the invitations was special for me. I personally wrote every single invitation and wrote something different to each person about why I wanted them to be there. I was making a personal connection to every single person . . .

Not everyone invited was able or expected to come. An invitation went to a friend doing volunteer work in Africa. A close friend from the university was unable to come, but sent the tallit (prayer shawl) Miriam wore during the service.

The Weekend

Friends of the family invited about thirty people—relatives, out of town guests, and Miriam's close friend to dinner on the Friday night before the ceremony. Although not normally observant, the hosts prepared for the Sabbath evening rituals of candle lighting, blessing the wine and blessing the bread. Miriam introduced them to the ritual of blessing the bread which she had learned at the women's group. "I felt like I gave them something. They loved it." The evening had a festive atmosphere. "Many of my parents' friends and my family came in from out of town. They hadn't been together for a very long time. These are friends of my parents since high school. This was a *simcha* to bring them together after a period of time." When, after four and a half hours, Miriam and her friend left to walk home, they were the first ones to leave. As they walked, they discussed Miriam's d'var torah and other things that were to happen the next morning.

Very early the next morning Miriam and her friend walked to the synagogue, put things in order, and talked until other people began to arrive. Services began as scheduled at 9:30. What was special for the bat mitzvah began with the Torah service at about 10:30. Family were given the honors of opening the Ark in which the Torahs are kept, being called to the reading of the Torah, lifting and dressing the scroll at the completion of the Torah reading, and closing the Ark after the Torah was replaced. It was important for Miriam that her grandmother have the honor of being called to the reading of the Torah. Since her grandmother cannot read Hebrew,

Miriam wrote out for her phonetically the blessings which are said before and after the Torah is read.

The leader of the women's group had the honor of calling people up to the reading of the Torah. As is the normal custom in this congregation, she chanted the formula "Rise up [first name] [second name] son of/daughter of [parent's first name] [parent's second name] and [other parent's first name] [other parent's second name]" when calling each person up, and chanted a blessing for each after their section of the Torah had been read.

As is the case at all bar and bat mitzvahs, the congregation became particularly attentive when Miriam was called up for the concluding aliyah. The blessing chanted after she concluded included a song about women rejoicing in the Torah which was written by the women's group leader. The Torah was then rolled and dressed, and Miriam chanted the haftorah. When she had completed the concluding blessing over the haftorah, the congregation, as is often the case at bar and bat mitzvahs in this synagogue, called out *Mazel Tov* (literally, "good luck," colloquially, "congratulations") and threw candies at her. Miriam was lead down from the bimah (the elevated platform on which the Torah is read) and most of the congregation joined hands, dancing through the aisles singing *Simmen Tov u' Mazel Tov* (a traditional song of congratulations).

The service resumed, the Torah was paraded through the synagogue and returned to the Ark, and Miriam returned to the bimah to deliver her d'var torah. While chanting her portions from the Torah and haftorah, Miriam, like the others who had the honor of being called to the Torah, had been facing the Ark. Now she was turned away from the Ark, towards the congregation, to deliver her talk.

The d'var Torah lasted about fifteen minutes. It was structured, as is conventional for a d'var Torah, as a commentary on the Torah and haftorah reading. In developing the commentary, quotations are used, events and personalities in the readings are discussed, and printed commentaries are quoted, but the intent is to use these sources in an original, personal way.

Miriam's d'var Torah discussed the women who were central to the content of the week's Torah and haftorah portions. The role of woman as mother was acknowledged and honored and the implications of the biblical reference to a prophetess as "a mother of Israel" explored. Motherhood was presented as implying more than the physical act of giving birth, as also including teaching and leadership. Different women leaders "mother" the "children of Israel" in different ways, some through scholarship and rationality, and some through emotions and ritual. By exploring the personalities of these biblical characters, contemporary Jewish women can find role models to guide their own relationships to tradition and contemporary Jewish life.

Miriam returned, accompanied by handshakes, kisses, and congratulatory wishes, to her seat, and the service continued for about another twenty minutes, to about 12:30.

The entire congregation was invited to a buffet lunch in the social hall. Congratulations and expressions of pleasure continued. Miriam had been concerned that "many people in my family didn't understand where I was coming from" before the bat mitzvah, "asking questions about why have a bat mitzvah, why does a woman have to have a ceremony." After the ceremony, from what people said and how they acted during the reception and through the rest of the day, Miriam felt that their questions had been answered and that they understood.

> My grandmother said to me . . . 'I don't understand why you have to observe Shabbat like that, just like in the shtetl'—like why do you regress like that?—I had to try and explain to her that I wasn't regressing, it was just getting in touch with something special, but she saw it as a definite regression. After my bat mitzvah, she said, 'Now I understand . . .'

Many other relatives expressed the opinion to her that they now thought that everyone should have their bar and bat mitzvah as an adult because Miriam's bat mitzvah, had shown its "real meaning" unlike many for thirteen-year-olds they've attended where the emphasis is on the party.

The celebrating continued that evening with a dinner party at Miriam's parents' home which lasted until about 1 a.m. More people attended than the night before. The night before was more for family, the night after more for friends.

There was no possibility of extending celebrations further because the next day Miriam had to leave the country as part of a group engaged in a Jewish communal welfare project. The awareness, shared by family, friends, and the congregation, that Miriam was to leave on this trip underscored the seriousness of her bat mitzvah. Her ritual acceptance of responsibility was followed the next day by action which was an extension of her continuing commitment.

Commentary

Miriam's bat mitzvah was a combination of the traditional and the non-traditional, a dual statement of integration into the group and of commitment to spiritual autonomy.

Integration into the Group

The rituals and the social events through the weekend contained many integrating elements. While an adult bat mitzvah is still unusual, the ritual of bat mitzvah and its theme of identification were familiar to family, friends, and congregation. The bat mitzvah dramatized the affirmation and reintegration of family ties, participation in a religious congregation, identification with Jewish women, and commitment to the broader ties of Jewish peoplehood.

FAMILY. Parents were involved early in the planning. Extended family were invited and their participation honored. The social events Friday and Saturday nights were hosted by family.

RELIGIOUS COMMUNITY. Ties to a religious community were symbolized by the decision to have the ceremony in the context of a normal synagogue service instead of arranging one in a private setting as is sometimes done. Miriam participated by doing things that are usually done at a bar or bat mitzvah—chanting the concluding section from the Torah and the weekly section from the prophets and giving the d'var Torah. All members of the congregation attending on the day of the bat mitzvah were invited to the reception after services, regardless of whether they had received a personal invitation.

JEWISH WOMEN. The role of the leader of the women's group in the ceremony and sharing the preparations with a religious friend were both symbolic and practical. The bat mitzvah dramatized participation in a *congregation* and in a community of religious *women*. These two groups share some members, but they are distinct. The special role of religious women in the synagogue ceremony indicated their importance to the bat mitzvah. The dramatization of identification with Jewish women was also linked to identification with the Jewish people in the d'var Torah. The conjunction of these two elements is discussed in the next section.

JEWISH PEOPLEHOOD. Identification with the Jewish people is a pre-supposition of Jewish liturgy. The traditional prayer book is written as communal worship in which each congregation expresses its prayers as part of the Jewish people. In addition to the traditional liturgy, this congregation, like most, recites a prayer for the State of Israel during the service.

The theme of identification with the Jewish people was strongly expressed in the d'var Torah delivered to the congregation. The d'var Torah was special for this occasion because it examined biblical precedents for the contemporary participation of women in Jewish life. Its focus was not on private and domestic virtues, although these were acknowledged, but on the special contribution women could make as leaders and public persons.

The exploration of the meaning of the bat mitzvah's Hebrew name—in the process leading up to the decision to have a bat mitzvah—was an important part of the dual integration into the social roles of "woman" and "Jew." The symbolic importance of the Hebrew name recalls the tendency in many mystical traditions to find a hidden significance in the names of things. In many religious traditions, mystics have approached the names of things as clues to their essence, seeing the name as a guide to the reality of the thing which is not apparent on the surface. Personal names, even more than the names of things, are symbolically rich. Carrying the name of a deceased relative—as is common among American Jews—in some mysterious way keeps that personality alive. Carrying the name of a biblical person—as is also common among American Jews—creates the potential for psychological identification with the biblical role model.

The naming patterns of American Jews add a twist to the mystical tendency to seek the essential personality in a person's name. Because the Hebrew name of most Americans is different from their "English" name, it is used only in special Jewish settings such as synagogue or family. The exploration of this name and public identification with it is a symbolic indication of the importance of these settings to one's identity. It is a symbolic drawing of boundaries in which the person says that his/her real name is the one connecting him/her to other Jews, not the one known to society at large.[6]

Spiritual Autonomy

The bat mitzvah also dramatized individualistic spiritual autonomy. The bat mitzvah was not held to fulfill a traditional or family obligation but as a personal choice. Miriam had become more ritually observant than her parents, who are affiliated with a Conservative congregation. She had not, however, identified herself with Orthodoxy, in which general compliance with standards of observance is mandatory, but with a style of religious experimentation and seeking which is perhaps best expressed in the following quote from the part of an interview in which the question of authority in Judaism was discussed:

. . . on a level of religion and feelings and spirituality, you always
have to have a teacher . . . to guide you and give you resources, but
you have to do it on your own because God is defined by your own
person. I really don't like the idea of people sitting in a large synagogue
and being passive. . . . Everyone has their own definition of God. You
can't let someone else dictate to you what the meaning of Judaism and
God is. . . . May people in large, large congregations feel safe because
they don't have to face the real meaning of why they're there because
the rabbi is doing it all for them . . .

The bat mitzvah was a sufficiently flexible ritual to allow the
introduction or emphasis of what was personally meaningful. Rather
than follow a routinized institutional script, Miriam made choices all
through the process—involving her family, finding a setting which
was open to what she wanted and adapting the ritual script.

The ritual script was adapted to express her personal experiences
as a woman, a Jew, a member of her family, a girl who had watched
while the boys had their bar mitzvahs, and an individual seeking
spiritual meaning in life. The decision to have a bat mitzvah crys-
talized around a desire to speak about the meaning of her Hebrew
name. The ceremony was arranged at a congregation where gender
distinctions are not made in ritualistic roles and where a d'var Torah
is given by a member instead of a sermon given by a rabbi. She
chose someone she personally respected to work with her on the
portions from the Torah and prophets. Handwritten, individualized
invitations were sent instead of printed ones. She used the occasion
to introduce her family to a variation on the blessing over the bread.
The leader of the women's group played a prominent role during
the Torah service, adding a song in honor of the occasion and leading
the dancing. Miriam used her d'var Torah to speak personally about
her connection to Judaism by talking to the congregation about the
biblical woman whose name she bears and the topic of women in
the Jewish community.

In choosing to have a bat mitzvah and incorporating what was
personally meaningful rather than following an institutionalized routine, the dual themes of identification with the group and individual
autonomy were both portrayed. In her relationship with her parents
and extended family, this dual theme had an especially emotional
resonance. The participation of her family in the bat mitzvah that
she arranged, and their positive comments about it afterward symbolized their acceptance of the religious direction she had taken.

Social and Theological Supports

While Miriam's bat mitzvah cannot be considered a typical adult bat mitzvah, it was not idiosyncratic. Another bat mitzvah a few months apart at the same congregation shared many characteristics—membership in the women's group, singing and dancing in the sanctuary after the recitation of the haftorah, a d'var Torah about the woman's Hebrew name, and personal symbolic gestures. The ritual variations chosen for these bat mitzvahs and the themes that they expressed connect them to approaches to Judaism found in a loose but active network of individuals and organizations. Miriam's way along the path that led to the particular bat mitzvah she had was structured for her by an interfaith network of individuals exploring spiritual issues, a loosely organized women's group, a sophisticated center for Jewish spiritual development and a congregation combining a commitment to gender equality and tradition.

The Jewish network developing a path of personal, voluntaristic spirituality reached many people through the three volumes of *The Jewish Catalogue* (Siegel, Strassfeld and Strassfeld, 1973), *The Second Jewish Catalogue* (Strassfeld and Strassfeld, 1976), and *The Third Jewish Catalogue* (Strassfeld and Strassfeld, 1980). These publications developed out of the *havurah* movement, but the approach to Judaism they contained appealed to many in the Jewish mainstream. This approach to Judaism is organizationally supported by the National Havurah Committee and its publication, *New Traditions*. It is also found in the "alternative" Jewish magazines *Moment*, *Sh'ma*, and the feminist magazine *Lilith* and in occasional articles in other publications. Personal contacts within mainstream denominational and educational organizations also sustain the network. Established synagogues, in addition to maintaining conventional services conducted by ecclesiastical specialists, have found ways of accommodating alternative services which are characterized by informality, lay participation, rotating leadership and experimentation with innovations and revived traditions (see, e.g., Furman, 1981).

The exploration of traditional Judaism in a search for personal meaning is found in Jewish theology as well as practice. The pioneering figure is Franz Rosenzweig (1886–1929; see Rosenzwieg, 1961, and also Martin, 1970), whose life and work powerfully articulated this approach in modern Jewish theology.

Individualism and Modern Ritual

The adult bat mitzvah which has been studied illustrates the blending of symbols of group integration and symbols of individual uniqueness. This blending expresses the desire to bring the external demands of group tradition and the sacredness which modern culture accords to individual autonomy into a harmonious relationship—a desire to experience religious-communal commitment as choice as well as fate. This bat mitzvah is used only as an illustration, suggesting where Luckmann's comment that "church religiosity" could continue as "one of the many manifestations of an emerging, institutionally nonspecialized social form of religion" might lead to research on the contemporary meaning of religious affiliation and participation.

In a society in which the individual has the structural freedom to build a personal identity around meanings appropriated from a wide variety of cultural sources, a religious tradition becomes one resource among others upon which an individual may draw. Some will choose not to draw upon it; others, to connect in a tentative way around life-cycle events such as birth, marriage and death. Others will choose a deep involvement as they confront the problems of personal meaning and social ethics.

Campbell (1978), argues that the search for meaning under the conditions of structural individualism in modern society leads to mysticism, belief in the possibility of spiritual growth, tolerance, and syncretism. This "spiritual and mystic" religiosity separates itself from established religions and seeks to replace them (ibid.:147). This form of religion has "no place for formal organization or communal ritual" (ibid.:150) and attaches no special importance to formal statements of belief" (ibid.).

The emphasis in Campbell's argument on personal, eclectic mysticism reflects the modern sacredness of the individual recognized by both Durkheim and Luckmann, but it underestimates both Durkheim's insistence on the social importance of collective ritual and the flexibility of institutionalized religion. Theology and practice may be adapted—and legitimated by a modern reading of basic sources—to accommodate a personal, selective, and tolerant pursuit of spiritual growth. In an age in which religion is chosen rather than given, the fact of choice and the meaning of that choice to the individual reshape religious rituals, leading to the simultaneous dramatization of integration into the group and individual spiritual autonomy.

Notes

The research for this paper was part of a project supported by a grant from the Canadian Social Sciences and Humanities Research council.

1. Hapgood, in 1902, reported that the rejection of Jewish ritual obligations among adolescent boys extended as far as the refusal to join their families for Friday night dinner (1976:27). Wirth discussed declining ritual observance in the 1920s (1956); Sklare and Greenblum (1967) picked up the theme in the 1950s. Cohen (1983) and Waxman (1983) in the early 1980s reviewed the changes through the twentieth century.

2. For a general statement of the relationship between modernization and self-awareness see Berger, Berger, and Kellner, 1973.

3. In Luckmann's words, "church religiosity" could continue as "one of the many manifestations of an emerging, institutionally nonspecialized social form of religion."

4. See Liebman, 1973 and Schoenfeld, 1987 for analyses of folk-elite tension in Judaism.

5. To preserve anonymity, her real names—Hebrew and "English"—are not used.

6. There are many, many instances in contemporary Jewish literature, e.g., Weisel (1982) and Cowan (1982), of the emotional importance of exploring one's Hebrew name while coming to terms with one's identity as a Jew. As the story by Wiesel indicates, the contrast between the public name and the private, hidden name suggests an analogy between American Jews and sixteenth century Iberian Marranos, an analogy developed polemically by Borowitz (1973).

References

Berger, Peter, Brigitte Berger, and Hansfried Kellner.
    1973 *The Homeless Mind: Modernization and Consciousness.* New York: Random House.

Borowitz, Eugene.
    1973 *The Masks Jews Wear.* New York: Simon and Schuster.

Campbell, Colin.
    1978 "The Secret Religion of the Educated Classes." *Sociological Analysis* 39,2:146–156.

Cohen, Steven M.
    1983 *American Modernity and Jewish Identity.* New York: Tavistock.

Cowan, Paul.
1982   *An Orphan in History.* New York: Doubleday.

Dawidowicz, Lucy.
1977   "Jewish Identity: A Matter of Fate, a Matter of Choice." pp. 3–31 in *The Jewish Presence.* New York: Harcourt Brace Jovanovich.

Durkheim, Emile.
1933   *The Division of Labor.* New York: Macmillan.
1975   "Individualism and the Intellectuals." pp. 59–73 in W. S. F. Pickering, editor, *Durkheim on Religion: A Selection of Readings with Bibliographies.* London: Routledge & Kegan Paul.
1976   *The Elementary Forms of the Religious Life.* London: George Allen and Unwin.

Furman, Frida Kerner.
1981   "Ritual as Social Mirror and Agent of Cultural Change: A Case Study in Synagogue Life," *Journal for the Scientific Study of Religion* 20(3):228–241.

Hapgood, Hutchins.
1976   [1902]. *The Spirit of the Ghetto: Studies of the Jewish Quarter of New York.* New York: Schocken.

La Fontaine, J. S.
1985   *Initiation: Ritual Drama and Secret Knowledge Across the World.* Harmondsworth, Middlesex: Penguin.

Liebman, Charles.
1973   *The Ambivalent American Jew.* Philadelphia: Jewish Publication Society of America.

Luckmann, Thomas.
1967   *The Invisible Religion.* New York: Macmillan.

Martin, Bernard.
1970   *Great 20th Century Jewish Philosophers: Shestov, Rosenzweig, Buber.* New York: Macmillan.

Rivkind, Isaac.
1942   *L'ot U'l'zikaron . . . (Bar Mitzvah: A Study in Jewish Cultural History)* Hebrew. New York: Bloch.

Rosenzweig, Franz.
1961   *Franz Rosenzweig: His Life and Thought.* Presented by Nahum Glatzer. New York: Schocken.

Schoenfeld, Stuart.
1987   (in press). "Folk Religion, Elite Religion and the Role of Bar Mitzvah in the Development of the Synagogue and Jewish School in America," *Contemporary Jewry* 9.

Siegel, Richard, Sharon Strassfeld, and Michael Strassfeld, editors
1973　*The Jewish Catalogue.* Philadelphia: Jewish Publication Society of America.

Sklare, Marshall and Joseph Greenblum.
1972　[1967]. *Jewish Identity on the Suburban Frontier, 2nd edition.* Chicago: University of Chicago Press.

Strassfeld, Sharon and Michael, editors.
1976　*The Second Jewish Catalogue,* Philadelphia: Jewish Publication Society of America.
1980　*The Third Jewish Catalogue,* Philadelphia: Jewish Publication Society of America.

Waxman, Chaim.
1983　*America's Jews in Transition.* Philadelphia: Temple University Press.

Weisel, Elie
1982　"Testament of a Jew from Saragosso." pp. 63–72 in *Legends of Our Time.* New York: Schocken.

Wirth, Louis.
1956　*The Ghetto.* Chicago: University of Chicago Press.

Part II

Arenas of Jewish Life

As a result of modernization, Jewish life was transformed from having a close connection with a communal body in a particular place and ties to similar communities elsewhere to something hard to pin down. Jews can opt out of organized Jewish life, even without formal conversion. They can ignore Jewish institutions. A whole range of people exist from the unaffiliated to people whose main concerns are Jewish. Most Jews work side by side with Gentiles and a majority may have Gentile neighbors even if some of these are segregated in their social lives. In North America, informal and flexible patterns of communal organization have developed. No single umbrella organization encompasses all of Jewry in the United States. While the situation in Canada is somewhat different, Jewish life there is also characterized by pluralism.

In such a context, it is better to speak of Jewish arenas rather than a Jewish community. Certain places are marked as arenas of Jewish activity, such as the synagogue, the Hebrew school, the community center, and the cemetery. One of these, the community center, and perhaps others, are not even exclusively Jewish. In many places, large numbers of Gentiles are members and participate actively in the athletic and other leisure-time activities of the Jewish community center, just as Jews may be members of the YMCA or YWCA. Choirs in Reform temples often include Gentile singers, while Jews participate in church choirs. Still, Reform temples and Jewish community centers consider the maintenance of a distinctive Jewish culture as a goal and they are distinguished as "Jewish." Additionally, some Gentile-owned food processing enterprises sell kosher goods and accept rabbinical supervision.

People move in and out of these arenas. Heilman (1976:229–233) has shown how some Orthodox Jews switch from standard English, which they use in their offices and places of work, to "Yenglish," a mixture of English and Yiddish, which they use while studying

Talmud in their synagogue. Conservative and Reform Jews may light Sabbath candles and go to the synagogue on "Shabbat" and then enter the world of "Saturday" by going shopping in the afternoon. For the most part, our ethnographies describe the Jewish part of the arena. In the previous section, there were descriptions of a Hebrew school and a small synagogue. Here we find descriptions of several such institutions.

The family is, of course, a key Jewish arena. For some Jews it is the one which is crucial and which colors attitudes toward all other institutions. Even if other ties have been broken, ties with one's kin may remain. While ritual is absent from many Jewish families, that is the crucible of identification. The family is also linked to the workaday world, as Silverman (below) shows.

The synagogue and the Hebrew school are for most Jews only part-time arenas. In fact, even while Jews are within the synagogue, they are engaged in activities which partake of the environmental culture. Synagogues must remain financially solvent. Thus the officers must bring business practices into this presumably sacred institution. As Schoem suggested, a congregational Hebrew school is expensive, even if it is run on the basis of low salaries for teachers. Its direction is thus limited by market forces. This is true of many aspects of synagogue life, as it is of other Jewish institutions, such as community centers, old age homes, and Jewish studies departments in universities. For many, these "facts of institutional life" undercut the value of tradition and community which these places represent. The actions of rabbis, teachers, and trustees often subvert their teachings.

The Jewish institutions are also means for conveying aspects of the majority culture. Forty years ago, Reform and Conservative rabbis would commonly devote sermons to reviews of high quality books and synagogue adult education programs dealt with general, as well as specifically Jewish, topics. German refugees might go to temples to help perfect their English by listening to rabbinic sermons. This suited a second generation Jewish community which was still highly segregated and where many had no college education. Synagogues, like *landsmanshaftn*, played an important role in acculturation to high middlebrow and middle class life.

Today synagogues and community centers are much more interested in preserving and propagating specifically Jewish themes. As Markowitz and others who have studied programs for the recent wave of Soviet emigres, judaization efforts are central thrusts in acculturation. This is also done for American-born participants in their programs.

The changes in institutional direction over time thus occur in a number of arenas, not only the landsmanshaftn. What Kliger shows so clearly is how distant the old hometowns in Europe became and how American these organizations seemed after twenty or fifty years. While the landsmanshaftn seem like organizations for a first-generation immigrant population, it could be argued that the same desire for a "home away from home" has been a prime mover for Jewish organizations in North America. Time and time again, Jews have moved from one place for economic opportunity and for pleasanter surroundings and then have built synagogues and other institutions which remind them of what they left behind.

A. I. Epstein (1978:71–74) finds a precedent for this in "Yankee City." By 1930, the immigrant leadership of the Jewish community was passing from the scene. The Depression was at its height. Most younger Jews were trying to show how American they had become and had stopped observing Jewish tradition with any zeal. Yet at the end of 1932, a campaign was begun to raise money to build a new synagogue. Within a few weeks, the campaign had succeeded in raising $100,000 and most of the younger men in the community had joined the new congregation.

This element of creating a new Jewish arena occurs on many levels. Jews who live far from their families will come together and hold a Seder. In new suburban areas or in SunBelt cities far from the Northeastern centers Jews will get together for lox and bagel breakfasts, Hanukkah parties, and the like. They may form social clubs and synagogues to reproduce the old patterns, albeit on a diminished scale. Those who work for large corporations, universities, or government agencies do not require the economic assistance provided by the older landsmanshaftn, but they do want a sense of continuity.

This also has been true of groups within the Jewish community. German Jewish refugees in the 1930s were not always comfortable in American synagogues and temples. In some cases, American Reform congregations provided them with rooms so they could hold their own services in a German style with a German rabbi. These sometimes became the core of new synagogues. This process persists. In a New York suburb, an Ashkenazic Orthodox synagogue hosts Sephardic Sabbath services, which were started by Syrian Sephardim moving out from Brooklyn.

In all of this it is hard to find a strong ideological or philosophical thrust. Miriam, the "adult bat mitzvah," found that there is very little discussion of religious issues among Jews (Schoenfeld above). The underlying ideology seems to be a need for roots in the past and of continuing tradition in some sense in the future. Those Jews who buy "Judaica" in order to ornament their houses clearly reflect this form of "symbolic ethnicity" as do Americans of other origins.

This need for roots and branches, however, should not be dismissed as superficial for it relates to ultimate issues of life and death. For many, the central ceremonies in Jewish rituals are the prayers commemorating the dead, said either as part of a year of mourning, on the anniversary of the death, or at special times during Festivals. Many Jews who do not attend the synagogue at other times come for such occasions as well as for weddings and bar and bat mitzvahs. Thus, Judaism is seen in terms of obligations to parents and to children, for past and future (see Wimberley and Savishinsky 1978; Zenner 1965, Markowitz above). Jewish burial, as Gradwohl and Gradwohl imply, is not only a material expression of Jewish identity but an existential statement.

The various authors in this volume suggest that Jewishness in America is found on a fragmented archipelago of arenas not in a cohesive community. Yet this is not the case for the more traditionalistic. Among these a Jewish religious viewpoint provides a guide to life in this bewildering world. Jewish categories, institutions, and practices are central, even if their lives are compartmentalized. In fact, those who follow the pathway of "the modern Orthodox," the secular world is an important compartment even if they must move between it and the world of the sacred on a daily basis. This compartmentalization, which was advocated by S. R. Hirsch, whose congregation survives, has provided many with a way to combine the two (Lowenstein, below). This way, however, involves conflicts between the sacred and secular worlds, too.

The other solution is to attempt to cut the community off from the outside world as far as possible. Self-segregation and the creation of a parallel communal structure has been most completely attempted by various Hasidic sects. The various Hasidim are not uniform in how to accomplish this task while living in a highly urban world. The Hasidim through their exotic outer appearance (and sectarianism) have attracted a fair amount of social scientific attention. Studying a community which attempts to close itself off also offers a special challenge. Such groups are often seen as people trying to live in a time past. Janet Belcove-Shalin points out that this impression is mistaken.

References

Epstein, A. I.
1978 Ethos and Identity: Three Studies in Ethnicity. Chicago: Aldine.

Heilman, Samuel
1976 Synagogue Life. Chicago: University of Chicago Press.

Wimberley, Howard, and Joel Savishinsky
1978 Ancestor Memorialism: A Comparison of Jews and Japanese. In Community, Self and Identity. B. Misra and J. Preston, editors, The Hague: Mouton, pp. 115–130.

Zenner, Walter P.
1965 Memorialism: Some Jewish Examples. American Anthropologist 67:481–483.

7

A Home Away from Home: Participation in Jewish Immigrant Associations in America

Hannah Kliger

Countrymen going to live in cities and international migrants from many different countries seek out people from their localities in their new homes. Regional associations and hometown clubs are found in Egypt, Nigeria, Peru, Mexico, and Canada. The landsmanshaftn of East European Jews in North America fit into this mold. Kliger in this article shows how these organizations helped Jewish immigrants adapt to American life and, in turn, how the regional organizations were changed by the American environment. It should be pointed out that while the landsmanshaftn are no longer as important as they were, their form and the need for which they were created continue to influence American Jewish life. Cousin clubs partook of landsman-shaftn. In addition, Jews who have moved from metropolitan centers to peripheral areas, whether in the suburbs or in the Sunbelt re-create Jewish clubs which can be seen as the new "hometown clubs," where they can be among others like themselves.

For readers of the New York Yiddish daily, *The Day*, on January 5, 1939 their newspaper presented an exchange of opinions on the following issue: Should an individual affiliate with a landsmanshaft, or rather with other organizations? The weekly column that regularly featured responses and photographs of "the man on the street," challenged by a roving Yiddish reporter to address pertinent issues of the moment, focused that day on participation in landsmanshaftn.[1] This Yiddish plural term refers to associations of Jewish immigrants who share common origins in an East European hometown.

Not only was the topic of landsmanshaftn deemed of sufficient importance for the 1939 Yiddish reading audience, but the question itself reflects the pervasiveness of landsmanshaft activity within that sector of the American Jewish community. The choice of where to belong was clearly dichotomized, posing the landsmanshaft against all other possible groups.

The published responses to the query reflect an array of concerns. One interviewee chose to draw a broader conceptualization of compatriot, moving beyond the boundaries of shared birthplace to say, "as long as I'm among Jews, it makes no difference if from Lodz or from Boiberik." A second statement reverts to a different criterion: "what good is a landsmanshaft if there are exploiters, bourgeois or dishonest people—a worker must belong with his class." Most of

JEWISH EASTERN EUROPE
1830 — 1914

-------- Provincial Border
— — — — Congress Poland
———— Pale of Settlement

0   100   200
                         km

the comments, however, favor belonging to a landsmanshaft, among *eygene*, among one's own, where familiar friends easily share memories of the old home and concerns about the new one, America. The meaning of participation in Jewish immigrant organizations, or landsmanshaftn, was intriguing to a newspaper editor in 1939. Yet, despite the appropriateness of studying landsmanshaftn in order to understand the process of ethnic socialization at a grass roots level, and although there are more of these than other institutions created to aid immigrants in their accommodation to American life, the landsmanshaft remains relatively unexplored by students of contemporary American Jewish life.

Approaching Research on Landsmanshaftn

The landsmanshaft sector has been discussed in several descriptive accounts (Baker 1978; Curchak 1970; Doroshkin 1969; Howe 1976; Levitats 1959; Weisser 1985). Master's essays contributed to the field (Applebaum 1952; Levinthal 1932; Milamed 1980; Soyer 1985). However, a comprehensive survey of landsmanshaft activities has not been made since the investigation led by Rontch, the results of which were published in Yiddish (Federal Writers Project 1938) and summarized in English (Rontch 1939). The 1938 data, gleaned from the questionnaire responses of approximately 2,500 organizations surveyed in New York, were gathered under the auspices of the Works Progress Administration. An accompanying volume described Jewish family clubs (Federal Writers Project 1939), which were later treated by Mitchell (1978).

The life experiences of landsmanshaft members have been neglected for too long. Landsmanshaft documents and publications form an important base for sociocultural and historical data from which to study how expressions of ethnicity change.[2] In addition, the Yiddish press has traditionally provided a forum for the presentation of the actions and priorities of these ethnic organizations.[3] In other words, the lives of ordinary people can be interpreted according to their own records and their own testimony. To this end, and in the spirit of *The Day*'s canvas of their readers in January 1939, I have conducted detailed in-depth interviews with landsmanshaft members to capture their voices in reconstructing landsmanshaft activity, past and present.[4] By integrating multiple approaches to analyze the development and current ongoing work of landsmanshaftn, we learn how ethnic voluntary associations "are not, in fact, pure heritages, but the products of the immigrants' efforts to adapt their heritages to American conditions" (Park and Miller 1921:120).[5]

Beginning in the 1800s to the present, landsmanshaft members founded synagogues, provided financial assistance and insurance benefits, supplied burial services and sent aid to their hometowns. One other important addition to the inventory of activities which landsmanshaftn undertake is the preparation of memorial (yisker) books. The publication of the yisker books, volumes usually prepared to honor the memory of townspeople killed in Europe during World War II, often replaced the self-help and relief functions of the landsmanshaftn once it became clear that plans to rehabilitate a town and its citizens were futile.[6] The group also serves as a social center for landslayt, people sharing loyalty to a common birthplace which they refer to as di alte heym (the old home) among themselves. These newcomers and their leaders organized themselves to help ease the process of adjusting creatively to their new culture in the context of familiar customs and traditions. Eventually, these organizations come to reflect the acceptance of American traits in their adoption of procedures similar to those of American clubs and fraternal orders, in trends in language use, and in the varying responses to issues and events.

In this essay, I explore the changing orientation of landsmanshaftn to their city or town of origin, to the United States, and to the State of Israel. The data highlight the growing Americanization of organizational behavior and the increased role of Israel as a focus of concern. In addition, the heterogeneous backgrounds of the leadership today is striking. How can we account for and interpret the continuity of landsmanshaft affiliation? We need to explain the pervasiveness of this participation throughout the Jewish community: for men and women, for various socio-economic classes, and among different generations, encompassing children of immigrants born in America before World War I and post-World War II immigrants and their offspring. In my interviews with representatives of landsmanshaftn from six European locations—Antopol, Bialystok, Czestochowa, Lodz, Minsk (White Russia) and Warsaw—the landsmanshaft emerged as an institution where American Jewish ethnicity persists.[7]

In studying the role of these immigrant organizations as transmitters of cultural continuity and change in the new country of settlement, the relationship of the researcher to the data at hand was constantly being considered. My own personal engagement with the issue of ethnic identity and Jewish community life, I feel, was an important component in carrying out the research. Furthermore, my concern for recording their story was unembarrassedly and openly demonstrated to the people I approached.

While I was pleased to find relatively little reticence on the part of those who were approached for interviews, my competence in Yiddish turned out to be a central factor in gaining entry into certain kinds of narratives and responses. Yiddish was the language preferred by some of the interviewees, but even when our exchange was in English, my knowledge of Yiddish clearly strengthened our bond and the ease with which we could talk. At the very least, it was intriguing enough to some who might otherwise not have so readily asked me to their homes, sometimes even extending an invitation to share a meal.

Although I had prepared a formal interview guide, my intent was for individuals to serve as much as possible as resource persons reporting on the history and activities of their organizations, rather than as respondents in an opinion survey. Topics discussed often deviated from the prepared outline, based on the interests and suggestions of the interviewees, thereby enriching the data beyond the preconceived list of subjects.

With regard to the dilemma of being an insider or outsider to the research situation, I felt caught somewhere between the two possibilities. I am an insider to the Jewish world, but an outsider to the experience of participating in American Jewish landsmanshaftn, a partner in their ethnic concerns, but a young observer of a world populated mainly by a more elderly subgroup.

Despite shared interests, some topics remained difficult to broach, usually financial matters and those parts of the interview directed to the events of World War II. In retrospect, my own position as a daughter of Polish Jewish Holocaust survivors influenced me to include these reflections, yet the choice seems both rational and necessary. Given my interest in the ties of American landsmanshaftn to the old hometown, it was necessary to ask about events during this crucial historical period. Nevertheless, I did not anticipate my informants' nor my own reactions to the process of recalling emotional and actual responses to that tragic destruction of a world that is no more.[8]

In the process of conducting my research, I also felt deep admiration for the individuals I met, who persevere in their attempts to affiliate and connect with their fellow human beings. They have taught me, more than they know, of the vital significance of sociability and fellowship.

As a result of contacting various Jewish organizations and community leaders in the New York area, a selected list of landsmanshaft activists was assembled. The two major national Jewish philanthropic and fundraising agencies, the United Jewish Appeal (UJA) and the State of Israel Bonds, have divisions that solicit funds from a variety of Jewish lodges, and they maintain the largest rosters of landsmanshaftn. I also turned to Jewish fraternal orders with branches based on locality, including the Workmen's Circle, Farband Labor Zionist Alliance, Jewish Cultural Clubs and Societies, the Independent Order Brith Abraham and Bnai Zion. I also located unallied societies whose work proceeds independently and without any affiliation with other fraternities.[9] A comparative dimension was added to my research by studying landsmanshaftn in Israel, where I conducted interviews with local representatives of landsmanshaftn stemming from the six sites in my sample.[10]

In the United States and Israel, interviews were mainly open-ended face-to-face meetings, ranging from thirty minutes to over three hours. Telephone interviews were made when personal interviews were not possible. In addition, I met with leaders of Jewish communal agencies which work closely with these societies, and also attended landsmanshaft gatherings. Throughout the fieldwork, the historical records and secondary accounts were continually consulted.

Yet another view of the nature and development of organizational dynamics was generated through weekly monitoring from January 1983 to December 1984 of the Yiddish press, as well as by scanning the Yiddish dailies for reactions to the Holocaust on the part of landsmanshaftn during the early years of World War II, 1939 through 1941. In conclusion, I have utilized a variety of methods in order to tap the richness of the data that exist on landsmanshaftn as vehicles for participation.

The Organizational Context for Participation

New York landsmanshaftn, despite their number and heterogeneity, can be arranged according to organizational types. In 1938, the WPA investigation offered a typology that is still useful today. The report begins with religious landsmanshaftn of people from a specific locality, the *anshey* or *khevre*, initially formed around a synagogue yet also offering mutual aid and financial benefits in a manner similar to the other groups.

The next classification, labeled societies, encompasses landsmanshaftn that did not identify themselves as religious organizations. Their names often include such terms as "Progressive," "Independent," "Sick and Benevolent Society," "Young Men's." The outgrowth of this category is the third unit in the typology, namely the women's societies. Either as auxiliaries to the mainly male-dominated landsmanshaftn, or else working independently in some instances, the women's organizations engage in social and charitable activities.

Landsmanshaftn also operated as locality-based branches of various Jewish fraternal orders. These parent organizations either affiliate with labor politics or Zionist principles, or else they may be non-ideological American Jewish fraternities.

The next class of landsmanshaft-type associations incorporates name societies and family circles. According to the 1938 study, these conform to much of the same organizational structure as the landsmanshaftn. However, these groups are identified in their titles with either a family name or that of a distinguished individual they wish to honor.

Other indications of affiliation with the town or city of origin were noted in the formation of separate associations that sent aid to the native community, particularly during pogroms and wartime. Relief organizations launched active fundraising campaigns, creating either coalitions of several independent landsmanshaftn or else acting as emergency committees whose aim was to support political prisoners in Poland. Finally, the WPA survey located landsmanshaft-type clubs whose members were linked by a shared occupation, while other organizations formed specifically to provide loans or credit.[11]

Of the classes of landsmanshaft bodies described in 1938, my survey shows that representatives of each subdivision can presently be found. Landsmanshaft practices persist—burial arrangements, philanthropic and self-help activities, and the provision of a social center for members—although we find varying degrees of adherence to these principles. This essay addresses why affiliation in this organizational context continues.

Participation and Fellowship

Respondents, when asked to describe their landsmanshaft, judge the organization in terms of the opportunity it provides for meeting with one another. Participants value the chance to voice their concerns and opinions, and to discuss and settle deliberations about organizational priorities and goals. Fellowship and companionship, they claim, contribute to the very preservation of the landsmanshaft and the devotion of its members.

The landsmanshaftn originated as hometown-based, hometown-oriented associations, but they owe their endurance in America to other factors. The connectedness and interactions with people here in America overshadow the links that exist with the old home. One daughter summarizes her mother's dedication to the Ladies Auxiliary of the Bialystoker Home for the Aged:

> The feeling for people. Not just the fact that she was born in Bialystok, because let me tell you that my mother was born in Bialystok, moved out of Bialystok when she was a baby, and she was a very young child when she came to the United States anyway.

She continues by explaining that organizational participation "was a way of getting together . . . The women came down and did the cooking, did the serving, did the cleaning . . . When this started, this was their Home." Her remarks leave open the possibility that she is referring not only to the facility, but also to the less tangible abstraction, "home."

Today, it is even clearer that ties to Bialystok and its institutions are not the sole criteria for participation. Members are typically women who live in the neighborhood of the Bialystoker Home, attracted to the social functions and charity work of the group. This development is viewed with mixed sentiments by the leaders: "They don't have the feeling we do, they're not Bialystoker . . ." but this "doesn't mean they cannot be involved in an organization."[12]

It is not uncommon to find that organizations no longer restrict *landslayt* status to fellow townspeople. This issue is highlighted in the observations of one delegate from the Lodz branch of her fraternal order, the Workmen's Circle: "They take in every member . . . because they need the people," with new candidates placed according to their request for a branch in New York that is geographically convenient for them, rather than one that is geographically connected to their origins in Europe. Yet, "people don't want to be wiped out entirely," and request the retention of their town name when a merger of several smaller branches occurs.[13]

The organization's computerized billing system identifies branches according to its specifications, however, filing them under only one name. For the computer, Branch 639 must therefore forfeit parts of its identity as the Workmen's Circle base for members from Warsaw, Mlawa, Tlumach, Rakov. For the president of this branch, the shortened title is not the problem. Which affiliation to select is the issue:

> I don't approve of all the place names. But some people insist on holding on . . . they still want a remembrance of home. But there's nothing to hold on to, not even the Jewish cemeteries . . . they, too,

have been destroyed. In other places, not a trace remains of Jewish life. So why cling to the name?[14]

Even in earlier years, according to the 1938 WPA survey, non-*landslayt* relatives and friends were welcomed into the landsmanshaft (Federal Writers Project 1938). Indeed, the existence of multiple societies from a single locale supports the idea that shared origins in the same birthplace is not the only binding factor.[15] Rather, the desire to meet regularly and affirm bonds of friendship is underscored by informants, even though many landsmanshaftn must contend with the geographic dispersal and old age of many present day members.

Formal ties of membership overlap with informal friendship patterns in today's more vital societies. This situation pertains in one organization, the Lodzer Young Men's Benevolent Society, established in 1902 and restored to a new level of vigor by arrivees from post-World War II Europe. Besides socializing in each other's homes weekly, a core of activists will linger and enjoy each other's company at the conclusion of the official program of their monthly meetings.[16] Another respondent summarizes: "What we discuss is unimportant, as long as we get a chance to talk with one another."[17]

As the previous example suggests, communication among members is one determinant of the durability of a landsmanshaft and its ability to pull members into its orbit. The opportunity to share talk about one's personal past, regardless of the organizational tasks at hand, is a major attraction. This is echoed in one informant's remarks:

> So they see each other once in a month, or maybe some of them meet once in three months. And also they come together, they have something to reminisce, to talk about . . . when you come together, you have a feeling to talk about. Otherwise, somebody once said to me, if you can't talk about who you are . . . who are you?[18]

A Lodz landsmanshaft leader affirms the sentiments that people were interested not so much in the hometown, but rather in other individuals who share similar problems and interests. The search for a common language is both metaphorically and in actuality an underlying motive for building community in the setting of the landsmanshaftn. In the words of one informant:

> I'm longer here than I was in Lodz. But when I hear somebody, a Lodzer, I feel it's a kin of mine. You feel like you could express yourself better . . . When I hear somebody talking my kind of language, so I ask them whether they're Lodzer.[19]

Other Yiddish speakers, including the American-born lands-manshaft leaders who are a generation removed from the chore of learning English, welcome the chance to encounter their special dialect of the language. They acknowledge the special bonds fostered when hearing the particular Yiddish tones of their hometown. "It was the greatest thing . . . It's like having a family."[20]

The landsmanshaft representatives I interviewed for this study span diverse categories. A sense of personal obligation, "a kind of trust that was handed down," and nostalgia motivates some leaders today to continue the family traditions of landsmanshaft participation.[21] For others, the perseverance to do the necessary organizational work is separate from any such commitments.

Most of the interviewees are men, but women are also represented in ladies auxiliaries and in independent ladies aid societies. They are often marked as keepers of landsmanshaft history, more knowledgeable than their husbands about the association because it was the women's families that had ties to the organization. A son-in-law would be recruited into the organization upon marriage, becoming a potential candidate for a leadership position. As one daughter recalls: "My husband got his marching orders when he asked my father for my hand in marriage."[22]

The landsmanshaft in America typically expands its boundaries to include spouses, relatives, and friends who supplement the original core of male immigrants originating from the same birthplace. Guild-like landsmanshaftn such as the Bialystoker Bricklayers, the Bialys-toker Operators Club, the Bialystoker Painters, and the Bialystoker Cutters Social Club characterize the occupational links binding some groups. Laborers were specifically attracted to landsmanshaft divisions of such national orders as the Workmen's Circle or the International Workers Order. Today's distribution of leaders is more diversified socio-economically, and includes accountants, store owners, house-wives, lawyers, bookkeepers, executives, and stockbrokers.

Changes in the nature of American landsmanshaftn and their leaders show that the boundaries of landsmanshaft identification are not fixed, but rather flexible. This elasticity, according to Smith, is related to the fact that voluntary associations and the ethnic communities of which they are a part are "not simply transplanting of Old World . . . loyalties, but reasoned efforts to deal with new challenges" (Smith 1979:1168). As consociations of immigrants in their new country of settlement, ethnic organizations exist with objectives that reach beyond allegiance to the old home. These associations are an appropriate place to examine the emergence of new forms of ethnic identity which develop as a means of social adjustment to new conditions.

Learning to be American in the Landsmanshaft

Most landsmanshaftn are formally established to provide a voluntary organization that expresses the common sympathies of fellow townspeople. Self-help and self-preservation are the watchwords of this initial organizational effort, and varieties of mutual aid are instituted by and for members. However, as the core grows and the landsmanshaft exhibits its durability in the new country, the original precepts are expanded to match the new social structural position of the group.

In its tenure as an immigrant organization, this adjustment occurs in several spheres, such as in language change, in the adoption of the formalities of American fraternities, and in organizational responses and agendas. The criteria for affiliation are extended beyond like-minded *landslayt* from a common European locale to include a more far-ranging field of potential members. So, too, are the limits of organizational platforms stretched to accommodate fresh imperatives. Gradually, the urgency of ensuring material assistance is reduced, and American landsmanshaftn reflect growing familiarity with the host culture.

One result of the continuance of the landsmanshaft community in America is that along with the concentration of efforts on behalf of the hometown, local charities and causes also receive the organizations' attention. Reconciling American and East European Jewish identities remains an ongoing task for these groups and their leaders. The process is complex and puzzling to the participants themselves: they claim special attachments to Jewry's East European past, yet see themselves as members of the American Jewish citizenry. The readiness of many informants to declare their "Americanness" is counterbalanced with the tendency to explain their motivation for joining the landsmanshaft with a rather simple statement: "But I am an Antopoler" or "My parents are from Bialystok," thereby claiming oneness with that identity concurrently with their American allegiance. This unresolved ambivalence is described by Soyer (1985), who relegates the landsmanshaftn to a position somewhere "between two worlds" during the first decades of this century.

In past years' deliberations about aid to the European hometown, as now with regard to efforts on behalf of Israel, it is the group's relation to American society that is pivotal. Despite their vigorous support of Israel, for example, there are American landsmanshaft leaders who have never visited Israel, nor is there a strong alliance with Israeli landslayt. In fact, generalized giving to Israel on the part of American landsmanshaftn has overtaken a sense of personal responsibility for the Israeli landsmanshaft affiliate. This adaptation of organizational principles away from hometown relief and mutual aid toward endorsement of Israeli causes can lead to new definitions of original landsmanshaft precepts: "We're using up the money for . . . the betterment of Israel and Jewishness."[23] The issue today is one of integrating the three aspects of members' concerns—their East European origins, support for Israel, participation as American citizens—within the boundaries of the landsmanshaft community.

To some degree, the generational distribution of landsmanshaftn members contributes to this intricacy; the composite includes immigrants, themselves, their children and grandchildren. In fact, there is not a direct correspondence between age and immigration, such that veteran landsmanshaft leaders may well be American born. Their non-immigrant position is what many of them emphasize, claiming not to be from "the other side," but American.

This was a common reaction on the part of informants which challenged me to reconsider my aim of comparing the orientation of different American landsmanshaftn to their city or town of origin, to the United States, and to the State of Israel.[24] Rather than the triangle of relationships which I anticipated, the associations' priorities are mainly shaped by the society in which the group presently resides. According to the data, this was the case even in earlier years when immigration and the old home were much more a part of recent memory. Even during the period of World War II, the landsmanshaftn seem more linked to American rather than European concerns. Interestingly, even the older immigrant leaders are seen as "very American" by the second generation heirs to these positions, who recall:

> I think that they were very American . . . And the fact that they had come to this country, and they had learned English, and they were able to go to work, join a union, they were able to educate their children . . . So their allegiance to America was very, very strong.[25]

The connectedness of members to their city or town of origin varies, as does awareness of the historical position of their organization's namesake in Europe. The younger American-born leaders of today's organizations may not necessarily know the geographical or historical dimensions of their communities. In the case of Lodz, one of my six sites, this major urban center is mistakenly referred to as a small town by some of the second and third generation members.

As for first generation immigrants, such as the survivors of the Holocaust who settled in New York in the 1940s, their Lodz is different from the city remembered by the pre-World War II settlers. The meeting of the newer immigrants with their American *landslayt* highlighted the differences between the two sectors, particularly in their expressions of affiliation as Jews of Polish descent now in America. In one example, a Holocaust survivor distinguishes between himself and his older sibling, a brother who left Poland to come to this country in 1920 and who is a veteran leader in the landsmanshaft to which they both presently belong, the younger brother having joined after the war: "He really knows little about Czestochowa, he's a Yankee."[26]

One Czestochowa survivor who came in 1947 feels the older immigrants, though they spoke of longing for their old home, really hold in esteem all that is American. To satisfy the Jewish interests which he and other like-minded colleagues share, a separate Czestochowa "Circle" was organized where "each gathering was a cultural event . . . there everything was, of course, conducted in Yiddish."[27] Thus, contact with the larger *landslayt* association may occur for major events, but a more intimate network is necessary for expressing one's own variety of Jewish ethnic identification.

In the case of Lodz, survivors from the city elected to join the existing Lodzer Young Men's Benevolent Society, but initially remained a separate faction. Yet another group of Lodz landslayt who choose to recall their home in Lodz only in terms of their incarceration in the Lodz Ghetto during World War II have named their independent landsmanshaft accordingly. For others, Lodz is remembered for its religious Orthodox community, whose commemoration and preservation is the basis for a separate organization.

The variable expression of ethnic identity in landsmanshaftn is especially highlighted when we focus on a period of time that tests links to the old and the new home. The early years of World War II represent such an era, when the rule of Nazism was already established, yet the full impact of German aggression had not yet precipitated America's entry into the war. We might expect that their claims of maintaining close ties with brethren in the country of origin would predispose the landsmanshaftn more than other members of the community to exhibit special awareness about the fate of European Jewry.

Overall, however, what has been suggested about the general public response by Americans seems true for the landsmanshaftn (see, for example, Grobman 1979; Lipstadt 1986; Wyman 1984). It does not seem that a coordinated plan of action was formulated, nor were these individuals exempt from the inability to recognize the severity of the situation in Europe. Minute books and meeting protocols of the time indicate discussions of routine affairs. In our sample, the active intervention of specific relief agencies coordinated by the landsmanshaftn of Lodz or Czestochowa is a notable exception, although their work really intensified in the years following the war.[28]

The efforts of landsmanshaftn during the war's span are recalled by many interviewees in terms of the patriotic activities of their organization. This could have included buying War Bonds, or sending packages to the servicemen overseas, who were then invited to join the organization free of dues obligations upon returning from the Army.[29] Pictures and letters of these men were printed in souvenir journals from dinners and anniversary balls that were held during the war years.

Actually, there is evidence from many years before the war that the hometown was becoming distant for the landsmanshaftn in America. Souvenir journals, compiled at regular intervals throughout an organization's existence, are a telling sign of the progression of affiliation, and can help explain the situation we find during World War II. For example, on the occasion of their twenty-fifth anniversary in 1927, we read the following message from the Lodzer Young Men's president to his readers:

> Twenty-five years ago, we were wedded to the idea of helping our brethren in Poland, of aiding and serving our needy and neighborly fellowman, and of preparing ourselves to become respected and active citizens of the United States of America. And now it is time, in our maturity, to contribute to the totality of American and Jewish life.

Twenty years later, in a similar album, members propose to change the name of the organization to U.S. Lodge of the Young Men's Benevolent Society, arguing that the once magical word Lodz will "discourage those who follow us from taking our places in the organization in future years." The proposal never materialized, but its very suggestion symbolizes what was discernible during World War II, the group's Americanization and distancing from the European hometown.

Further research is needed to establish the interplay of factors that contributed to landsmanshaft responses during and after the war, as news of the grim details of destruction came through and surviving witnesses joined the community here. To what extent, we might ask, did the landsmanshaft reclaim its unique link with European Jewry? A related task is to understand the way in which that bond is transposed to a strengthened affiliation with Israel.

> Before the war they used to raise money for Lodz . . . And, naturally, the war changed the whole thing. There were no more people left in Lodz, so from supporting needy people in Poland, we supported Israel. And now Israel is the main purpose of any fundraising, any function we have in the organization.[30]

Today Israel is almost universally accepted as a major purpose of organizational charity by American landsmanshaftn. Once they financed the institutions and needs of their hometowns; today, their names appear on projects and buildings in Israel.

It is not unimportant that in its earlier days, the landsmanshaft was a spontaneous experiment in self-government and self-sufficiency, but also a deliberate reaction to the exclusion of East European Jewish immigrants from certain sectors and certain benefits of their society. Today's participation in landsmanshaftn is perhaps more than ever a voluntary association of individuals who may actually pick from a variety of possible alternative organizational affiliations. Given the options which are available to ethnic group members in a pluralist society, what effect does the choice of membership in landsmanshaftn have on how individuals and groups learn norms and values?

An initially unexpected finding, but one which was repeatedly encountered, is the tendency to join and sometimes lead several groups. Landsmanshaft members are also members in the Masons, the Knights of Pythias or other clubs; women enter the synagogue sisterhood, Hadassah, Pioneer Women, or ORT. "Most of the delegates you see at the various meetings all wear different hats."[31] On the other hand, the landsmanshaft is the sole organizational venture for some. One such officer, a lawyer, recounts the lessons he learned:

> It was a good training ground to become a politician . . . It was like sitting in the Assembly, or the Senate, or Congress and trying to rally the forces behind your issue . . . Actually, I cut my teeth with the Bialystoker Young Mens . . . I saw what they were doing, and I realized how I could do it.[32]

Another leader, who held positions in several organizations, reserves a special place for her landsmanshaft: *Never vet zayn greser keyn zakh vi di landsmanshaftn.* . . . (Never will there be a greater achievement than the landsmanshaftn. . . .)[33]

Conclusions

New developments in the structure and function of landsman-shaftn have consequences for the meaning of participation. Fieldwork in New York City shows that the way in which landsmanshaftn orient themselves as an ethnic unit reflects their position in American society today. This study of the current status of a selected group of New York landsmanshaftn, because it also considers a view of their past existence, points up how professed interests of an organization change and adapt to meet the demands of new conditions and new members.

It must be emphasized that landsmanshaftn do not merely provide a setting for leisure time pursuits or for the acquisition of certain kinds of material benefits. In today's society, these ethnic organizations are creative adjustments to urban life. They offer a context in which to discern the rules of the larger society. As the adaptive structural base in which such learning occurs, landsmanshaftn are integral to the life of the individual member, to the immigrant-based community, and to the society as a whole.

Though rooted originally in ties to the old home, the new country of settlement is a significant influence on the direction which landsmanshaftn take. These groups must conform to the larger culture while nurturing their own special bond. Adaptations in the meaning of landsmanshaft membership occur as the original hometown-based motive for affiliation shifts to a concentration on support of local American charities, for example, or philanthropic work for Israel.

In general, it is important to remember that these goals are reinforced by being presented regularly and repeatedly by the Jewish community's schools, synagogues and communal agencies. The tenor of social and political norms also reflect the historical circumstances and new social conditions of post-World War II American Jewish life. The once stricter interpretation of the landsmanshaft as a gathering of fellow townspeople has been modified, but will it widen to include acceptance of the term *landslayt* as a designation for fellow Jews?

The way in which many present landsmanshaft leaders perceive the future of their organizations indicates the inclination to devalue the link to a common birthplace or residence in Eastern Europe. Their own distance from the European hometown, especially but not only for those born in America, accounts for this approach. Such an attitude is also encouraged by the Yiddish press, the major voice for landsmanshaft affairs, which emphasizes a broader shared base of concerns to unite landsmanshaftn with the American Jewish community as a whole.

An even stronger sentiment expressed by landsmanshaft activists is their pessimism about the viability of this form of organization. In this respect, my expression of interest in their organization was often met with surprise. In reflecting on this situation, it seems at least possible that the very minimal level of dissemination of news about landsmanshaft activities in the English-language Jewish press, the media at large, and in other community institutions supports the commonly held notion, accepted by some of the participants themselves, that these associations have lost their purpose.

This evaluation of landsmanshaft affiliation is one of the outcomes of the tendency within the American Jewish community to reinforce the silence about the past and present status of landsmanshaft participation. One consequence of such practices is that landsmanshaft identity is learned to be experienced as nostalgia, with the special ties of ethnicity subordinated to the realm of past memories. Nonetheless, there are signs of landsmanshaft organizational growth in new contexts, in addition to the continuity and evolution of already established groups. The landsmanshaft sector, even in its reduced state of activity today, remains a vital and diverse segment of contemporary American Jewry.

Notes

1. When this newspaper ceased publication on December 28, 1971, it was by that time officially known as *The Day–Jewish Morning Journal*, having merged with the *Jewish Morning Journal* in 1953. For a discussion of this newspaper's position in light of the history of the New York Yiddish press, see Goldberg, 1972.

2. I would like to thank members of the staff of the YIVO Institute for Jewish Research in New York, particularly Susan Milamed and Rosaline Schwartz of the YIVO's Landsmanshaft Archive project. A description of the holdings is found in Schwartz and Milamed 1986. I also extended my archival search to the American Jewish Historical Society in Waltham, the American Jewish Archives in Cincinnati, and the New York Public Library's Jewish Division.

3. See Gertner et al 1983, Lopata 1954, and Soltes 1924 for discussions of the role of the ethnic language press in immigrant communities.

4. The self-reports of landsmanshaft leaders were gathered during August 1983 to August 1984 in Philadelphia, New York, and Tel Aviv. This fieldwork

was made possible through the generous support of the Annenberg School of Communications, University of Pennsylvania, the Memorial Foundation for Jewish Culture, the National Foundation for Jewish Culture, and the Penn-Israel Exchange Program at the University of Pennsylvania.

5. Instructive guidelines on the role of voluntary associations may be obtained from comparative studies on the associational life of numerous ethnic minorities. See John Bodnar, "The Formation of Ethnic Consciousness: Slavic Immigrants in Stillton" in *The Ethnic Experience in Pennsylvania* (Lewisburg: 1973), pp. 309–330; Richard N. Juliani, "The Social Organization of Immigration: The Italians in Philadelphia," Unpublished Ph.D. dissertation (University of Pennsylvania, 1971); Helena Z. Lopata, *Polish Americans: Status Competition in an Ethnic Community* (New Jersey, 1976); Mary C. Sengstock, "Social Change in the Country of Origin as a Factor in Immigrant Conceptions of Nationality," in *Ethnicity*, 4 (1977), 54–70; Mary B. Treudley, "Formal Organization and the Americanization Process with Special Reference to the Greeks of Boston," in *American Sociological Review*, 14 (1949), 44–53; Elena S. H. Yu, "Filipino Migration and Community Organizations in the United States," in *California Sociologist*, 3 (1980), 76–102.

6. See Kugelmass and Boyarin (1983) for a listing of published *yisker* books and excerpts from selected volumes.

7. The selection of the sample was not intended to produce a survey or even a cross-section of landsmanshaftn. The absence of any one central coordinating bureau for landsmanshaftn, as well as limitations on accessibility to some groups and their officers, made it unlikely that a completely representative sample could be attained. For a fuller description of the research design and the study population, see Kliger (1985).

8. As my fieldwork progressed, it became increasingly evident that I would need to evaluate my relationship to the nature of the research process and the questions which I posed to my interviewees. I am indebted to Charles R. Wright for encouraging me to pursue this self-reflective path.

9. My thanks to the many individuals who offered their guidance in helping me generate my interview population, especially staff members of the Council of Organizations of the United Jewish Appeal-Federation Campaign and Israel Emergency Fund, and of the Israel Bonds Greater New York Committee's Department of Organizations-Fraternal Division.

10. For a fuller discussion of contrasts between the Israeli and U.S. groups, see Kliger (1985).

11. The pioneering study of the Yiddish Writers Union of the Federal Writers Project provides the material for this summary. A longer account of the typology of landsmanshaftn is found in numerous works (Federal Writers Project 1938; Federal Writers Project 1939; Rontch 1939).

12. Interview, Bialystoker Ladies Auxiliary.

13. Interview, Workmen's Circle Lodzer Ladies Branch 324B.

14. Interview, Workmen's Circle Warsaw-Mlaver-Tlumatcher-Rakover-Opatoshu Branch 386–639.

15. For example, the recently published *Bialystoker Memorial Book* (Shmulewitz 1982) cites forty-six organizations of descendants from Bialystok.

16. Interview, Lodzer Young Men's Benevolent Society.

17. Interview, Workmen's Circle Bialystoker Branch 88.

18. Interview, Lodzer Young Ladies Aid Society.

19. Interview, Workmen's Circle Lodzer Ladies Branch 324B.

20. Interview, Warshauer Benevolent Society.

21. Interview, Ochoter Warshauer Young Men's Progressive Society.

22. Interview, Ochoter Warshauer Young Men's Progressive Society.

23. Interview, Antopoler Young Men's Benevolent Association.

24. This approach was borrowed from the study of Polish-American voluntary associations conducted by Lopata (1954).

25. Interview, Warshauer Benevolent Society.

26. Interview, Czenstochauer Young Men.

27. Interview, Chenstochover Circle of Brooklyn.

28. See YIVO Landsmanshaftn Archives, Record Group 987: United Czenstochauer Relief Committee, and Record Group 966: United Lodzer Relief.

29. Interview, Lodzer Friends Benevolent Society.

30. Interview, Lodzer Young Men's Benevolent Society.

31. Interview, Minsker Young Friends Benevolent Association.

32. Interview, Bialystoker Young Men's Association.

33. Interview, Antopoler Ladies of Harlem.

References

Applebaum, Karl
    1952   A History of the Jewish Landsmanschaftn Organizations in New York City. Unpublished MA thesis, New York University.

Baker, Zachary M.
    1978   Landsmanshaftn and the Jewish Genealogist, Toledot 2:10–12.

Bodnar, John E.
    1973   The Formation of Ethnic Consciousness: Slavic Immigrants in Stillton, *In* The Ethnic Experience in Pennsylvania. John E. Bodnar, editor, pp. 309–30. Lewisburg: Bucknell University Press.

Curchak, Mark P.
1970   The Adaptability of Traditional Institutions as a Factor in the Formation of Immigrant Voluntary Associations: The Example of the Landsmanshaftn, The Kroeber Anthropological Society Papers 42:88–98.

Doroshkin, Milton.
1969   Yiddish in America: Social and Cultural Foundations. New Jersey: Associated University Presses, Inc.

Federal Writers Project.
1938   *Di yidishe landsmanshaftn fun nyu york* (The Jewish Landsmanshaftn of New York). New York: Yiddish Writers Union.

Federal Writers Project.
1939   *Yidishe familyes un familye krayzn fun nyu york* (Jewish Families and Family Circles of New York). New York: Yiddish Writers Union.

Goldberg, B. Z.
1972   The Passing of The Day—Jewish Morning Journal, Midstream 18:12–38.

Grobman, Alex.
1979   What Did They Know? The American Jewish Press and the Holocaust, 1 September 1939–17 December 1942, American Jewish History 68:327–52.

Higham, John, editor.
1978   Ethnic Leadership in America. Baltimore: The Johns Hopkins University Press.

Juliani, Richard N.
1971   The Social Organization of Immigration: The Italians in Philadelphia. Unpublished Ph.D. dissertation, University of Pennsylvania.

Howe, Irving.
1976   World of our Fathers. New York: Harcourt Brace Jovanovich.

Kliger, Hannah.
1985   Communication and Ethnic Community: The Case of Landsmanshaftn. Unpublished Ph.D. dissertation, University of Pennsylvania.

Kugelmass, Jack and Jonathan Boyarin.
1983   From a Ruined Garden: The Memorial Books of Polish Jewry. New York: Schocken Books.

Levinthal, Helen Hadassah.
1932   The Jewish Fraternal Order: An Americanizing and Socializing Force. Unpublished MA thesis, Columbia University.

Levitats, Isaac.
1959   The Jewish Association in America, *In* Essays in Jewish Life and Thought Presented in Honor of Salo Wittmayer Baron. Joseph Blau et al., editors, pp. 331–49. New York: Columbia University Press.

Lipstadt, Deborah.
1986   Beyond Belief: The American Press and the Coming of the Holocaust 1933–1945. New York: The Free Press.

Lopata, Helena Znaniecki.
1954   The Function of Voluntary Associations in an Ethnic Community, Polonia. Unpublished Ph.D. dissertation, University of Chicago.
1976   Polish Americans: Status Competition in an Ethnic Community. New Jersey: Prentice Hall.

Milamed, Susan.
1980   Proskurover Landsmanshaftn: A Case Study in Jewish Communal Development. Unpublished MA thesis, Columbia University, 1980.

Mitchell, William E.
1978   *Mishpokhe:* A Study of New York City Jewish Family Clubs. The Hague: Mouton Publishers.

Park, Robert & Herbert A. Miller.
1921   Old World Traits Transplanted. New York: Harper and Row.

Rontch, I. E.
1939   The Present State of the Landsmanschaften, The Jewish Social Service Quarterly 15:360–78.

Schwartz, Rosaline and Susan Milamed.
1986   From Alexandrovsk to Zyrardow: A Guide to YIVO's Landsmanshaftn Archive. New York: YIVO Institute for Jewish Research.

Sengstock, Mary C.
1977   Social Change in the Country of Origin as a Factor in Immigrant Conceptions of Nationality, Ethnicity 4:54–70.

Shmulewitz, I., editor.
1982   *Der Byalistoker yisker-bukh* (The Bialystoker Memorial Book). New York: The Bialystoker Center.

Soyer, Daniel.
1985   Between Two Worlds: The Jewish Landsmanshaftn and Questions of Immigrant Identity, Unpublished MA thesis, New York University.

Treudley, Mary B.
1949   Formal Organization and the Americanization Process with Special Reference to the Greeks of Boston. American Sociological Review 14:44–53.

Weisser, Michael R.
  1985   A Brotherhood of Memory: Landsmanshaftn in the New World.
         New York: Basic Books, Inc.

Wyman, David S.
  1984   The Abandonment of the Jews: Americans and the Holocaust
         1941–1945. New York: Pantheon Books.

Yu, Elena S. H.
  1980   Filipino Migration and Community Organizations in the United
         States, California Sociologist 3:76–102.

8 Family, Kinship, and Strategies for Upward Mo~

Myrna Silverman

In this paper, Myrna Silverman points out the way in which Jewish families and kin have supported each other in their adaptations to the American environment. She here supports the view that ethnic and kinship solidarity have been of particular aid to those who have used small business as the ladder for higher social and economic status. Paradoxically, as Schoem points out, Jewish success in this realm has undercut the preservation of the culture from which the social cohesion originated. Silverman uses family and community history in her account of the Davidson-Kalson family.

Introduction

Kinship plays an important role in both remote, primitive societies and urban-industrial societies. Families may be a source of economic support for their kin and can also perform mediating and socializing functions for their members. Particularly, a kin network can aid in a member's survival and adaptation to urban, complex societies. If the family member has "the credentials," the network can assist him or her in achieving both individual and family goals (Sussman 1977:15; Leichter and Mitchell 1967:65).

Generally, studies on family and kinship have challenged the usefulness of kinship bonds in the attainment and maintenance of middle-class status (Parsons 1943; Gans 1962; Goode 1970; Schneider and Smith 1973). At the same time, studies have questioned using ethnicity to identify or define behavior patterns in middle-class life (Gans 1962; Schneider and Smith 1973; Sandberg 1974). Encouraged by supporting empirical data from studies by Aiken and Goldberg (1969); Whitten (1969); Leyton (1970); Ianni (1972); Hammel and Yarbrough (1973); and Levy (1973), my study of Pittsburgh's East European Jews questions both of these assumptions (Silverman 1976).

This case study of a three-generation Jewish family describes the formation of a close-knit unit of family and kin who pooled their economic resources to sponsor the upward mobility of their members. During the upward climb, their ethnicity was an asset because it determined who should be included in this resource pool. It also provided the basis for repeated family gatherings; hence, the continuous renewal of kin ties.

The potential for using family, kin, and ethnicity as strategies for upward mobility greatly depends on how the members of an ethnic group are received where they live, what resources are available to them, and what the opportunities are for attaining upward mobility.

A study of Pittsburgh's Jewish community between 1972 and 1974 provided the opportunity to interview Jewish families whose predecessors had immigrated or migrated to Pittsburgh, Pennsylvania from East Europe at the turn of the century.[1] The Davidson-Kalson[2] family was selected as an example of a family that was prepared to assist its members in their pursuit of economic mobility. The family made use of its ethnic heritage and value system to reinforce family solidarity and continue interaction between members.

Pittsburgh's Jewish Community: A Brief History and Overview

Pittsburgh's earliest Jewish settlers were German Jews whose influx into the Pittsburgh area from 1840 to 1860 appears to have coincided with the development of the city as a critical center of economic development and an important link between eastern and western sections of the country (Wilson, in Feldman 1959).

By the 1870s immigrants to Pittsburgh and the country as a whole had begun to change from largely northern Europeans to southern and eastern Europeans. Lithuanian Jews were one of the first groups of East European Jews to come to Pittsburgh. With few exceptions, these immigrants came in small groups or individually, husbands frequently preceding their wives and families (Feldman 1959:61). Between 1890 and 1892, more Jews settled in Pittsburgh than at any previous time during the nineteenth century. They were met by Jewish immigrant aid societies, established by the German Jews, that aided in their settlement and pursuit of jobs (Feldman 1959:42–59).

By 1897 there were approximately 10,000 Jews in Pittsburgh (Feldman 1959:64); by 1905 approximately 15,000; and in 1917 approximately 40,000 (Cooper 1918:198).

Most of these Jews settled into "the Hill," an area adjacent to the central business district. Unlike many of the East European peasants who were coming at the same time, these Jews were able to adapt fairly well to the conditions of an urban environment and an urban economy. Because Jews had frequently been forbidden to own land or enter public employment in eastern Europe, they engaged primarily in small-scale commerce and handicrafts, usually in urban areas (Bienenstock 1950:240). In Pittsburgh and in many of the smaller communities around the city, such skills were readily transferable and many of these immigrants became shopkeepers and petty traders. Also, since it was commonly believed at the time that "a Jew cannot work," opportunities to compete with other ethnic populations as unskilled laborers were rare. Apparently even Jewish mill owners refused to hire Jews because of this stereotype (Pine 1940:45–46). Thus the primary mode of economic adaptation for Pittsburgh's Jews became the self-owned business or trade. Many East European Jews started as itinerant peddlers in small working-class communities, the mill and mining towns in and around Pittsburgh. Others formed cottage industries such as the production and marketing of stogie cigars.

As they became economically successful, Jews began to develop more Americanized patterns of housing, religion, and social interaction. The first evidence of this change was a movement out of the Hill to other communities not associated with their past. However, they continued to sustain their ties to their families in the Hill through frequent visits, participation in ethnic rituals, and economic support for their poorer kin.

Migration out of the Hill followed the traditional patterns of succession and replacement (Warner and Srole 1945). Migration was eastward, generally along the major lines of public transportation, to the areas of Oakland, East End, and Squirrel Hill. Gradually, as new neighborhoods became associated with upward mobility and more recent immigrant groups moved into the ghettoes and neighborhoods of primary settlement, the majority of the city's Jews moved into these newer areas. Some of those who had settled and worked in the small mill towns outside Pittsburgh and the working class communities in Pittsburgh also moved into these areas. Generally, they responded to their environments in new ways by developing new synagogues that emphasized Conservative Judaism instead of the traditional Orthodox synagogues established by their fathers.

By the 1960s, Squirrel Hill's Jewish population had swelled to 65% of the city's Jewish households. The different sectors of the Jewish population then formed a unified, though still not homogeneous, ethnic community of 45,000 Jews. The next shift in the Pittsburgh Jewish population was to the suburban areas east and south of the city, then connected by highways and tunnels with the city center. Pittsburgh's suburban Jews were unlike others throughout the country since they did not form separate and distinct communities.

However, they did fulfill the need of the younger generation to move away from the "gilded ghetto"[3] to areas of status and prestige, but of lower Jewish density.

Much of Pittsburgh's Jewish migration to the suburbs appears also to have been a short-term response to the desire for cheaper housing, de-ghettoized areas, segregated schools, and to particular phases in the life cycle. Movement back into the city to areas adjacent to or in the Jewish neighborhood occurred as families matured or achieved sufficient resources to maintain a household in the city.

The occupational patterns of this generation were also beginning to change. Until the mid-1940s, the economic patterns of the group as a whole had created an image of Jews as a particular occupational group, both locally and nationally. Almost 30% of the workers were employers or self-employed, including self-employed professionals, as compared to 21.8% for the country as a whole in 1930 (Taylor 1941:78).

The high proportion of Jews in the professions was a significant change in the second generation of Jewish Americans. Given the complex status system of *yikhus*, where wealth and/or learning intertwined to produce prestige or status within the Jewish community, it was not unusual that many male children of eastern European immigrants chose to pursue careers through the educational system.[4] One of the best routes to success and esteem was through pursuit of a professional career, both within the Jewish community and in the larger economic and social system. Moreover, many other routes to occupational mobility were blocked by anti-Semitic policies (Higham 1957).

Although many Jewish women worked in family businesses and supported the economic activities of the earlier generations, their economic activities were rarely reported. In 1986, the United Jewish Federation's Community Report cited that 28.5% of Pittsburgh's Jewish women were working full-time, while 24.8% were employed part-time. Forty percent of those who worked in the city of Pittsburgh worked in business-related services, the arts, and blue-collar occupations. Following the patterns of Pittsburgh Jewish men, two-thirds of whom are self-employed, one-fifth of the women are self-employed (U.J.F. 1986:18–19).

In terms of broad trends, the Pittsburgh Jewish community is representative of the American Jewish population. Like the rest of the country, its population is aging. Its over-65 population (21%) is the second largest in the country (Miami is first), and nearly double the United States' national average (UJF 1986). Like other Jewish and non-Jewish communities, the size of the household is 2.5 persons and there continues to be an increase in single-parent families and the population of single people. Due to changes in the occupational structure of the nation as a whole, reduced discrimination, and an alteration in the patterns and goals of Jewish Americans, the migration of the Jewish population away from major centers of Jewish settlement, and from the Northeast in particular, has increased (Goldstein 1971). Occupational options for Jews are increasing and many older family businesses are being sold for lack of an heir. Greater residential mobility is also evident for the third and fourth generations. Settlement still remains primarily within the city's boundaries, however, and those Jews located in suburban communities and outside the city still keep close ties to the "mother" community.

Because of Pittsburgh's particular demographic and ecological factors, certain limitations and incentives for the form and expression of its Jewish community have been established. Religious diversity characterizes this community as the proliferation of Orthodox, Conservative, Reformed, and Reconstructionist branches of Judaism, and other institutions continue to compete for membership. The movement toward Reform has grown in the 1980s although Conservative Judaism represents the largest segment of the community (UJF 1986).

The conservatism of Pittsburgh's Jewish community is also demonstrated by its amazing geographic and social stability over several generations. Peer groups continue to live in the same neighborhoods and participate in the same activities and organizations as their parents. Families continue to have close ties with friends over a span of three generations despite dispersal throughout the city and suburbs. Knowledge of family and kinship relationships is intensive and extensive among native Pittsburgh Jews. Ethnic community stratification, informal social groupings, and ethnic leadership continue to be controlled by native Pittsburghers whose networks and personal ties are old and enduring.

Strategies for Upward Mobility: The Case Study of the Davidson–Kalson Family

The study of the Davidson-Kalson family illustrates some of the factors that motivated Pittsburgh Jewish families to enter into reciprocal economic changes. The conditions and constraints that led to the development of this type of family are: (1) similar limits to socioeconomic mobility; (2) a resource pool of skills, labor, or capital; (3) shared goals, values, and ideologies about the path to success and its rewards; (4) a continuous reciprocal exchange of resources among kin; (5) social and ritual activities with extended kin; and (6) the localization of some members of the extended family. The case study below illustrates these conditions.

The Davidson–Kalson Family

> Bernie Davidson is one of five brothers; four are still living. Their parents were poor Rumanian immigrants who settled in a small mill town west of Pittsburgh. Bernie is also part of a large matrilateral family, the majority of whom have settled in and around Pittsburgh.
>
> The Davidson-Kalsons developed a highly effective and closely knit kin group around a set of brothers-in-law (Max Davidson and Harold Kalson), and their children. The impetus for their solidarity came from the close affective bonds between the brothers-in-law and their wives (who were sisters), economic assistance from an uncle, and a family business that pooled the groups' efforts and provided for their needs. Social, emotional, ethnic, ritual, and occupational solidarities reinforced the economic interdependencies of this kin group.
>
> The segmentation of this group of kin from the larger extended family began in the early 1920s when Bernie's father Max Davidson and his maternal uncle, Harold Kalson, both originally peddlers, became partners in the Dankay Dress Shop in Bradley, Pennsylvania. They borrowed money from Max's half-brother Baruch and established the business in 1926. It was a good time for the emergence of small businesses; many East European immigrants and blacks were migrating to the area to work in the mills and needed ready access to food and clothing. By the time the partnership was dissolved forty-four years later, it had expanded to fifteen stores in the small towns surrounding Pittsburgh. (Silverman 1976)

The development of bonds between the Davidsons and the Kalsons occurred as a result of their cooperation in a family business. Like other East European Jews who entered the country in the late 1800s and early 1900s, Max Davidson and Harold Kalson were faced with limited options for their socio-economic advancement. A stigma was attached to these Jews, as it had been in their former homes in East Europe, excluding them from economic and social options in the American system (Handlin 1954; Higham 1957; Vorspan and Gartner 1970; and others). In fact, their options were even more limited in Pittsburgh. Since the primary mode of economic adaptation for Jews at that time was the self-owned business or trade, kin became a critical resource to these enterprises, providing opportunities for the family as a whole.

Family businesses were also ideal adaptive devices for immigrant Jews in Pittsburgh: they kept kin close by, provided jobs during hard times, had a cheap and loyal labor force, and allowed Orthodox Jews to keep their traditional religious customs. Some family businesses lasted only a short time, or were a prelude to the development of other longer-lasting businesses. Mr. Kalson had attempted several enterprises before joining with Max Davidson, first in a small variety store and then in the successful Dankay Dress Shop.

It was not uncommon for brothers-in-law rather than brothers to start out in business together. Often they had more in common because they were the same age and at the same stage in the life cycle. This was the case with Max and Harold: both had migrated from villages in Rumania and both had married sisters. They also shared similar goals, values, religious beliefs, and ideologies about the appropriate path to success and its rewards.

Beginning as peddlers, each decided to settle in one of the small mill towns south of Pittsburgh where they had established a clientele during their years as itinerant peddlers. The Dankay Dress business represented an opportunity to pool skills, labor, and capital. Both Mr. Davidson and Mr. Kalson were skilled traders; both were willing to invest their labor (and later that of their children) to develop the business as a successful enterprise. But, at least at the beginning of this venture, they also needed capital.

> Bernie commented, "You never thought of going to a bank if you needed money. You always went to a relative." Bernie's Uncle Baruch, who was the first in the family to immigrate to Pittsburgh and had become a legal counselor and real estate investor, was a frequently used resource. Everyone considered him to be the wisest as well as the wealthiest member of the family at that time. "Whatever Baruch said was the way it was." Besides contributing capital to the development of the Dankay Dress Shop, he lent money and gave advice to Max and Harold whenever they needed it. (Silverman 1976)

Baruch's investment in Max and Harold was repaid many years later when he was housed and cared for in the Davidson family home.

The identification with the ancestral country was extremely important for Max and Harold's generation since it defined their language (there were different dialects of Yiddish spoken throughout Europe), their food preferences, their religious practice, and even their customs and manners. The Davidson–Kalson family's attachment to their Rumanian traditions extended even to their choice of burial ground in the Rumanian Cemetery. Ethnic identity, therefore, in this first generation, was a critical factor in choosing (and excluding) kin.

The first generation selected the mode of economic adaptation. They also established which family members were to be involved in pooling resources, reciprocating goods and services, and setting the ground rules for the appropriate path to success. Specific types of resources were shared during these early years. In the David-son–Kalson family,

> another shared resource was housing and food. The Davidsons owned a large house in Bradley and frequently during Bernie's childhood kin on both his mother's and father's side moved in. His Uncle Baruch and his wife's mother, *Bobbeh*[5] Morris, the family matriarch, both spent their last years in their home.
>
> While they were growing up, Bernie and his brothers and cousins worked in the stores without pay in order to support this "family" venture. When "the boys" needed money, they worked in the mills.
>
> The retail business was a "rough business." The Davidsons and Kalsons expected their sons to do better and urged them to go to college and obtain professional training as doctors or lawyers. Bernie's oldest brother was the first of his generation to try. Encouraged by this family and supported by three of his uncles, he graduated and entered a professional field. The others, Bernie, his brothers Donald and Ivan, and his cousin Larry (Harold Kalson's son), all followed his example. The store was doing well by then and with the assistance of the G.I. bill and the family, they all succeeded. (Silverman 1976)

The second generation, Bernie Davidson and his brothers and Larry Kalson, identified with the values and goals established by their parents and supported the family venture through their unpaid labor. They continued to invest in this group by obtaining income from sources outside of the business and pursuing occupational goals that met with the approval of their families.

The economic scene had changed by the 1930s and 1940s when Bernie and his generation were seeking jobs and beginning their careers. In contrast to the earlier generation, the mills were willing to employ Jews and other marginal groups. In fact, small businesses, such as the Dankay Dress Shop and others, were flourishing in the mill communities. Other members of the Davidson–Kalson family had opted to settle and open businesses in these small towns. Many of these communities were at the peak of their development; industry was flourishing in western Pennsylvania and therefore the community merchants were also flourishing.

> Bernie and his brothers all married Jewish women, and they all settled in the area around Bradley after they finished their professional training. Two now live in Pittsburgh, a few blocks from each other. One lives

in a nearby town. One remained in Bradley where he serves as legal and medical advisor to his parents, in addition to his many other services for them.
Many of the members of Bernie's matrilateral family have had successful careers in commerce, optometry, and medicine. The majority setttled in the valleys and small towns near to their parents' homes and businesses where they had both family and ethnic community support for their endeavors. One of the few close kin who moved away was Harold Kalson's son. (Silverman 1976)

Because members of the same extended family often lived in the same area, there was strong incentive for continued interaction. Family residential patterns crystallized and had their greatest effect on family cohesion and interaction when successful immigrants and their children were settling into new neighborhoods associated with their upward climb (Silverman 1978). Many Jews began to buy or build homes that would house their large extended families, and, as children married, they generally moved into residences in the same neighborhoods as their parents. In some cases, married couples remained with their elderly parents to care for them and eventually became the owners of the "family" house. In other cases, family houses were converted into multiple dwellings to house several members of the extended family or were sold to younger family members.

The Davidson sons married and, with the exception of one who remained in the local community, they moved closer into Pittsburgh. This pattern of movement into Pittsburgh, particularly for the second and younger generation, was quite common. The distance between the family home and Pittsburgh was not great (an hour's drive at most) and frequent and routine visits to the family home, at least once a week, sustained family ties and closeness.

Harold Kalson's children differed from the Davidsons. Harold had a son and a daughter. His son pursued a professional career similar to his cousins. However, following his training, he settled in Texas. Harold's daughter Elaine remained in the mill town where she married and raised her children. Both children contributed to the development and maintenance of this kin group in specific ways. As did her cousins, Harold's daughter worked in the family business, particularly after her divorce. Since it was rare for females to be included in the management of a business, Elaine did not become manager of the store until all male claims to the business had been relinquished and the partnership was bought from the Davidsons. Harold's son, Larry, continued to maintain his family ties, not only through participation in major rituals such as bar mitzvahs,[6] and family events, but also as an economic support. When his sister needed financial assistance following her divorce, he and his cousins provided the needed funds.

Ethnicity, religious ritual, and social activities were major factors in maintaining cohesion among the Davidson family, particularly because the extended family did not remain in the same neighborhood.

> Kin solidarities were encouraged and reinforced not only by these continuous exchanges but by family ritual and ethnic observances, such as the Passover *Seder*,[7] by formal family organizations, and by the daily interaction of family members. Because his grandmother and other significant kin lived at his house, Bernie grew up in close contact with his kin. His mother's siblings and their children frequently came to visit his grandmother, *Bobbeh*. During World War II, an attempt was made to formalize these kin gatherings through a family club, called the Morris Family Club. All the descendants of *Bobbeh* Morris and her husband's first wife, some ten children and their spouses and, when they were alive, twenty-two grandchildren, were included. They had regular meetings, a set of officers, and various activities such as summer picnics, *Hanukkah*[8] parties, and the like. The club met for the last time early in the 1960s at the wedding of one of *Bobbeh*'s great-grandchildren. (Silverman 1976)

Kinship clubs in the past served a number of purposes other than social interaction. They maintained kin group solidarity, minimized differences among kin in religious expression, occupation, education, or degree of economic success. By making known family members' needs and resources, they eased the adjustment of families to the demands of the urban industrial environment, i.e., increased mobility and loss of face-to-face interaction. And, as Mitchell notes, kinship groups fit well into the American industrial system, jeopardizing neither business nor friendship contacts (Mitchell 1969:231, 255; Mitchell 1961).

One of the most critical and enduring components of Jewish kinship relationships is economic. It is often the basis for differentiating between close and distant kin, and between kin and non-kin. It is responsible for developing and continuing family solidarity, and largely accounts for the rapid upward mobility of the family as a whole, particularly those specific subgroups who received a greater share of the resources.

"There is an economic aspect to every social relationship," Sahlins reminds us (1968:81). But the nature of the economic relationship depends on the closeness of the social relationship. "Thus, from a relative, 'you can get it wholesale,' and, from a close relative, perhaps for free" (Sahlins 1968:81).

Over three generations, the continuous exchange of goods and services among kin helped them to survive, adapt quickly, and possibly advance into more rewarding economic sectors of the local economy. In turn, these patterns of economic exchange defined one's effective kin.

The type and nature of the exchange varied with the changing needs of each generation. Those in business could provide goods to their relatives at a discount or as gifts on appropriate occasions. Professionals, who were increasing in number, could provide countless services ranging from guidance or apprenticeship for younger kin to free advice. Families supported the business and professional ventures of their kin. A lawyer became the "family lawyer" and was frequently consulted as the "wise man" in the family. Even when "fringe benefits" were minimal, it was expected that the family architect, doctor, or merchant would be used rather than "a stranger" or an "outsider." Families in business were expected to find jobs for kin in need, even if non-kin applicants were more qualified.

> The development and maintenance of their [the Davidson-Kalson family] life style often depended on the generalized reciprocity of resources and services. When Bernie was growing up, economic reciprocity within the kin group was extensive. Since at this time all his kin shared the same marginal economic circumstances, money was usually borrowed from the richest.
>
> Religious rituals and symbols overlapped the economic solidarities among kin. When Bernie and his brothers were bar mitzvahed, his Uncle Harold bought them each their first suit, and his Uncle Daniel (his mother's brother), a jeweler, gave them each a gold ring. Many of Bernie's cousins shared in this same ritual, further emphasizing the solidarity of the kin group.
>
> When Mr. Davidson's oldest son died during World War II, Mr. Kalson and Mr. Davidson purchased twenty-four lots in the Rumanian cemetery for the family. Six lots went to each family and the remaining twelve to the Morrises. Although there is no well-defined plan, it is assumed that all the Kalsons, Davidsons, and Morrises, and their spouses, will be buried there or in nearby plots. It will be the "family cemetery." (Silverman 1976)

In the drive for upward mobility, those whose goals did not coincide with the core group, or who did not seek status or socioeconomic achievement, moved or were pushed to the periphery of the family. While such kin might be ignored for a time, they were not forgotten. When the core group achieved their own immediate goals, these relatives were often supported through summer jobs, gifts, employment in positions lower than those of the core group, and the like. Family members associated with these kin in such ways as attendance at (or acknowledgement of) life crisis events. They did not participate in the "resource pool" of the core kin.

Many changes occurred in family patterns, economic patterns, and ethnic expression by the third generation. Because of increased economic security, aging patterns, new economic and social alternatives, and altered goals, family members no longer lived so close to each other. Spreading out into newly built apartments, suburban areas, other cities or areas of the country, few extended families shared the same household or neighborhood. Family clubs have diminished in frequency and size since older members have moved away, died, or lost interest in the family club and have not been replaced by younger family members, who do not find these organizations suitable to their needs. Even economic activities changed because the third generation was allowed more freedom, both by their families and by the larger society, in their choice of occupation. Family businesses became less common and old ones often have been sold to non-kin or have closed their doors.

In addition, the pressures that drove the first generation no longer exist for the third generation. Economic survival is rarely a problem for them; their success (or that of their parents) has allowed them greater freedom to pursue activities not within the grasp of earlier generations. Ethnicity continues to be associated with the practice of religious rituals, the observance of holidays, and the adherence to codes of conduct appropriate to Jews. In addition, by the 1960s and 1970s, ethnicity was expressed through an identification with Israel and the use of Hebrew phrases rather than Yiddish. *Shabbat Shalom* (meaning Sabbath Peace) replaced the familiar *Gut Shabbes* (Good Sabbath) as the salutation at the Sabbath service.

Sanctions on the infringement of cultural rules have become less severe. Intermarriage no longer causes a severe break in family relations, and divorce has become more frequent among Jews as it has in American society in general. The pursuit of careers outside the home or the traditional area of community voluntary activities has altered the patterns of female activity, but not as a substitute for the traditional goals of marriage and parenthood. The economic and social success of one's children is still important, and families continue to strive for their children's "improvement," culturally, socially, and economically.

By the 1970s, the [Davidson-Kalson] family as a whole were upper middle-class in their life styles, goals, occupations, and income. That is, for the most part, they owned homes of varying degrees of lavishment in the "better" sections of Pittsburgh and its surrounding towns. Most owned two automobiles, were taking "expensive" vacations, sending their children to private day schools and "elite" colleges, and participating "generously" in the Jewish community in fund raising and contributions. Many today are leaders of Jewish institutions and organizations in their respective communities. Only a few in this family "didn't make it."

The pattern of sharing homes with kin continued into Bernie's generation. When he was divorced from his first wife, Bernie lived with his brother and his family. Since then, he and Sharon (his second wife) have housed kin who were going to school in Pittsburgh. Vacations or short trips are often spent at the homes of kin or in their apartments at resorts when they are not being used.

Conclusions

The bonds that hold families together are tenuous ones. When the family elders die, when young kin start to move away, when a family business loses its function as the focal point of family support, the closeness of extended family bonds are threatened.

Without the presence of the senior generation, or the emergence of an acceptable substitute to cement family bonds, the Davidson family may segment into smaller kin groups, just as their parents segmented from their larger matrilateral group.

The loss of the Davidson family home as a focal point for kin interaction actually had a greater impact than the dispersal of kin in two separate communities. Without the structural and ideological solidarity provided by the parents, petty conflicts in the family can become exaggerated. Economic needs are not critical as they were twenty five years ago, although exchanges of wealth still occur to maintain the economic equilibrium of the family.

The preservation of family support systems engaged in economic reciprocity requires a delicate balance between the needs of the nuclear family and those of the larger kin group. Strong bonds of affection underlie the establishment of this relationship and must be maintained if the family unit is to continue to share its resources. With the coming marriage of Bernie's daughter and two of his nephews, there will be many opportunities for reciprocal exchanges between the brothers and their nieces and nephews. The maintenance of an upper middle-class lifestyle is demanding and expensive. As long as the brothers place some value on their image as "a successful family," and, on their loyalties to one another, economic exchanges will occur and the family will maintain its solidarity.

The Davidson case study illustrates several significant features in the organization of closely knit family systems. First, it suggests that a family may have to limit the size of its kin group in order to be effective as a resource pool. Too large a group, such as the entire matrilateral family, might diffuse and drain the group's resources, providing too little to be of benefit to anyone. Second, a crisis such as the loss of a sibling may be a stimulus for continued group solidarity by forcing the family to make plans for a family plot in a cemetery. Third, alignments within the group, such as those among siblings, are frequently (though not always) incentives for strong family support systems. They may even extend to cousins as was the case in Bernie's family. Finally, the development of closely knit support systems are strengthened and enhanced by ethnic symbols such as holiday rituals, life crisis events, and by secular activities such as those identified with the traditional heritage or family clubs which tend to keep kin networks open.

It is important to remember that not all families are equally prepared to share their resources; nor do all families have members who can take advantage of family resources and opportunities. Perhaps more significantly, some family members may not choose to enter into a system of exchange with family and kin in order to support their upward mobility.

The Davidson-Kalson family provides an example of a family that elected to use their family, kin and ethnic identity to support their upward drive for success. Exclusion from the general opportunity structure, frequent economic exchanges, a family business, a common set of cultural, ethnic, and religious values, and settlement within the local area were among the factors that stimulated and enriched this process.

Notes

Acknowledgments. The research on which this paper is based was carried out with support from the Institute on Pluralism and Group Identity of the American Jewish Committee. I am grateful to Lee Silverman and Monica C. Frölander-Ulf, who read and commented on earlier drafts of this paper. My deepest gratitude is to the Pittsburgh Jewish families who shared their lives with me.

1. The case study presented in this paper is among those drawn from a sample of 26 individuals who were selected from the membership of a Conservative Jewish synagogue in Pittsburgh. They were selected because they all were descendants of East European Jews who had migrated or immigrated to Pittsburgh, Pennsylvania, between 1800 and 1920 and because they all consisted of a minimum of three generations of kin living in or around Pittsburgh, up to a 60-mile radius. The methods employed in this phase of the research were those of traditional anthropology, that is, participant observation, the collection of genealogies, and open-ended interviews on specific topics.

2. The Davidson-Kalson family is a factual case study. However, their names and other details in their lives have been changed in order to protect their privacy.

3. This refers to the second generation of economically successful Jewish settlements (Kramer and Leventman 1960).

4. See also Zborowski and Herzog (1952:71–87) and Bienenstok 1950 for details on the concept of *yikhus*.

5. *Bobbeh* (or bobbe, baba) is an affectionate name for grandmother (Rostin 1970).

6. Bar Mitzvah (Mitzva) is a *rite de passage* symbolizing the transition from childhood to adulthood for males in the Jewish religion, at or after the age of thirteen (Rostin 1970).

7. Passover is one of the three major festivals of the Jewish year, commemorating Israel's deliverance from enslavement in Egypt 3,200 years ago, as recounted in the Book of Exodus. On the evenings of the first (and for more Orthodox Jews) the second nights of Passover, a *Seder* or ritual service is held.

8. *Hanukkah* is the eight-day holiday commemorating the destruction of the Second Temple and of the victory of the Jewish Maccabees over the Syrians.

References

Aiken, M. and D. Goldberg
    1969   "Social Mobility and Kinship: A Reexamination of the Hypothesis," *American Anthropologist* 71:261–270.

Bienenstok, T.
    1950   "Social Life and Authority in the East European Jewish Shtetl Community," *Southwest Journal of Anthropology* 6:238–254.

Cooper, C. E.
    1918   "The Story of the Jews in Pittsburgh," *The Jewish Criterion* May 31.

Feldman, J. A.
  1959 The Early Migration and Settlement of Jews in Pittsburgh,
        1754–1894. Pittsburgh: United Jewish Federation of Pittsburgh
        and Pittsburgh Council of B'nai B'rith.

Gans, H.
  1962 Urban Villagers, New York: Free Press.

Goldstein, S.
  1971 "American Jewry 1970: A Demographic Profile," in M. Fine and
        M. Himmelfarb, editors, American Jewish Yearbook 72:3–88. Phil-
        adelphia: The Jewish Publication Society of America.

Goode, W.
  1970 World Revolution and Family Patterns, New York: Free Press.

Hammel, E. A. And C. Yarbrough
  1973 "Social Mobility and the Durability of Family Ties," Journal of
        Anthropological Research 29:145–163.

Handlin, O.
  1954 Adventure in Freedom: Three Hundred Years of Jewish Life in Amer-
        ica. New York: McGraw-Hill.

Higham, John
  1957–1958 "Social Discrimination Against Jews in America, 1830–1930."
             Publication of American Jewish Historical Society, 47:1–33.

Ianni, F.
  1972 A Family Business: Kinship and Social Control in Organized Crime.
        New York: Russell Sage–Basic Books.

Kramer, J. and S. Leventman
  1960 Children of the Gilded Ghetto. New Haven: Yale University Press.

Leichter, H. J. and W. E. Mitchell
  1967 Kinship and Casework. New York: Russell Sage Foundation.

Leyton, E.
  1970 "Composite Descent Groups in Canada," in C. C. Harris, editor,
        Readings in Kinship in Urban Society. New York: Pergamon Press,
        pp. 179–186.

Levy, S. B.
  1975 "Shifting Patterns of Ethnic Identification Among the Hassidim,"
        in J. Bennett, editor, The New Ethnicity: Perspectives from Ethnology.
        St. Paul, MN: West Publ. Co., pp. 25–50.

Mitchell, W. E.
  1961 "Descent Groups Among New York City Jews." Jewish Journal
        of Sociology 3:121–28.
  1969 Cognatic Descent Groups in an Urban-Industrial Society. Un-
        published Ph.D. dissertation, Columbia University.

Parsons, T.
1943   "The Kinship System of the Contemporary United States." *American Anthropologist* 45:22–38.

Pine, K.
1943   The Jews in the Hill District of Pittsburgh, 1910–1940. Unpublished MS Thesis, University of Pittsburgh.

Rosten, L.
1970   *The Joys of Yiddish*. New York: Pocket Books.

Sahlins, M. D.
1968   *Tribesmen*. Englewood Cliffs, NJ: Prentice-Hall.

Sandberg, N.
1974   *Ethnic Identity and Assimilation, the Polish American Community: Case Study of Metropolitan Los Angeles*. New York: Praeger.

Schneider, D. M. and R. T. Smith
1973   *Class Differences and Sex Roles in American Kinship and Family Structure*. Englewood Cliffs, NJ: Prentice-Hall.

Silverman, M.
1976   Jewish Family and Kinship in Pittsburgh: An Exploration into the Significance of Kinship, Ethnicity and Social Class Mobility. Unpublished Ph.D. dissertation, University of Pittsburgh.

Silverman, M.
1978   Class, Kinship and Ethnicity: Patterns of Jewish Upward Mobility in Pittsburgh, PA. *Urban Anthropology*, Vol. 7 (1), 1978, pp. 25–43.

Sussman, M.
1977   "Family, Bureaucracy and the Elderly Individual: An Organizational Linkage Perspective" in *Family, Bureaucracy and the Elderly*, Ethel Shanas and Marvin B. Sussman, editors, Durham, NC.: Duke University Press, pp. 2–21.

Taylor, M.
1941   The Jewish Community of Pittsburgh, December 1938. Pittsburgh: Federation of Jewish Philanthropies.

United Jewish Federation
1963   *The Jewish Community of Pittsburgh: A Population Study*.
1975   *A Demographic Study Report*.
1986   *1986 Community Report: Jewish Population Study of Greater Pittsburgh*.

Vorspan, M. and L. P. Gartner
1970   *History of the Jews of Los Angeles*. Philadelphia: Jewish Publication Society of America.

Warner, W. L. and L. Srole
1945   *The Social Systems of American Ethnic Groups*. New Haven: Yale University Press.

Whitten, N. E., Jr.
   1969   *Class, Kinship, and Power in an Ecuadorian Town.* Stanford, CA.:
          Stanford University Press.

Zborowski, M. and E. Herzog
   1952   *Life Is With People.* New York: Schocken Books.

9 The Hasidim of North America: A Review of the Literature

Janet S. Belcove-Shalin

In this review article, Janet Belcove-Shalin shows how many of the problems found in the social scientific study of American Jews are recapitulated in the smaller area of Hasidic studies. She stresses that most social scientists have tended either to underline the changes which have occurred in North American Hasidic life or to look for continuities between the East European *shtetl* and the "Rabbivilles" of our suburbs. She correctly stresses that there is a dynamic relationship between continuity and persistence on the one hand and change and discontinuity on the other. The Hasidim have reconstituted their once-rural communities in North American metropolitan areas after the destruction and desolation caused by Sovietization and the Nazi genocide. They have skillfully mobilized their limited resources to build new frameworks in an environment which has led others toward assimilation.

A burgeoning Hasidic movement electrified Eastern Europe in the latter half of the eighteenth century, uncovering what A. J. Heschel called "the ineffable delight of being a Jew" (Heschel 1949:75). Although its original momentum languished after the 1860s, its special place in the modern history of Judaism was firmly established. Ever since, Hasidism has been the subject of numerous historical explorations, philosophical disquisitions, and popular accounts. In the academic world, the study of Hasidism was cultivated chiefly by humanistic scholars, whose interest in the subject dates back to the nineteenth century tradition of *Wissenschaft des Judentums*. The social scientific study of Hasidim, by contrast, is of a relatively recent origin. It was not until the last two decades that social scientists began to pay more than perfunctory attention to Hasidic communities of the New World, or for that matter, to the whole area of Jewish studies.[1]

In the last two decades, ethnographic studies of Hasidic life in North America have definitely reached a take-off point. The yield so far has been comparatively small, but it is encouragingly diverse, and it increasingly reflects the methods, theories, and themes of contemporary social science. The following review does not pretend to be exhaustive. However, I hope that it is representative of the emerging trends in the field. I begin with the review of the theoretical and methodological premises underlying contemporary Hasidic studies. Next, I examine five substantive areas of research: charismatic leadership, recruitment practices, cultural performance, self-identity, and tradition and social change. This paper concludes with an agenda for future research.

Methodology

The methods most often used by researchers studying Hasidim are participant observation, personal interviews (both structured and unstructured), visual materials, and life histories. The specific application of these methods reflects the peculiarities of fieldwork among Hasidim.

"Hanging out" at the yeshivas, synagogues, and other locales where Jewish men frequently congregate is one way of establishing contacts and securing future informants (Shaffir 1974, 1978; Mintz 1968). Access is greatly facilitated by the ethnographer's identity. In the Hungarian community of Williamsburg where most of the early studies were conducted, all researchers were men, which is understandable given the fact that only male ethnographers had the luxury of idling about in exclusively male domains. The same behavior would be judged immodest and unseemly for a woman. Furthermore, all researchers were Jewish. Given the insulated nature of the Williamsburg Hasidic community, it is unlikely that the Hasidim would have allowed a Gentile to mingle among them. In fact, the main reason Hasidim would associate with the Jewish ethnographer at all was their hope to intensify his faith. Contrary to common wisdom, an appreciable number of researchers were not the grandchildren of immigrants, fully secure in their American identity, but first generation-born Americans and new immigrants. Having come from a similar religious and ethnic background, these people had far more in common with their subjects of research than most ethnographers. Although they were not Hasidim, and therefore not native to the way of life they were studying, their orthodox roots suggested that they were not altogether strangers. Shared languages and customs, no doubt, stimulated entree into a seemingly impenetrable community. Having too much in common with the members of a Hasidic community under study, however, often proved to be an impediment (Poll 1962), while full-scale membership could effectively preclude the researcher's ability to gather data (Belcove-Shalin 1988). It should be noted that these difficulties of affinity have not proven to be decisive factors for the fieldwork of native ethnographers in other Orthodox communities. Heilman's (1973) study of a modern Orthodox synagogue, in which he was a member, and Helmreich's (1982) research on a "Strictly Orthodox" or Lithuanian-style yeshiva where he had once been a student, have involved an entirely different constellation of role playing and values. As the focus of ethnographic research eventually shifted toward the less insulated Russian Lubavitcher Hasidim of Crown Heights, and more recently, to the Polish and Galicianer communities in and outside New York City, being a male and an observant Jew proved to be less crucial for gaining access to the members of a Hasidic community. The difficulties of finding an entree into a Hasidic community, as well as the ethical and methodological problems encountered along the way, are discussed in Shaffir 1985, Gutwirth 1978a, 1978b, and Belcove-Shalin 1988.

Interviews with Hasidim are typically conducted in English, Polish, Czech, Hebrew, or Hungarian, depending on the linguistic background of a particular person and community under investigation, and of course in Yiddish, the vernacular of East European Jewry. In a technique called "Simultaneous Usage of Multiple Languages" (1962), Solomon Poll deliberately mixed several languages when talking to the Williamsburger Hasidim. The purpose here was twofold: to assure better understanding of the question by the respondent and to demonstrate the researcher's familiarity with local culture, all of which helps to lower social barriers.

Few ethnographers have published their questionnaires (Rotenberg 1978) and research guides (Mintz 1968) or discussed their construction as well as their value. Mintz offers a guide for selection of topics to be covered during an interview. His own questionnaire is based on materials developed by Abram Kardiner and Ralph Linton for the Columbia University Research in Contemporary Cultures project, and an analysis of fifty Hasidic stories from which inferences were drawn regarding the values and beliefs of the Hasidic community. Both Kamen (1985) and Gutwirth (1978b) discuss the limitations of the questionnaire method. While the questionnaire disseminated by Kamen among Bobover yeshiva students was helpful in eliciting demographic and occupational data, the fact that it was censored by school administrators, that an unwilling student body plagiarized each other's responses, and that some of the respondents filled out the forms incompletely (if at all), drastically reduced its value and virtually precluded any "balanced conclusions." Gutwirth asserts that even though the questionnaire is a valuable tool for eliciting demographic data, it is sorely inadequate for comprehending the relationships the Hasidim have with the dominant community in which they live and work. Instead, he urges a greater reliance on participant observation, open-ended interviews, archival research, and the content analysis of indigenous documents.

In appreciation for the multiple environs in which the Hasidim interact, Mitchell and Plotnicov (1975) employ a "contextual methodology," the purpose of which is to delineate Hasidic activities holistically. This method, the authors claim, is not novel; it harks back to traditional field research in which organic relations between social forms were explored. Singer (1978), by contrast, accentuates the "local context" in an attempt to determine how the size, history, geographic location, ethnic composition, and regional values of the community shape its recruitment style and determine its effectiveness. This approach tends to alter a common view of the community as an autonomous entity by bringing to the fore its complex interaction with the outside world. It belongs to a body of work which views the ethnic entity as "fuzzy at the fringes" with its boundaries, loyalties, and labels in a state of flux (LeVine and Campbell 1972).

While a number of ethnographers have included photographs in their work, few attempts have been made so far to use the image as the prime vehicle for capturing the Hasidic ethos. In the words of Kranzler (1972:76), visual methods add "a depth dimension of creative penetration that allows for a more realistic comprehension and reconstruction of the total image" (Kranzler and Herzberg 1972:76). Successful instances of this method are Epstein's (1977) videotape of the expressive behavior of the Bobover Hasidim's *purimshpiyl* (Purim play),[2] Kranzler and Herzberg's (1972) photo essay of community life among the Hasidim of Williamsburg, Cohen and Garvin's (1970) volume that traces a year in the life of several Brooklyn Hasidic communities, and Warshaw's (1976) study of Lubavitcher religious life. These pieces form a link in the long tradition of photo studies of Jewish life begun in Eastern Europe in the nineteenth century (Dobroszycki and Kirshenblatt-Gimblett 1977).

The role of life histories in ethnographic research is discussed by Gutwirth (1972a) and Kranzler (1961). Oral reports, Gutwirth stresses, are an invaluable complement to written history. He urges ethnographers of Jewish communities to record first-hand accounts of pre-war Europe as long as they are still vivid in the minds of Holocaust survivors. Taking a lead from Thomas and Znaniecki, authors of the classic study of the Polish immigrants in the United States (1919:6), Kranzler collected the life histories of members of Hasidic communities. Social institutions, he insists, are better understood if individuals' personal accounts augment abstract studies of formal organizations.

The comparative method is used sparingly by students of Hasidic life. Levy (1975) highlights the differences between the sub-communities of one Hasidic dynasty. Kranzler (1961) compares three main phases of institutional development in the now Hasidic community of Williamsburg. Gellerman (1977), Shaffir (1983), Mintz (1979), and Gutwirth (1972b, 1973) compare the culture and society of various Hasidic groups. Berger (1980), Zylberberg (1984), and Gutwirth (1976b) draw comparisons between Hasidic and Gentile religious communities. Bosk (1974), Sharot (1982), and Freilich (1962) highlight the differences and similarities between the Hasidim and other Jewish movements and social organizations.

To sum up, surveys and statistical analyses have never been popular methods in Hasidic ethnography. As individuals, Hasidim make such elusive subjects that it is doubtful one could ever get representative samples. The traditional techniques of participant observation and interviewing, along with the recording of life histories and visual representations of Hasidic life have proven to be the most useful techniques. While these methods have remained fairly standard, the sort of individual engaged in fieldwork has radically changed. As research moved into the more liberal, non-Hungarian communities, women and non-Orthodox researchers have joined the ranks of ethnographers of Hasidic life.

Theory

A variety of theoretical perspectives inform Hasidic studies, even though much of theory here remains implicit and is clearly subordinate to the task of ethnographic description.

Functionalism remains a predominant theoretical paradigm in Hasidic studies, perhaps reflecting its influence on the social science in the last few decades. Seeing society as a unified system, functionalists consider an institution or activity to be functional if it contributes to the cohesiveness and stability of the social whole. This precept was first clearly enunciated by the French sociologist, Emile Durkheim, who saw in the religious community a "unified system of beliefs and practices [that] exerts a cohesive integrating influence upon the actions and thoughts, both public and private, of its members" (Quoted in Poll 1962:248). A number of Hasidic ethnographers have built on Durkheim's insights. Gutwirth (1972b; 1973; 1976a) and Singer (1980) emphasize the integrative functions of ritual and lore which serve as potent means of generating mutual sentiment. The role of charismatic Hasidic leaders in unifying religious communities is brought to the fore by Bosk (1979), Rubin (1964), and Berger (1980). Poll (1962) analyzes how economic and religious spheres reinforce each other in Hasidic communities.

If Marxism has had any impact on Hasidic studies, it is mostly as a negative frame of reference. Poll (1962), Rubin (1972), and Kranzler (1961), each of whom wrote monographs on Williamsburg Hasidim, turn the Marxist notion of historical materialism on its head by showing how the Hasidic belief system molds Hasidic economic behavior. According to Poll, Jewish law and custom largely determine production and consumption in Hasidic communities. The status of a member of the Hasidic community reflects not so much the individual's profession and income as "the frequency and intensity of [his] religious observance" (117). Similarly, Rubin attempts to show that cultural rather than economic sanctions serve as primary agents of social control, and Kranzler criticizes a cultural ecology approach, insisting that cultural institutions rather than economic and ecological factors spurred the revitalization of Hasidic communities in Williamsburg. The thesis of the primacy of belief over socio-economic relations has not gone unchallenged. It is called into question by Gutwirth who concludes from his studies of the socio-economic relations among Hasidim (1978b) and between Jews and Gentiles (1972a) that the Hasidic lifestyle is conditioned by the community's economic activity.

Reflecting the broader trends in the social sciences, Hasidic studies began to shift in the 1970s away from the positivist-functionalist paradigm toward a symbolic-interpretive one. This latter theoretical perspective is based on the assumption that "man is an animal suspended in webs of significance he himself has spun" (Geertz 1973:5). The focus of research grounded in this interpretative tradition is on the flexible structure of meaning, as distinguished from the immutable structure of impersonal social norms. As seen from this perspective, the task of the ethnographer is to investigate the multitude of ways in which we make sense of our social universe. Gellerman (1977), Levy (1975), Epstein (1987, 1977), and Belcove-Shalin (1983, 1984, 1988) are the most explicit in their commitment to this model. Many others, however, trace their roots to the same tradition. Shaffir (1974, 1978) grounds his ethnographic description in symbolic interactionism, a theoretical framework developed by G. H. Mead. Berger (1980), Bosk (1979), Sharot (1982), and Rubin (1964) trace their theoretical roots to the work of Max Weber, the father of interpretive social science. Most of these authors use Weber's notion of charismatic authority and its routinization as a foil for their own

ethnographic research. Rotenberg (1978, 1983, 1986) builds on Weber's notion of the Protestant work ethic in his reconstruction of the
Hasidic and Protestant lifestyles, although he draws some of his
ideas from Freud, Durkheim, and Marx as well.

Standing somewhat apart from the rest of the field is the work
by Bosk (1974) who relies on a cybernetic model to delineate structural
imbalances in Hasidic action systems. This model is used to analyze
three Jewish movements, Hasidism, Messianism, and Rabbinism,
which vied for power and influence in eighteenth century Eastern
Europe.

As one can gather from the above, the strength of Hasidic
ethnography lies in its ethnographic exposition rather than in its
theoretical innovation. To this end, various theoretical perspectives
have been utilized to shed light on ethnographic data, rather than
the other way around. Although Hasidic ethnography reflects many
of the theoretical trends that sprung to life in the social sciences in
the last thirty years, only recently has it begun to apply with any
rigor non-positivistic conceptual frameworks. With the exception of
Shaffir's work that studiously utilizes the model of symbolic interactionism, hardly any project could be cited that draws on such
approaches as ethnomethodology, dramaturgical analysis, labling theory, exchange theory, or phenomenological sociology. By the same
token, psychological anthropology and feminist studies are clearly
under-utilized by researchers in the field. Finally, one has to note
with some irony that the sociology and anthropology of religion has
been conspicuously absent in the area of Hasidic studies (Leibman
1981, 1982). One hopes that inquiries into belief, ritual, the sacred,
and the profane will assume their due place in the area of Hasidic
studies.

Charismatic Leadership

While the history of Judaism is dotted with charismatic personalities, it was not until the rise of Hasidism that a Jewish mass-
movement emerged that was based on a popular devotion to charismatic leaders—saint-mystics or *rebbes.* So drastic was this break
with normative or rabbinical Judaism that the allegiance to a rebbe
was considered by the Hasidim's detractors to rival their devotion
to Torah. Today, few ethnographic studies of Hasidic communities
fail to discuss the role of the charismatic rebbe. The more significant
of them (Berger 1980; Sharot 1982; Bosk 1974; Rubin 1972) derive

inspiration and a conceptual framework from Max Weber's writings on charismatic authority and the routinization of charisma.

Most of the discussions of charismatic leadership among Hasidim are philosophical and historical in nature.[3] Sharot (1982) describes the decentralization of charismatic authority and the emergence of Hasidic communities which initially evolved around a rebbe and were subsequently legitimized through the process of succession. The sections on the rebbe's court, which describe the creation of an administrative staff and financial support networks in early Hasidic communities, offer numerous concrete examples of this process.

Bosk (1974) takes issue with Weber's conceptualization of charismatic leadership. In his opinion, Weber emphasized ethical prophecy at the expense of exemplary prophecy and paid scant attention to the ways in which charismatic individuals manipulate their symbolic environment. In this connection, Bosk describes the rebbe's revolt against the dominant rabbinical tradition that yielded the mystical symbolic code of the Lurianic Kabbala, which in turn helped to elevate the rebbe to the status of a model personality. Although this study offers valuable insight into the textual origins of Hasidic charismatic leadership, it raises a number of questions concerning the ways in which charisma is actually routinized. How is charismatic authority realized once the initial surge of enthusiasm dies away and traditional rabbinic traits begin to reassert themselves? What conventions and institutions help to perpetuate charisma? An important clue that Bosk offers in this respect is the legitimation which the office of the Hasidic rebbes acquired after it became hereditary.

The dynastic pattern of succession is examined at length by Rubin (1964). He analyzes two "behavioral clusters" distinguishing all Hasidic communities and contributing significantly to their widespread appeal and longevity: allegiance to the rebbe, and an emphasis on expressive modes of behavior. Rubin's work is of particular interest because the author takes issue with the prominent historian, Simon Dubnow, who believes that the creative phase of Hasidism ended soon after the movement's inception. By arguing that each rebbe has the ability to sustain the joy and ecstasy of his forefathers, and highlighting the volunteeristic aspects of Hasidic life (which are generally overlooked in the analysis of community behavior), Rubin comes to the conclusion that routinization does not necessarily imply bureaucratization, that it can actually be a source of innovation and creativity.

Berger (1980) is another ethnographer who challenges Weber's classical formulations and resists the polarization of charismatic and traditional authority. To make his point, Berger compares the charismatic leadership of the Hasidic rebbe with that of the Rev. Sun Myung Moon, leader and founder of the Unification Church. Both leaders, he insists, exemplify alternative types of charisma, the former one being based on wonder and religious mysticism and the latter one on scientific rationality.

Curiously enough, Berger is the only researcher who deals (even if somewhat gingerly) with the other forms of authority outlined by Weber, i.e. traditional and legal-rational authority. A full-scale study that contrasts rabbinical authority with that of the Hasidic rebbe's is yet to be conducted.

Recruitment

Throughout their history Jews have been the target of numerous attempts at conversion and assimilation. Rarely did this beleaguered community have the wherewithal to stem the tide of acculturation, much less for proselytizing. Today the situation has changed. The Lubavitcher Hasidim are particularly renowned for their well-organized campaigns for recruiting non-observant Jews into a religious way of life. Undaunted by man or machine, they have the reputation for their skillful use of technology in spreading the word of God among potential converts. To save Jewish souls, the Lubavitchers have established Chabad Houses, oases of Yiddishkeit, in communities with large unobservant Jewish populations. Mitchell and Plotnicov (1975), Singer (1978, 1980), and Shaffir (1978, 1974) all explore the dimensions of Lubavitcher proselytizing in these satellite communities, away from the Lubavitchers' Brooklyn headquarters at 770 Eastern Parkway.

Mitchell and Plotnicov (1975) show that proselytizing is an activity with religious and mystical significance for Lubavitcher Hasidim. Returning a Jew's soul to his people is considered a special *mitzvah* (a divine commandment and good deed) among Lubavitchers. No Jew, Hasidim believe, is without a spark of *Yiddishkeit* (Jewishness) in his soul, and if it can be awakened, perhaps some day he may embrace his faith fully. Furthermore, when all Jews observe God's commandments in their entirety, the Messiah will come. Proselytizing, then, is seen as a way to hasten the arrival of the messianic era.

The techniques of recruitment are varied. Mitchell and Plotnicov (1975) describe the efforts of the Lubavitch Youth Organization in Pittsburgh which broadcasts a weekly ½ hour radio program, conducts discussions at local university campuses, and most importantly, operates a fleet of "Mitzvah Mobiles," which are staffed by Lubavitcher students who distribute Jewish ritual objects, teach women to light the Sabbath candles and men to don *tefilin* (phylacteries). Initiated by the Lubavitcher Rebbe at the time of Israel's Six Day War, the teffilin campaign is an enterprise for which the Lubavitchers are particularly renowned (Singer 1978; Shaffir 1978, 1974). Singer's (1980) study focuses on folklore as a means of proselytizing. Story-telling, he argues in his study of the Lubavitchers of Los Angeles, is an excellent agent for conversion because it taps shared sentiments of identity, common anxieties of persecution, and helps create a festive atmosphere at Chabad House, the prime site of recruitment.

The results of Lubavitcher proselytizing are varied. Mitchell and Plotnicov (1975), as well as Shaffir (1978, 1974), report that despite a massive campaign, few non-observant Jews in Pittsburgh or Montreal have actually joined Orthodox ranks. Singer cites a better success rate in Los Angeles where the Lubavitchers, fighting what they consider to be a last-ditch effort to rescue masses of secularized youth, launched a particularly aggressive campaign.

The traditional assumption that proselytizing aims chiefly at recruiting the non-Orthodox Jew, is questioned by Shaffir (1978, 1974). In the process of recruiting or "witnessing" among non-Orthodox Jews, he maintains, the identities of young impressionable Lubavitchers are reinforced. Contrary to common wisdom, these youngsters' commitment is not at all based on their prowess at this venture, for very few outsiders are actually proselytized. When a Lubavitcher proclaims his faith by engaging another in conversation on the importance of Torah, mitzvot, and *Ahavas Yisroel* (love for one's fellow Jews), he is, in fact, persuading himself. Drawing upon the work of such social interactionists as G. H. Mead, Shaffir asserts that a person can become the object of his own activity, for just as he acts toward others, he acts socially toward himself.

This provocative study raises some interesting questions. Since witnessing is a collective effort, what of the effect one Lubavitcher's proselytizing has upon another? Shaffir cites Cooley's notion of "the looking-glass self" which implies that an individual's self-esteem and identity are contingent upon the response of others, but fails to apply this insight to his case. Furthermore, what role does the response of the non-observant Jew play in identity consolidation? Could the hostile reactions of the outside world eventually erode Lubavitcher self-confidence? To what extent can identity affirmation be construed as the result of repeating one's message, some sort of auto-indoctrination, as Shaffir asserts, and to what extent is it also a product of the positive interaction with one's peers and potential converts? The interplay between proselytizing as both a recruitment technique and social construction of reality promises to be a rich vein for future research. So far, most studies of Hasidic recruitment have taken place among Lubavitcher Hasidim, which is understandable given the fact that when the tefilin campaign was initiated some decades ago, Lubavitcher proselytizing activity was unique in the annals of modern Judaism. In recent years, however, other communities have developed their own outreach programs. The most prominent among them is that of the Bostoner Hasidim (Brussel 1975). Their *Shabbatones* (Sabbath get-together) are quite prominent, and by all accounts, quite successful. Even Belz, one of the more traditional Hasidic communities, is beginning to attract a number of baalai tshuvah into their community. Witnessing might well be the wave of the future among ultra-Orthodox Jews.

Cultural Performance

Expressive behavior, or what anthropologists call cultural performance, is the area of Hasidic studies that overlaps most closely with traditional humanistic scholarship. What makes ethnographic accounts different is that the ethnographer perceives such expressive conduct as dance, music and storytelling not so much as instances of artistic virtuosity than as the expression of community values. As religious rituals, cultural performances are highly charged symbolic codes designed to gear the participants to the sacred. As social activity, they confer status on the virtuoso, valorize social norms, and contribute to the overall integration of the community. Cultural performances also serve as acculturative mechanisms: they are the pores through which foreign ways and customs are reconciled with the Hasidic tradition.

Despite the fact that the Hasidic tale has been considered by many to be "the greatest creative expression of Hasidim" (Scholem 1941:349), few ethnographers have given it the systematic treatment it deserves. The exceptions to this trend are Mintz (1968), and more recently, Eliach (1982) and Singer (1980). The collections of legends prepared by Mintz and Eliach are gathered from the various Hasidic courts of Brooklyn. Mintz includes in his introduction a discussion of the context and functions of storytelling, the different genres of Hasidic legends, and the sources of these tales, noting that with the revitalization of Hasidim on American shores, places which are a part of the American landscape and experience have made their way into Hasidic stories. This integrative quality is evident in Eliach (1982) who presents a selection of legends based on the narrators' Holocaust experience. Her volume is noteworthy as the first edition of tales in which both men *and* women serve as protagonists. Despite their similarities, these works differ sharply in their orientation. Mintz's study has been inspired by the Boasian Culture and Personality School, as exemplified by Boas' and Benedict's study of mythology, which integrated accounts of everyday attitudes and the oral literature. Mintz is careful to distinguish this approach from the literary one pioneered by Martin Buber and Louis I. Newman, whose editorial decisions, in his view, transfigured the Hasidic tale to such a point where they offer a largely inadequate picture of Hasidic life. His goal, by contrast, is to present the tales "completely and accurately," so that the final product would allow "the reader to evaluate the analysis for himself." Eliach, on the other hand, belongs squarely to a literary tradition. She has carefully selected the tales with an eye to the "inner spiritual strength" of the Hasidim (xix) and partially rewritten them "in a consistent literary style so as to give the tales of cohesive form and structure" (xxiii). Her emphasis is not so much on ethnographic "documentation," as on "art" (Ibid). Singer (1980), who shares Mintz's ethnographic animus, focuses on the values of the tales' protagonists. His primary objective is to show how folklore communicates implicit norms and values and thereby helps to initiate the non-observant into Hasidic life.

Of all the mediums of Hasidic expression, dance has been the least systematically explored. To the best of my knowledge, Gellerman (1977) is the only one to have described women's dance style in three Hasidic communities and explored the way in which each dance pattern reflects alternative ethoses. By contrast, music has received a good deal of scholarly attention. A collection of hundreds of *nigunim* (melodies accompanying Hasidic dance), along with a full-scale analysis of the form-structure of this genre is gathered by Hajdw and Mazor (1974).[4] Brief overviews of the nigun's ethos and melos are presented by Pasternack (1972) and Avenary (1964). A comparative study of the music of Hasidim and that of jazz artists is made available by Katz (1970). Koskoff (1978) throws into clear relief a thesis implicit in most of this research, namely, that the Hasidic musical repertoire reflects the practice of appropriating foreign melodies. Specifically, she analyzes the types of tunes Lubavitchers are likely to adopt, the contexts and agents of acculturation, and the manner in which songs are altered to make them acceptable to the ways of this ultra-Orthodox community. The discussion of the mystical and cultural significance of the nigun transcends the purely musicological analysis of Hasidic tunes and is relevant to the study of Hasidic acculturation in general.

Most studies of Hasidic cultural performance have concentrated on a particular dramatic genre to tap this community's ethos and world view. On the other hand, Epstein's (1987) description of the Bobover Hasidim's Purim celebration is reminiscent of what Barbara Myerhoff called a "definitional ceremony" in which members of a community make sense of themselves by "show[ing] themselves to themselves" through multiple performative enactments (1987:143). Bobover Hasidim invest Purim with meaning specific to their experience and religious tradition. This cultural mirroring is most evident in the way the Bobovers redefine what for most Jews is a thoroughly spirited festival of drama, song, and dance into a day of atonement. Reflecting their Kabbalistic heritage, Purim is transformed into a Yom Kippur.

It is rather ironic that the study of cultural performance has remained such an underdeveloped area of Hasidic research, for it was precisely the Hasidim's emphasis on expressive modes of worship that was so instrumental to their revolt against rabbinism in the eighteenth century. A systematic analysis of dramatic genres can be an important tool in the arsenal of ethnographers studying the Hasidic ethos.

Hasidic Identity

Considering the vast amount of impassioned prose written on the subject of "Who is a Jew?", it is somewhat surprising how little attention has been paid so far to the Hasidic identity. A few authors have researched the way in which Hasidim perpetuate their communal identity through an analysis of kinship ties. Levy (1975), Berger (1977), and Berger-Sofer (1984) examine the ways in which Lubavitcher men *and* women (this latter group having received short shrift by ethnographers) maintain their ethnic solidarity by manipulating genealogical relations. Berger-Sofer's study, which probes the interrelationship between the kinship network of the Lubavitcher dynasty and the historical context, delineates the diminishing role played by the women in the kinship network in the context of a rise in numbers of male offsprings. The expansion of Lubavitcher Hasidim during its fourth generation, she believes, catalyzed the changes in the dynastic kinship network. In her analysis of modern-day marriages among Lubavitcher Hasidim, Levy finds that hypergamous relations are preferred over hypogamous ones because a woman is expected to follow the traditions of her husband. In point of fact, hypogamous marriages are quite rare, due in part to the particularly limited contact women have outside the Lubavitcher environment.

Most scholars appear to take the cultural characteristics of the Hasidic community for granted, viewing them as immutable and self-evident. Those few who have spelled out these traits concentrate on the timeless qualities deeply rooted in Hasidim's past. For Pinsker (1975), piety is the most prominent constitutive characteristic of a Hasidic community. Poll (1962) makes a similar observation, although he goes a step further, delineating four basic attributes which, he insists, all Hasidim share: a particular appearance, value system, ecstatic ritual behavior, and devotion to a rebbe. This typology, to use Weber's language, is in the nature of an "ideal type" or pure case, i.e. it highlights the qualities inherent in a Hasid's Hasid (if such a person could ever be found in reality) and so, clues one in to the normative values of the Hasidic community. Poll does not stop with the delineation of cultural attributes. By looking at the frequency and intensity in the outward expression of religiosity, he divides the community into six social classes—a procedure intended to bridge culture and social structure.

More recently a quite different approach to the subject of identity gained prominence in Hasidic studies, this one emphasizing the intentional and interactional component of the Hasidic identity. Instead of treating an individual as an instance of a class, this approach attempts to show how the individual transgresses social boundaries and, willingly or unwillingly, spills over classificatory categories. This emergent, variable nature of the Hasidic identity is emphasized in the works of Levy (1975) and Belcove-Shalin (1988). Levy examines the methods by which Lubavitcher Hasidim manipulate cultural forms to create a strong sense of community. The significant word in the last sentence is "create." A Hasid's identity is seen here not as fixed but as "floating," something that can be strategically activated and situationally deployed through the manipulation of symbols. Belcove-Shalin confounds the image of Hasidim as self-content pietists in her analysis of the fierce undercurrent of spiritual struggle among Hasidim as they position themselves on ever-new thresholds of piety, without ever being able to claim to have succeeded fully.

Concerted attempts to "bracket" the taken-for-granted aspects of Hasidic reality characteristic of this approach, help to explicate the volunteeristic component of the Hasidic identity. The focus of attention here is on what social scientists refer to as micro-structures: the everday activities, states of consciousness, and frames of reference in terms of which individuals construct their social selves. One hopes that eventually these inquiries would also include the *Hasidista's* (Hasidic woman's) identity, which so far has received only scant attention.

Tradition and Social Change

Scholars and commentators have always been fascinated with the Jews' extraordinary capacity to absorb alien ways into their own unique cultural system without loosing their ancient moorings and severing their ties with tradition. Anthropologists and sociologists describe this process of adaptation as "acculturation." The thing that strikes the external observer first and foremost in the Hasidic lifestyle is how faithful contemporary Hasidim are to their century-old tradition. Several studies focus on this remarkable continuity of the Hasidic tradition, and specifically on the ways in which Hasidism have reconstituted themselves in the New World.

Kranzler (1961) shows how despite conditions of urban decay which precipitated the flight to suburbia, Hasidim have entrenched themselves in Williamsburg and regenerated the social institutions and lifestyle they had formed in Hungary. The Hasidic yeshiva is one such institution that enables the Hasidim to perpetuate their norms and customs. Kamen (1985) demonstrates how yeshivas have provided a total environment in which young impressionable minds are socialized into the ways of their forefathers through the study of Torah, how Hasidic rituals are learned to create a special bond of loyalty between the rebbe and his future followers, and how students are schooled in jobs deemed compatible with the community's world view, all of which assures continuity in the Hasidic lifestyle.

In one of the earliest studies of this kind, Freilich (1962) compares the cultural life of the Eastern European shtetl with that of "Rabbiville," a suburban Hasidic community outside New York. His purpose is to illustrate the many age-old symbols and values which Hasidim from Rabbiville transplanted from the Old World and which in many ways are remarkably similar to the life in the Pale of Settlement shtetl. Freilich uses the model of the shtetl first advanced by the Columbia University Project on Contemporary Cultures. Out of this project came a number of important studies, including the popular *Life is With People*, which focused on the cultural continuities between shtetl lifestyles on both continents. Despite its heuristic value, this approach has serious limitations, one of which is the tendency to distill all of Ashkenazic Jewry into one overarching pattern (Kirshenblatt-Gimblett forthcoming). Two stereotypes of shtetl life, in particular, are perpetuated in Freilich's study: Rabbiville is portrayed as an autonomous, isolated, and timeless entity that suppresses the political activism, economic relations, demographic processes, and modes of acculturation which link this community to its township, state, and nation. The impression one frequently gleans from the studies done in this tradition is that one deals with a home of former shtetl dwellers, whereas in fact a good number of European Hasidim came from cities and had fully adapted themselves to an urban existence. Indeed, Rabbiville is not an isolated rural community, but rests on the perimeter of metropolitan New York City.

More recent studies of Hasidic communities are free from the constrictions of the shtetl paradigm and highlight the community's texture and transformations. Both Shaffir (1976, 1983) and Mintz (1979) document how Hasidim have developed a knack for the art of politics. In his study on Hasidic yeshivas, Shaffir writes how daring the Hasidim are at innovating a secular curriculum that fulfills existing government requirements, thus enabling their community to receive municipal funding and at the same time, protects their religious values. Similarly, Mintz pinpoints the ways in which the Hasidim of Williamsburg have evolved into shrewd culture brokers, skilled in lobbying techniques which help them to obtain favorable rulings from the local government.

Shaffir (1986) and Gutwirth (1972b) discuss the evolution of alternative social structures and novel social relations in Hasidic communities. In one of the few studies of the Hasidic family, Shaffir documents the impact of external influences on the nuclear unit, and so, shows how malleable this "pillar" of tradition actually is. Gutwirth discusses the ways in which the ultra-Orthodox of Antwerp and Montreal have united to form viable and expanding religious communities, despite the differences in their religious orientation and national backgrounds.

Poll (1962) and Jochnowitz (1968) explore the ways in which the Hasidic vernacular, Yiddish, has evolved since the Hasidim settled in the United States. Yiddish is regarded by linguists as a "fusion language" on account of its remarkable ability to absorb new words and grammatical constructions, even creating novel words from the roots and affixes of different linguistic traditions (Weinreich 1980). Normally Hasidim eschew the language of the people whom they perceive as a threat to their religious integrity (Poll 1965). Thus Hungarian Hasidim discourage subscribing to non-Hasidic Yiddish newspapers and associating with Yiddish speaking but non-religious persons. Still, important linguistic changes occur even within the Yiddish-speaking communities. Jochnowitz points out that despite the presence of multiple dialects in the Lubavitcher neighborhood of Crown Heights, children show a remarkable fidelity to North-Eastern (Belorussian) Yiddish, and unlike their parents speak a genderless Yiddish. Both Jochnowitz and Poll note that while men are more likely to communicate in Yiddish (the language of yeshiva instruction), women are more apt to speak to one another in English or in the language of their place of birth.

Most studies of Hasidim present a somewhat idealized view of Hasidic society which minimizes the discordant facets of community life. This portrayal is in keeping with the shtetl paradigm in which the tone is overwhelmingly sentimental and romantic. Yet there are reports of deviance and types of change among Hasidim which could be potentially disruptive to the community. Rubin (1972), for one, conveys the stringencies and hard-headedness for which the Satmar are well-known, as well as the explosive tensions which uneasily rest just below the surface. Only the Satmarer rebbe, it seems, can keep a lid on this churning cauldron. Recognizing that deviance and defections are not uncommon in this community as it adapts itself to American culture, Rubin pinpoints various modes of social control the Hasidim use in their dealings with unruly members.

Few studies explicitly deal with the process of cultural and social innovation. In the early sixties, Poll described a strategy he termed "sacralizing secular activites" by which the Hasidim utilized the paraphernalia of modern culture for religious ends. Thus an automatic timer can be transformed into a *shabbos zeiger* or sabbath clock by a click of a switch which automatically turns on and off the lights; heavy-gauge stockings serve as special symbols of modesty when worn by Hasidic women; a refrigerator becomes a facilitator of kashrut. Twenty years later, Belcove-Shalin (1983, 1984) described a common strategy of "sanctification" which the Hasidim use to hallow the profane in the service of the Lord. Like Poll's model, Belcove-Shalin's account has a functional component, since sanctification can be viewed as an acculturative impulse that enables the Hasidim to adopt new conventions and accommodate social change. Nonetheless, her approach differs in some signficiant respects. Whereas Poll applied his model exclusively to material culture, Belcove-Shalin focuses on activities and persons as well. The latter tack, which emphasizes the importance of intentionality and the definition of the situation, helps to reveal the dialectical interrelationship between sanctification and separation, the dual strategies used by Hasidim to absorb alien cultural forms and to maintain their separate existence.

In sum, the study of tradition and social change is an important area of Hasidic ethnography which has already produced a number of interesting insights. I wish to stress, however, that a typical study in this area tends to focus either on tradition or on social change. As a result, one side of the coin is often emphasized at the expense of the other (as is the case, for example, with Freilich's work which pushes the thesis of continuity to its logical extreme). It is the dialectics of continuity and discontinuity that is of primary theoretical importance in this field of scholarship, and one hopes that future projects will be more explicit in their concern with the interplay between these two conflicting imperatives.

Conclusion

The social scientific study of Hasidic communities has made significant strides since the time when the socio-linguist, Joshua Fishman, lamented, "What about the recently formed Hasidic enclaves in sections of Brooklyn? They are still virtually unknown territory to the American social scientist" (1958–1959:98). Research over the last two decades has generated a small body of work representative of many a theme and perspective that guide modern social science. Today, the legitimation of these studies and Jewish research in general has received further impetus from academic journals, endowed chairs, and publication series cropping up at major universities, as well as the growing number of papers presented at academic conferences. This last point is particularly noteworthy. For the first time in the history of the American Anthropological Association, an entire panel was devoted to Hasidic life during the eighty-fifth annual meeting. The papers presented at the Hasidic session titled, "Lubavitch: The Hassidic Mystique," highlight a number of fertile areas of scholarship and innovative methods of research including: (1) The micro-analytical approach to social life; (2) performative aspects of self-presentation (Jayanti 1986; Goldberg 1986); (3) women's experiences (Kaufman 1986; Koskoff 1986; Goldberg 1986); and (4) Hasidic proselytizing and the enhancement of one's faith (Pastner 1986). To varying degrees, these studies utilize models from the humanities for their inspiration, rather than from the positivistic social sciences. Perhaps this is a sign that ethnographers are returning, albeit in a metamorphosed fashion, to their humanistic roots. Armed with new ideas and methods, they may find themselves in a position to shed a new light on the "ineffable delight of being a Jew," which as Heschel noted long ago, is the key to a Hasidic way of life.

Notes

I wish to express a special debt of gratitude to Dmitri N. Shalin for his comments on earlier drafts. I also want to thank A. T. Kirsch, James A. Boon, and Carol J. Greenhouse for their input on balance and tone, and particularly, Barbara Kirshenblatt-Gimblett for her concrete suggestions.

1. The discussion in this paper refers exclusively to Western social science and does not apply to a separate tradition of Eastern European Jewish ethnography. The focal point of research in Eastern Europe (Soifer 1978) was folkloristic and historic. Sh. An-ski was probably the most prominent among Eastern European ethnographers of this century. Between 1911 and 1914 he conducted several expeditions to the Ukraine during which he gathered a plethora of valuable materials, including tales, songs, and photographs.

2. This tape is available at the YIVO Institute of Jewish Research, N.Y.

3. A notable exception to this trend is the work of Zalman Schachter (1981), a scholar and a Hasid, who adopts a psychiatric perspective to give a definitive analysis of the *Yehidut* (Encounter) transaction by which the rebbe counsels his Hasid. Much of the rebbe's prestige rests upon the success of these sessions.

4. Although these tales were collected in Israel, the authors' conclusions are valid for the study of Hasidic music in any part of the world, and so, have been included in this review.

References

Avenary, Hanoch
    1964   The Hasidic Nigun: Ethos and Melos of a Folk Liturgy. Journal of the International Folk Music Council. 16:60–63.

Belcove-Shalin, Janet S.
    1982   Notes From the Underground: Fieldwork in Hasidic Boro Park. Paper presented at the eighty-first American Anthropological Association Meetings in Washington, D.C.
    1983   Rituals of Sanctification in a Hasidic Community. Paper presented at the eighty-second American Anthropological Association Meetings in Chicago.
    1984   The Dialectics of Separation and Sanctification Among the Hasidim of Boro Park. Paper presented at the National Jewish Folklore Conference, Living Tradition: Jewish Folk Creativity and Cultural Survival.

1988   Becoming More of An Eskimo: Fieldwork Among the Hasidim of Boro Park. *In* Between Two Worlds: Essays on the Ethnography of American Jewry. Jack Kugelmass, editor, Ithaca: Cornell University Press.

Berger, Alan L.
1980   Hasidism and Moonism: Charisma in the Counterculture. Sociological Analysis 41(4):375–390.

Berger, Rhonda Edna
1977   An Exploration into the Lubavitcher and Hasidic Leadership Kinship Alliance Network. YIVO Institute for Jewish Research Working Papers in Yiddish and East European Jewish Studies, #27. New York.

Berger-Sofer, Rhonda
1984   Political Kinship Alliances of a Hasidic Dynasty. Ethnology 23(1):49–62.

Bosk, Charles
1974   Cybernetic Hasidism: An Essay on Social and Religious Change. Sociological Inquiry 44(2):131–144.
1979   The Routinization of Charisma: The Case of the Zaddik. Sociological Inquiry 49(2–3)150–167.

Brussel, S. G.
1975   Continuity and Change: A Study of the Hasidic Community of Boston. Ann Arbor: University Microfilms International.

Cohen, Arthur A. and Garvin, Philip
1970   A People Apart: Hasidim in America. New York: E. P. Dutton.

Dobroszycki, Lucjan, and Barbara Kirshenblatt-Gimblett
1977   Image Before My Eyes: A Photographic History of Jewish Life in Poland. 1864–1939. New York: Schocken Books.

Eliach, Yaffa
1982   Hasidic Tales of the Holocaust. New York: Avon Books.

Epstein, Shifra
1977   The Celebration of a Contemporary Purim in the Bobover Hasidic Community. Ann Arbor: University Microfilms International.
1987   Drama on a Table: The Bobover Hasidim Piremshpiyl. *In* Judaism: Viewed From Within and From Without. Harvey E. Goldberg, editor, pp. 195–217. Albany: State University of New York Press.

Fishman, Joshua A.
1958–1959   American Jewry as a Field of Social Science Research. YIVO Annual of Jewish Social Science 12:70–102.

Freilich, Morris
1962   The Modern *Shtetl:* A Study of Cultural Persistence. Anthropos 57:45–54.

Geertz, Clifford
1973   The Interpretation of Cultures. New York: Basic Books.

Gellerman, Jill
1977   The *Mayim* Pattern as an Indicator of Cultural Attitudes in Three American Hasidic Communities: A Comparative Approach Based on Labananalysis. YIVO Institute for Jewish Research Working Papers in Yiddish and East European Jewish Studies, #26. New York.

Goldberg, Robin
1986   The Story of Dvorah Leah: Fundamental Myth For Lubavitcher Hasidic Womanhood. Paper presented at the eighty-fifth American Anthropological Association Meetings in Philadelphia.

Gutwirth, Jacques
1972a Les Juifs en Europe de l'Est: Problematique inter-ethnique. *In* Actes du Premier Congres International d'Ethnologie Euro-peenne. Paris: Institut d'Ethnologie, Microfiches 71–080–50.
1972b The structure of a Hassidic Community in Montreal. Jewish Journal of Sociology 14:43–62.
1973   Hassidim et Judaicite a Montreal. Recherches Sociographiques 14(3):291–325.
1976a Les Pains Azymes de la Pâque chez les Hassidim. Objets et Mondes 16(4):137–138.
1976b Rapport de Mission aux Etats-Unis (1975–1976). Report to the Centre National de Recherche Scientifique, dated Nov. 1.
1978a L'Enquete en Ethnologie Urbaine. Herodote 9:38–55.
1978b Fieldwork Method and the Sociology of Jews: Case Studies of Hassidic Communities. Jewish Journal of Sociology 20(1):49–58.

Hajdw, A. and Y. Mazor, in collaboration with Bathja Bayer
1974   The Hasidic Dance—*Niggun*—A Study Collection and Its Clas-sificatory Analysis. *In* Yuval. Israel Adler and Bathja Bayer, editors, pp. 136–266. Jerusalem: Magnes Press.

Heilman, Samuel C.
1973   Synagogue Life: A Study in Symbolic Interactionism. Chicago: University of Chicago Press.

Helmreich, William B.
1982   The World of the Yeshiva: An Intimate Portrait of Orthodox Jewry. New York: The Free Press.

Heschel, Abraham Joshua
1949   The Earth is the Lord's. New York: Farrar Straus Giroux.

Jayanti, Miriam
1986   The Chabad Telethon: Public and Private Faces of a Hassidic Outreach Group. Paper presented at the eighty-fifth American Anthropological Association Meetings in Philadelphia.

Jochnowitz, George
  1968   Bilingualism and Dialect Mixture Among Lubavitcher Hasidic Children. American Speech 43(3)182–200.

Kamen, Robert Mark
  1985   Growing Up Hasidic: Education and Socialization in the Bobover Hasidic Community. New York: AMS Press.

Katz, John
  1970   Chasidism in Jazz. Journal of Synagogue Music 2(4):28–33.

Kaufman, Debra
  1986   Experiencing Chassidism: A Woman's Perspective. Paper presented at the eighty-fifth American Anthropological Association Meetings in Philadelphia.

Kirshenblatt-Gimblett, Barbara
  The Study of Jewish Folklore and Culture, forthcoming.

Koskoff, Ellen
  1978   Some Aspects of Musical Acculturation Among Lubavitcher Hasidim. YIVO Institute for Jewish Research Working Papers in Yiddish and East European Jewish Studies, #32. New York.
  1986   The Sound of a Woman's Voice: Gender and Music in an American Hasidic Community. Paper presented at the eighty-fifth American Anthropological Association Meetings in Philadelphia.

Kranzler, George
  1961   Williamsburg: A Jewish Community in Transition. New York: Philipp Feldheim.

Kranzler, George, and Arthur Herzberg
  1972   The Face of Faith: An American Hassidic Community. Baltimore: The Baltimore Hebrew College Press.

Leibman, Charles, S.
  1981   The Sociology of Religion and the Study of American Jews. Conservative Judaism 34(5):17–33.
  1982   The Religious Life of American Jewry. In Understanding American Jewry. Marshall Sklare, editor, pp. 96–124. New Brunswick: Transaction Books.

LeVine, Robert A. and Donald T. Cambell
  1972   Ethnocentrism: Theories of Conflict, Ethnic Attitudes, and Group Behavior. New York: John Wiley and Sons.

Levy, Sydelle Brooks
  1975   Shifting Patterns of Ethnic Identification Among the Hassidim. In The New Ethnicity: Perspectives from Ethnology. John W. Bennett, editor, pp. 25–50. St. Paul, MN: West Publishing Co.

Mintz, Jerome R.
1968   Legends of the Hasidim: An Introduction to Hasidic Culture and Oral Tradition in the New World. Chicago: The University of Chicago Press.
1979   Ethnic Activism: The Hasidic Example. Judaism 28(4):449–464.

Mitchell, Douglas and Leonard Plotnicov
1975   The Lubavitch Movement: A Study in Contexts. Urban Anthropology 4(4):303–315.

Myerhoff, Barbara
1987   Life, Not Death in Venice: Its Second Life. In Judaism: Viewed from Within and from Without. Harvey E. Goldberg, editor, pp. 143–169. Albany: State University of New York Press.

Pasternack, Velvel
1972   Chasidic Music. Congress Bi-weekly 33:14–18.

Pastner, Stephen L.
1986   Recruiting for Hashem in the Wilderness. Paper presented at the eighty-fifth American Anthropological Association Meetings in Philadelphia.

Pinsker, Sanford
1975   Piety as Community: The Hasidic View. Social Research 42:230–246.

Poll, Solomon
1962   The Hasidic Community of Williamsburg. New York: Free Press.
1965   The Role of Yiddish in American Ultra-Orthodox and Hassidic Communities. YIVO Annual of Jewish Social Science 13:125–152.

Rozen, David Joel
1980   The Village of New Square: A Study of Health in the Hasidic Community. Ann Arbor: University Microfilms International.

Rotenberg, Mordechai
1978   Damnation and Deviance: The Protestant Ethic and the Spirit of Failure. New York: The Free Press.
1983   Dialogue with Deviance: The Hasidic Ethic and the Theory of Social Contraction. Philadelphia: ISHI.
1986   Hasidic Contraction: A Model for Interhemispheric Dialogue. Zygon 21:210–217.

Rubin, Israel
1964   Chassidic Community Behavior. Anthropological Quarterly 37(3):138–148.
1972   Satmar: An Island in the City. Chicago: Quadrangle Books.

Schachter, Zalman
1981   The Encounter: A Study of Counselling in Hasidism. Ann Arbor: University Microfilms International.

Scholem, Gershom G.
1941 Major Trends in Jewish Mysticism. New York: Schocken Books.

Shaffir, William
1974 Life in a Religious Community: The Lubavitcher Chassidim in Montreal. Toronto: Holt, Rinehart & Winston of Canada.
1976 The Organization of Secular Education in a Chassidic Jewish Community. Canadian Ethnic Studies 8:38–51.
1978 Witnessing as Identity Consolidation: The Case of the Lubavitcher Chassidim. In Identity and Religion: International, Cross-Cultural Approaches. Hans Mol, editor, pp. 39–55. Beverly Hills: SAGE Publications Inc.
1983 Hassidic Jews and Quebec Politics. Jewish Journal of Sociology 25(2):105–118.
1985 Some Reflections on Approaches to Fieldwork in Hasidic Communities. Jewish Journal of Sociology 27(2):115–134.
1986 Persistence and Change in the Hasidic Family. In The Jewish Family: Myths and Reality. S. M. Cohen and Hyman, editors, pp. 187–199. New York: Holmes and Meier.

Sharot, Stephen
1982 Messianism, Mysticism, and Magic: A Sociological Analysis of Jewish Religious Movements. Chapel Hill: The University of North Carolina Press.

Singer, Merrill
1978 Chassidic Recruitment and the Local Context. Urban Anthropology 7(4):373–383.
1980 The Use of Folklore in Religious Conversion: The Chassidic Case. Review of Religious Research 22(2):170–185.

Soifer, Paul E.
1978 Soviet Jewish Folkloristics and Ethnography: An Institutional History, 1918–1948. YIVO Institute for Jewish Research Working Papers in Yiddish and East European Jewish Studies, #30. New York.

Speigler, S.
1965 Fact and Opinion: Hasidism "Integrated" into Williamsburg YMHA. Journal of Jewish Communal Service 41(3):300–304.

Stern, Stephen
1986 "Returning" To Orthodox Judaism as a Career. Paper presented at the eighty-fifth American Anthropological Association Meetings in Philadelphia.

Thomas, William I. and Florian Znaniecki
1919 The Polish Peasant in Europe and America. Boston: The Gorham Press.

Warshaw, Mal
1976   Tradition: Orthodox Jewish Life in America. New York: Schocken
       Books.

Weber, Max
1963   The Sociology of Religion. Boston: Beacon Press.

Weinreich, Max
1980   History of the Yiddish Language. Chicago: University of Chicago
       Press.

Zborowski, Mark and Elizabeth Herzog
1952   Life is With People: The Culture of the Shtetl. New York: Schocken
       Books.

Zylberberg, Jacques
1984   Nationalisation et denationalisation: le Cas des Collectivetes Sac-
       rales Excentriques. Social Compas 31(4):409–426.

10 Separatist Orthodoxy's Attitudes Toward Community—The Breuer Community in Germany and America

Steven M. Lowenstein

In this article, Steven Lowenstein, a social historian, implicitly describes the strategies of identity and acculturation utilized by German Separatist-Orthodox Jews. Lowenstein points out some of the paradoxes in Hirschian orthodoxy. While upholding the Jewish tradition, it did so by proclaiming the rights of individuals to withdraw from the Jewish community in Germany. While sharing the rejection of religious liberalism with Hasidim and other Orthodox Jews, the Hirschians accepted modern secular culture. In their accommodations to pre-Nazi Germany and to the changing conditions in the Manhattan neighborhood of Washington Heights, the Hirschians have shown the kind of resilience which Spicer has called a "persistent cultural system." This quality has provided them like their Hasidic co-religionists, with success in New York City neighborhood politics.

Samson Raphael Hirsch and his Separatist Orthodox followers have bequeathed two apparently contradictory legacies to later generations. On the one hand, Hirschian Orthodoxy proclaimed a confessionalization of Judaism almost as radical as that of his Reform opponents. For Hirsch, Judaism was primarily a religion, and the national and communitarian elements in Judaism had a justification only insofar as they contributed to their religious purpose. For this reason, Hirsch recognized only communities led by the Orthodox as legitimate and denied the need for all Jews in a particular locality to be members of the same organic *kehilla*. [Kehilla is the traditional Jewish term for the organic Jewish community. In the pre-modern world, the kehilla combined functions usually associated with a religious body (hiring clergy, upkeep of houses of worship and religious education) and those more commonly associated with local government (taxation, regulation of Jewish commerce, etc.). Every

Jewish community, no matter what the size and number of synagogues, had a single local kehilla].

Yet, the same Hirschian Orthodoxy which denied the supremacy of the organic kehilla over ideological religious differences, produced one of the only successful attempts to transplant the kehilla structure to the United States. This paper will attempt to show the connection between the rejection of the geographically-based kehilla in Germany by the Hirschians and their successful creation of a kehilla in the United States. It will also explore the extent to which Hirschian separatism precludes or permits co-operation with non-Orthodox forces to promote common goals.

Orthodox Jewry has had to react to a radical change in the relationship between Jewish tradition and Jewish community in the modern world. Before the great changes which began in Western Europe in the late eighteenth century, the Jewish community had been an autonomous self-governing body with considerable powers of internal discipline. The kehilla had its own communal courts in which the halachic determinations of the official communal rabbinate could be enforced. The community was an important instrument for the enforcement of traditional norms against any who might try to flaunt them.

This function of the community began to change in Western Europe (especially in Germany) in the course of the nineteenth century in two important ways. First, the community lost most of its power to make legal decisions in civil matters as well as the right to enforce its decision with fines and excommunication. Second, at a somewhat later date, most large urban communities passed out of the control of traditionalist forces into the hands of laymen who sympathized with the new religious Reform movement. Orthodoxy had to handle a double challenge—first to retain the loyalty of Jews without the use of coercive power and second to come to grips with an official Jewish community in which their point of view no longer predominated.

Samson Raphael Hirsch and the Ideology of Separatism

The lifework of Samson Raphael Hirsch was devoted at least in part to tackling these twin challenges. Hirsch, through his writings, tried to make traditional Judaism attractive to individual educated German Jews, having given up the idea of using the coercive power of the Jewish community. In attempting to meet the challenge of an official community dominated by Reform, Hirsch also made use of this new individual approach. Using tactics which marked a sharp break from traditional attempts to use coercion, Hirsch argued that the rights of Orthodoxy were a matter of freedom of conscience (Liberles 1985:208).

This new approach was most evident in Hirsch's championing of the famous Prussian secession law of 1876. Until that year, Prussian law had required that all persons born as Jews automatically be members of their local Jewish community. Only one Jewish community was permitted in each locality, grouping all Jewish residents. All members of the community were required by law to pay taxes to the community for the upkeep of its various institutions including all local synagogues. The only way one could withdraw from the community was to renounce one's Jewishness.

Champions of Hirschian Orthodoxy teamed up with extreme Jewish liberals to procure a new law which permitted withdrawal from the Jewish community without withdrawal from Judaism. Hirsch had declared that it violated the conscience of an Orthodox Jew to be forced to pay for the upkeep of Reform religious worship. He declared that the differences between Orthodoxy and Reform were greater than those between Catholicism and Protestantism (Liberles 1985:208 quoting Denkschrift 1873:6). An even more extreme statement of Hirsch's view that Reform Judaism was a separate and foreign religion is quoted in the memoirs of Saemy Japhet. Japhet refers to a sermon given by Hirsch in which he stated: "Rather be buried in Sachsenhausen [in the Christian cemetery] under the sign of another faith than in communion with those [reformers]." (Japhet:1948:117).

These statements clearly show that Hirsch viewed Judaism in confessional terms and that he rejected any argument of the value of forming a unified community based on common ethnic and national interests. In a pamphlet published in 1870 Hirsch said "Religious unity has not existed for some time and wherever it is missing the enforced unity of the community . . . is nothing but an empty form." (Liberles 1985:202). In the words of one observer: "Hirsch considered the community as nothing else but a religious association of like-minded people." (Heinemann 1948:125).

In fact, for Hirsch, 'klal yisrael' [the collectivity of the Jewish people] was a religious concept only, including only those Jews who fulfilled the religious purpose of their peoplehood. Hirsch therefore said it was the liberal Frankfurt Gemeinde and not Hirsch himself who violated the Mishnaic maxim 'al tifrosh min hatsibur' (do not withdraw from the community). In a memorandum of 1858 to the Frankfurt Senate the *Israelitische Religionsgesellschaft* [Hirsch's community] had stated "We are not the separators . . . but the last remnant that has remained true to the traditional shrines of Judaism." (Liberles 1985:179). By rejecting Orthodoxy the Reformers had, in the eyes of the Hirschians, given up their status as a legitimate Jewish community.

After passage of the new law, Hirsch declared it the religious duty of all members of his congregation to declare their withdrawal *(Austritt)* from the Jewish community of Frankfurt and to belong exclusively to Hirsch's *Israelitische Religionsgesellschaft*. He even declared that the first question after death "When you appear before God would be 'Are you *ausgetreten'* ? (Have you left the community)." Japhet 1948:117).

Hirsch's attitude brought him into conflict with Seligmann Bamberger, another leader of German Orthodoxy, a man far more traditional in his intellectual and cultural position than the Westernized cultured Hirsch, who declared that withdrawal was not required if the liberal majority provided for the religious needs of the Orthodox (Japhet 1948:115; Heinemann 1948:128; Liberles 1985:220–224). It also does not seem to have convinced the majority of his own membership, most of whom continued a double membership in the Frankfurt Jewish community and in the Hirschian community. "When the official list was published, it was disclosed that of 355 members of the *Religionsgesellschaft*, only 85 had left the mother institution. . . . We cannot get away from the fact that 75% of the congregants did *not* obey the command of their rabbi." (Japhet 1948:119).[1]

Hirsch's *Religionsgesellschaft* in Frankfurt was, on the one hand, a voluntary community. One was not born into it as were the members of the Frankfurt Gemeinde; rather one joined it because one believed in its uncompromising Orthodox point of view. On the other hand, it performed all the functions of the main community. It had its own cemetery, its own mikve, kashrut supervision, schools, synagogues, yeshiva, and charitable organizations. Frankfurt between 1879 and 1938 had in fact two kehillot existing side by side.

In contrast to Bamberger and other German Orthodox leaders in Germany, Hirsch rejected, as a matter of principle any co-operation with non-Orthodox religious movements or organizations. Hirsch believed in what he called independent Orthodoxy. Hirsch's followers founded the society of Orthodox rabbis whose constitution denied membership to any members of the general association of German rabbis which grouped both Orthodox and Liberal rabbis.[2] His followers founded such other separatist federations as the Prussian Federation of Orthodox Congregations and the Free Association for the Interests of Orthodox Jewry.[3] In the twentieth century they supported Agudath Israel with its motto of an independent Orthodox voice while rejecting any co-operation with Zionism or the Mizrachi [religious Zionism]. This zealous guarding of independence and non-cooperation continued until the Nazis made it impossible in the late 1930s.

The Reconstruction of Hirschian Separatism in New York (the Breuer Community)

The destruction of the German Jewish community forced many followers of Hirschian Orthodoxy to flee Germany and come to the United States. Many of these followers chose to settle in the Washington Heights section of New York City, where a large colony of refugees from Nazi Germany came into existence in the late 1930s and early 1940s. The German Jews who settled in Washington Heights numbered over 20,000 and they founded over a dozen refugee synagogues. Three of these synagogues followed Hirschian principles of Separatist Orthodoxy.[4]

By far the largest and most influential of these congregations was K'hal Adath Jeshurun, or, as it was popularly known, Breuer's. Although the founders of the congregation were not themselves from Frankfurt,[5] the congregation soon acquired a large nucleus of former members of the Frankfurt *Religionsgesellschaft*. With the appointment of Rabbi Joseph Breuer, the grandson of Samson Raphael Hirsch, as rabbi of the congregation, the kehilla acquired the mantle of successor of Hirsch's *Religionsgesellschaft*. The customs of the Frankfurt community were adopted. Rabbi Breuer himself had a great influence in introducing these practices. One interviewee remarked that Rabbi Breuer himself molded the congregation "to be a Frankfurt kehilla." He introduced all Frankfurt minhogim. Before introducing Frankfurt melodies or other customs he was careful to ask permission to do so. Many of the organizational traditions of the Frankfurt Separatist Orthodox community were also introduced.

K'hal Adath Jeshurun grew to become one of the largest and most influential congregations in Washington Heights. It developed a ramified system of institutions and in 1952 built a synagogue with over 1,100 seats. In the forty years since its founding it exerted an ever greater influence on Jewish life in Washington Heights until it became the dominating force in the life of that community. Many came to equate it—erroneously—with the entire Washington Heights German community.

Within five years of the founding of K'hal Adath Jeshurun in 1938, the congregation began to acquire all the trappings of a full-blown kehilla on the European model. The congregation's leadership consciously rejected the American model of the congregation dedicated only to worship and social activities. It aspired to be a "kehilla kedosha." To quote an article by Simon Schwab, Rabbi Breuer's assistant and later successor: "The so-called Orthodox congregation which serves certain religious and social needs of its congregants . . . still does not become a kehillo unless it comprises all facets of Jewish communal life. . . . The true kehillo is an independent entity and not beholden to any non-Torah authority, not associated with any board, federation, roof-organization . . . which is not absolutely and exclusively identified with the Law of the Torah. . . . For almost four decades our kehillo has aspired to live up to such a mandate . . . We have a right to consider the existence of our kehillo a historic phenomenon." (Schwab 1977).

The Breuer community administered, in addition to its own synagogue, the following institutions: a school system beginning with nursery school, continuing through elementary and high school through a teachers' seminary for women and a beth midrash for men which granted semicha (rabbinic ordination), a mikva (ritual bath), a complex system of kashrut supervision covering butcher shops, bakeries, manufactured products, etc., its own rabbinic court, separate burial societies for men and women, a sisterhood, various charity societies including a free loan society, a golden age club and a kosher luncheon club for the elderly.[6] It was also closely associated with the local branch of Agudath Israel which ran a very active youth program for the congregation (Landsman 1969: 12–18, 35, 40, 45, 47, 49). The congregation even had its own Blue Cross-Blue Shield plan (Landsman 1969:45). The 1968 report of *K'hal Adath Jeshurun* gives an idea of the farflung congregational activities.

The worship aspects of the congregation were also complex since they included two full-time rabbis, a dayan [rabbinic judge], a volunteer men's choir, two cantors, a shamash [sexton] and other functionaries. To run such an operation required considerable administrative resources and skills and a large mainly volunteer bureaucratic structure. A good example of the bureaucratic structure of its volunteer apparatus is the description of the functions of each of the nine members of the synagogue committee published in *Mitteilungen*–Apr/May 1968:

1) maintenance of synagogue and lighting, 2) purchase, etc. of utensils, 3) requests for seats, 4) gifts and donations, 5) supervision of yahrzeit lights, 6) distribution of tefillaus, [leading prayers], kaddeshim [the right

to recite the mourner's prayer] 7) registration of weddings, 8) ordering of mitzwaus [synagogue honors], 9) control of zedokoh [charity] boxes.

The congregation was administered by an elected board many of whose members were elected for term after term. The congregation had the same president from 1942 until 1980. Though the board was the chief administrative arm of the congregation, it rarely took action on any matter without consulting the rabbinate of the congregation. In the words of one communal leader, "In an American congregation the rabbi was afraid of the president; in our congregation, the president was afraid of the rabbi. He was a real leader, you know."[7]

Why Could Hirschians Reconstruct an Organic Community in America Where Others Failed?

The success of the Breuer congregation in creating a cradle to grave community covering all aspect of Jewish life, where others failed can be directly related to the nature of its predecessor in Frankfurt. The European organic kehilla had been based on birth and payment of communal taxes by government decree. It was an institution whose membership was not totally voluntary. It was therefore difficult to carry over into America, where all synagogue membership was voluntary. An American synagogue was a private club, with little or no control over kashrut, education, burial, or the like and with no power to tax or judge its members. The immigrants in America, freed of the community's power to tax, were unwilling to see the creation here of any institution which would gain such powers.

The experience of the Frankfurt Separatist Orthodox had been different in Europe. The Prussian secession law of 1876 had freed them to belong only to a community to which they had an ideological commitment. No one could be forced to belong to the *Israelitische Religionsgesellschaft*. Yet this voluntary association was an organic community like its larger rival the Gemeinde of Frankfurt. Like its rival, it taxed its members, ran a cemetery, schools, synagogues and other communal institutions like a full-fledged kehilla. The Breuer group was thus virtually the only group in America which had had a European tradition of an organic community based on voluntary ideological commitment. They were thus able to carry over such a community to voluntaristic America with little difficulty.

The other major groups which were able to create a similar sense of community in America (though with a far greater sense of separateness from general American life) were Hasidic groups. They, like the Breuer community, had had an organic authority structure, in this case based on the institutionalized charisma of the rebbe rather than on a *Religionsgesellschaft,* which was based on ideological and personal loyalty rather than on the accident of being born in a certain town. These types of voluntary commitment could be carried over to America whereas the geographically based organic kehilla could not be.

Continued Separatism in America

The Breuer kehilla retained its commitment to the principle of *Austritt* (secession) in America as in Germany. It refused to belong to any roof organization with any ties to the non-Orthodox. It remained firmly tied to Agudath Israel and vehemently rejected Mizrachi and any other pro-Zionist organization. It refused to collect money for the Jewish Federation, the UJA, Israel Bonds or any other such pan-Jewish organization. It withdrew from the Union of Orthodox Jewish Congregations of America, because of the Union's membership in the "multi-denominational" Synagogue Council of America. In the April/May 1967 issue of its bulletin *(Mitteilungen),* the congregation issued the following statement: "We must deplore the unfortunate fact that the Union of Orthodox Jewish Congregations is still remaining within the Synagogue Council, i.e., in partnership with reformed and conservative Congregations. Many years ago, our Kehilla left the Union for this reason. . . ."

On the neighborhood scale, too, the Breuer community remained fiercely independent. The congregation set up its own yeshiva [religious day school] when the local Orthodox day school displayed the Zionist flag (Landsman 1969:11). Its relationship with its neighbor Yeshiva University remained cool at best and were sometimes close to hostile. "It [the Breuer community] was faced with the choice of identifying itself with Yeshiva University, its neighbor in Washington Heights, and the world of modern Orthodoxy, or with the European Yeshivah world with which it had been aligned in Europe. It chose the latter." (Liebman 1965: 71). In 1982 when a collateral member of the Breuer family [not a member of the Breuer community of Washington Heights] gave money to Yeshiva University on the condition that one of Yeshiva's schools of Judaica be named "the Isaac Breuer school," the Breuer community reacted not with delight but with outrage. They were horrified by the "misrepresentation" involved with the linking of the Breuer name with an institution of a different ideological stripe than that of the congregation.

The Breuer community rarely worked together with other Orthodox congregations in the neighborhood. When attempts were made in 1956 (Beth Hamedrosh Hagodol 1956)[8] and again in 1962 (Hakohol 1962) to set up a Va'ad Harabanim [rabbinic council] of Orthodox rabbis in Washington Heights, the Breuer congregation refused to join, at least in part because the new organization intended to create a kashrut commission [to supervise the kosher supervision in the neighborhood], which would have infringed on an important function of the Breuer kehilla.

The rejection of co-operation with non-Orthodox or less Orthodox roof organizations, did not in theory at least, imply a rejection of the whole non-Breuer Jewish world. In fact, the Breuer community maintained good relations with the yeshiva world and with Agudath Israel, both of which shared many of their separatist ideas (though the Breuer people were more open to western culture than either of these two groups). They raised money for Israeli yeshivas, for Soviet Jewry (through its own organization) and for Shaare Zedek Hospital in Jerusalem. In an interview, one of the leaders of the Breuer community makes a distinction between the idea of separatism and the rejection of 'klal yisrael': "*Austritt* does not mean that you consider the non-Orthodox Jew as a stranger. You are trying to pull him to you, not eject him from you. Only the manifestations of non-Torah life are not recognized, which means the rabbi, the synagogue . . . I have never associated with a non-Orthodox rabbi, but with a non-Orthodox Jew who is willing . . . to be guided by me . . . I will always work."[9] The Breuer congregation could thus take an interest in the whole Jewish world but reject any association with non-Orthodox religious movements.

Neighborhood Crisis and Tactical Modification of Separatism

The rejection of non-Orthodox religious organizations was shaken only in times of severe crisis. When the Nazis came to power in Germany, virtually all Jewish organizations joined in the Reichsvertretung (representation of German Jews), but the Hirschian Orthodox kept their distance because of disagreements on educational policy. In 1934 the Agudah withdrew from the German-Jewish roof organization (Reichsvertretung der deutschen Juden) (Dawidowicz 1975:244). The Frankfurt *Israelitische Religionsgesellschaft* remained separate from the Gemeinde until forced to merge with it by the Nazis after the November 1938 "Kristallnacht" pogrom (Dokumente 1963:256–257). A crisis seemingly much milder which hit the Breuer community in the 1970s brought about a much more striking and voluntary change in the practice of *Austritt*. In the course of the late 1960s and 1970s, the Washington Heights community in which the Breuer community was located underwent massive demographic change. The Black and Hispanic population of the neighborhood increased from less than 25% to over 75% during the period. Many younger Jews moved away, leaving a Jewish population that was increasingly made up of the elderly. Rabbi Schwab strongly opposed moving from the neighborhood and, in fact, his congregation continued to build facilities in the neighborhood. Though he could not command the type of loyalty that Hasidic rebbes had over their flocks, he was able to slow down out-migration in his congregation considerably. Even today, the congregation has over 600 families resident in the Heights and its average age is far below that of all other congregations in the neighborhood.[10]

The demographic change threatened the continued existence of the Jewish community of Washington Heights. Unlike the situation of the 1930s, the congregation is no longer in the position of being able to reconstruct itself elsewhere. Its younger members are already probably too Americanized for that. Therefore, not to survive in Washington Heights probably means the demise of the Hirschian community and by implication the weakening of the influence of its doctrine. Curiously, for the Breuer community this threat may be severer than even that of early Nazism.

Because of the threat, the community did something which seems totally at variance with its philosophy of *Austritt*. It founded and dominated a Jewish Community Council of Washington Heights which includes all the important Jewish organizations in the neighborhood including Reform and Conservative temples. Of the twenty-four congregations listed as belonging to the council, nineteen were Orthodox, three were Conservative and two were Reform. (Jewish Community Council: 28) It has thus decided that the survival of the Washington Heights community is important enough to sit together, concerning political and social matters at least, with representatives of movements they considered illegitimate.

The Breuer community gradually increased its political and communal activities as the demographics of its immediate neighborhood began to change. It tried to prevent any projects or militant movements which would speed the change in the neighborhood's makeup or precipitate white flight. One of the incidents which impelled the

Breuer community to cooperate on a neighborhood-wide basis was the proposal to build a public housing project and public school directly across the street from the Breuer synagogue.[11] Such a project was perceived as a direct threat to the community. Other more general issues such as the rise of minority militancy in public school policy, the increase in neighborhood crime and the detereoration in housing conditions were also factors which drove the community to political action.

The degree of involvement by a community once famous for its "splendid isolation" is remarkable. The Breuer community co-sponsored a Jewish slate for the local school board which won almost every school board election in the 1970s; it created a neighborhood car patrol, luncheon club for the aged, members of the congregation sat on the local planning board and a member of the synagogue was even chosen Democratic district leader (Katznelson 1981:153–176; Schorscher 1972: 19–21).[12] Finally in 1973 the Community Council was created. It takes care of a host of functions designed to keep the Jewish presence in the neighborhood viable. Among these are social welfare programs and referrals, programs to settle and integrate Soviet Jews in the neighborhood, programs to buy and rehabilitate apartment houses, etc. The council maintains a close contact with the local planning board and with various local organizations sponsoring projects for neighborhood improvements. It has shown considerable skill in channelling potentially threatening projects into less dangerous directions (Jewish Community Council, n.d.).

The Council is officially a coalition of more than forty neighborhood Jewish organizations. In fact, the Breuer influence is predominant. The executive director is a member of the congregation, as is the president. Other members also hold important posts. In the words of one non-Breuer leader, "They put so much effort into it that others are pushed out." The superior organization and dedication of the Breuer kehilla as well as their relatively large number of younger people skilled in the ways of American organizational life have given them the edge over all other forces in the neighborhood's Jewish community.

The coalition with non-Orthodox forces thus tends to be advantageous to the Breuer community without any of the threats to its independence which had been feared in Germany. In Frankfurt, the Hirschians had been a minority who could not protect their religious interests within the community. In Washington Heights they have become the dominant group. Their co-operation with the non-Orthodox in the Council is mainly on political and social issues, though the council does engage in such religious activities as providing for the religious needs of recent Russian immigrants and strengthening the local day schools. The willingness of the Breuer community to co-operate with the YMHA, and non-Orthodox congregations does represent a significant concession despite the fact that the Council is mainly political and social. The Council lists and presumably refers interested people to activities of these and other non-Orthodox organizations (Jewish Community Council, n.d.). Although the Orthodox congregations were very reluctant even after the founding of the council to give legitimacy to the Reformers, the council has on occasion even met on the premises of the Reform temple.

Though the founding of the council does not represent a conscious reformulation of the idea of *Austritt*, it does show the degree to which an Orthodox group can use flexible tactics. The flexibility seems possible only under circumstances like those which now obtain in Washington Heights. First there must be a crisis which threatens the continuance of the community, and, second, the Orthodox forces have to be so strong that their agreement to work together with the non-Orthodox never means that they are actually following the policies of the non-Orthodox.

The Breuer community has shown great political and organizational skill in trying to preserve the Jewish community of its neighborhood. It has been willing to show a surprising degree of tactical flexibility, but it has done so only because it was well aware that it in fact retained power in its own hands.

Hirschianism was able to preserve the institutional framework of the old organic kehilla while rejecting the idea of membership of all local residents regardless of ideology. The Breuer community preserved both the separatism and the kehilla structure but in the face of a crisis made many concessions in its political and communal activity in order to preserve its existence. In many ways these concessions and the political activities themselves show to what extent the congregation has become Americanized. Yet the ideal of *Austritt* has been modified but not given up. Perhaps, in the end, the creation of the Washington Heights Community Council is simply a more subtle way of fulfilling the definition of *Austritt* given by a Breuer leader, "with a non-Orthodox Jew who is willing to be guided by me, I will always work."

Notes

1. See also the fuller treatment of this issue in Liberles (1985:215).

2. "Followers of Samson Raphael Hirsch's secessionist policy formed in 1906 the Verein der orthodoxer Rabbiner that denied membership to any rabbi

no matter how traditional who had joined the General Association of Rabbis (Allgemeiner Rabbiner-Verband)." Followers of Bamberger had founded the less exclusive *Vereinigung traditionell-gesetzestreuer Rabbiner* in 1897 (Altmann 1974:37).

3. In 1886 S. R. Hirsch created the *Freie Vereinigung fuer die Interessen des orthodoxen Judentums*, in 1920 the *Bund gesetzestreuer jüdischer Gemeinden Deutschlands* (Halberstädter Verband) and shortly thereafter, the *Preussischer Landesverband gesetzestreuer Synagogengemeinden* (Schwab, 1950:89, 113, 114).

4. They were K'hal Adath Jeshurun, founded in 1938 (first rabbi–Joseph Breuer), Agudas Yeshorim, founded 1939 (first rabbi–Philipp Biberfeld) and Kehillath Yaakov, founded 1942, (first rabbi–Leo Breslauer).

5. In an interview under the auspices of the Research Foundation for Jewish Immigration, an early leader states that none of the three founders of the congregation were from Frankfurt. In an interview under the same auspices another leader states "the majority of members of the community were not Frankfurt people at all."

6. The Moriah Nutrition Program for the Elderly declared in its bulletin *(Moriah Voice)*, that it was a "project of Agudath Israel of America in cooperation with K'hal Adath Jeshurun").

7. Interview at Research Foundation for Jewish Immigration (Names withheld on request of the Research Foundation.)

8. copy at Agudah Archives.

9. Interview at Research Foundation for Jewish Immigration, 1971.

10. (Oppenheim 1977:2) shows that in 1977 there were 922 households affiliated with the congregation of which 612 lived in Washington Heights-Inwood. Of the respondents (heads of families), 36.1% were over 65 as compared to 41.4% of heads of families counted in the 1970 census of the immediate neighborhood (Health Area 2.22). In my own mail survey of three non-Breuer "German-Jewish" congregations in Washington Heights made in 1983–1984, 488 of 775 respondents and their spouses (63%) were born in 1915 or earlier. In Oppenheim's survey of Breuer's congregation, 21.8% of respondent head-of-households were under 35 (as against 12% in Health Area 2.22 as a whole). Whereas children under age 18 were only 13.2% of the population of Health Area 2.22, they made up 30.2% of the populations of the Breuer congregation households who responded to Oppenheim's survey (pp. 3–4). Breuer congregation respondent households had an average size of 3.01 as against an average of 2.08 for Health Area 2.22 as a whole.

11. The construction of P.S. 48, grades one to four on the east side of Broadway at 185th Street (across the street from Breuer's) seems finally to have been approved after a sixteen year fight in June 1984. Even then an attempt was made by a group calling itself "Friends of Washington Heights" to prevent or delay the building of the school (Garcia 1984).

12. Sidney Stern who was leader of the Washington Heights Progressive Democrats was a member of K'hal Adath Jeshurun.

References

Altmann, Alexander. "The German Rabbi, 1910–1939," *Yearbook of the Leo Baeck Institute* 19 (1974).

Bulletin of Beth Hamedrash Hagodol of Washington Heights, March–April 1956.

Dawidowicz, Lucy. *The War Against the Jews, 1933–1945*, (New York: Bantam edition, 1975).

Denkschrift über die Judenfrage in dem Gesetz betreffend den Austritt aus der Kirche (Berlin, 1873).

Dokumente: Kommission zur Erforschung der Geschichte der Frankfurter Juden, *Dokumente zur Geschichte der Frankfurter Juden, 1933–45*, (Frankfurt am Main, 1963).

Garcia, Rudy. "PS 48 One and Two get Nod for Construction," *Uptown Press*, no. 32 (July 5–25, 1984).

Hakohol (Bulletin of Congregation Beth Israel of Washington Heights), Summer 1962.

Heinemann, Isaac. "Supplementary Remarks on the Secession from the Frankfurt Jewish Community under Samson Raphael Hirsch," *Historia Judaica* vol. 10., no. 2 (October 1948).

Japhet, Saemy. [published without author's name] "The Secession from the Frankfurt Jewish Community under Samson Raphael Hirsch," *Historia Judaica* vol. 10, no. 2 (October 1948).

Jewish Community Council (n.d.). *Directory of Programs and Services*, issued by the Jewish Community Council, Preservation and Restoration Corp., Washington Heights-Inwood.

Katznelson, Ira. *City Trenches, Urban Politics and the Patterning of Class in the United States*, (New York: Pantheon Books, 1981).

K'hal Adath Jeshurun: *Annual Report of K'hal Adath Jeshurun*, 1968

Landsman, Dan. *K'hal Adath Jeshurun Inc. (A Frankfort on the Main oriented-Kehillah), Its schools and institutions*, (Yeshiva University, MA thesis, September 1969).

Liberles, Robert. *Religious Conflict in Social Context, The Resurgence of Orthodox Judaism in Frankfurt am Main, 1838–1877* (Westwood, CT, London: Greenwood Press, 1985).

Liebman, Charles. "Orthodoxy in American Jewish Life," *American Jewish Year Book* 65 (1965).

Mitteilungen Bulletin of K'hal Adath Jeshurun.

Oppenheim, Adolph D. "Membership Survey on Preferences regarding relocation, branch development and preservation of Washington Heights area, prepared for the Board of Trustees of K'hal Adath Jeshurun," July 26, 1977.

Schwab, Hermann. *The History of Orthodox Jewry in Germany*, (London, 1950).

Schwab, Simon. "[Kehillo Kedosho]", *Mitteilungen, Bulletin of K'hal Adath Jeshurun*, (Sept/Oct/Nov. 1977).

Sorscher, Yehuda. "The Kehilla—A Community Stabilizer," *The Jewish Observer*, vol. 8, no. 7 (September 1972), pp. 19–21.

11

That Is the Pillar of Rachel's Grave unto This Day: An Ethnoarchaeological Comparison of Two Jewish Cemeteries in Lincoln, Nebraska

David Mayer Gradwohl
Hanna Rosenberg Gradwohl

Lincoln, Nebraska is the smallest Jewish community and the one furthest from major metropolitan centers considered in this volume. David and Hanna Gradwohl apply archaeological, ethnological, and historical methods in showing how the Jewish graves and cemeteries reveal the varying cultural orientations of the Jews of West and Central European origins on the one hand and the East European Jews on the other in that Midwestern city. The respective outward-looking and inward-looking stances of these two groups are parallel to Heilman's conclusions regarding the ownership of Jewish objets d'art. Still it is noteworthy that the more "conservative" Jews of Lincoln probably resemble the "less observant" consumers of Judaica in New York City.

Rachel died, and was buried on the way to Ephrath—the same is Bethlehem. And Jacob set up a pillar upon her grave; that is the pillar of Rachel's grave unto this day. (Genesis 35: 19–20)

Since biblical times and, indeed, farther back according to archaeological evidence, gravestones have been one way of marking the burial places and honoring the memory of the deceased. In their form and manner of embellishment, gravestones are material symbols of personal identities. Cemeteries thus provide a basis for studying not only cultural traditions through time but also the manner in which individuals identify themselves within the groups of which they are members.

The essential proposition we are exploring is whether or not the cemeteries of a Reform Jewish temple and a Conservative/Orthodox Jewish synagogue in a midwestern city of the United States parallel the different theological orientations and historical origins from which the members of those two institutions came. In one case, we have a group deriving largely from Western Europe. The seeds of their liberal religious beliefs and practices were germinated in the Old World and brought to speedy florescence in North America via the Pittsburgh Platform upon whose codified principles the Reform Jews founded their temple. In the other case, we have a group which came mostly from Eastern Europe. These people established a synagogue whose *minhagim* or customs followed much more strictly the tenets of Orthodox Judaism. Their traditional beliefs and practices, less subject to change, were deeply rooted in the authority of the Torah and its rabbinical interpretations such as the Talmud and the Mishnah. If one were able to walk into the Reform temple in 1900 (or, for that matter, even today), one would hear a somewhat different liturgy and see some contrasting material forms than one would observe in the Conservative/Orthodox synagogue. One might hypothesize that similar distinctions exist in the burial grounds of these two institutions. Given this background information, one can ask several questions: Is there any relationship between the non-material or cognitive domains of the institutions involved and the material cultural remains in the cemeteries? Are there separate material cultural associations in the cemeteries which can be correlated with the temple as distinguished from the synagogue? Are there material representations on specific gravestones which reflect individual and differing personal Judaic identities?

The purpose of this paper is to describe and compare the two Jewish cemeteries in Lincoln, Nebraska, using the techniques of ethnoarchaeology.[1] Mount Carmel Cemetery and Mount Lebanon Cemetery were established during the late nineteenth century (Figure 1). Mount Carmel Cemetery, originally known as the Chebra B'nai Jehuda Cemetery,[2] has served as the burial ground for Orthodox and Conservative Jews whose families live in and around Lincoln (Figure 2). Historically these Jews have been primarily affiliated with the Tifereth Israel Synagogue in Lincoln, although the Mount Carmel Cemetery Association is a separate legal entity and the graveyard is available, at least theoretically, to any Jew who is a member of that Association, regardless of other affiliations. On the other hand, the Mount Lebanon Cemetery has been the location of interments for Reform Jews whose families live in the vicinity of Lincoln (Figure 3). Historically and legally the Mount Lebanon Cemetery has been linked to the Temple B'nai Jeshurun. The geographic settings of Lincoln's two Jewish cemeteries and the nature of the gravestones within these two mortuary areas reflect, we believe, important socio-cultural developments among Jews in the United States. The data shed light on the relationship of cognitive patterns and change to material culture and the nature of intra-group variations in America.

The following discussion is divided into six sections. First, we explain our investigative model and techniques. Second, we provide a brief background summary of the history of Jews in the United States as the context in which our particular case study is set. Third, we review salient points pertaining to the history of Jews in Lincoln, Nebraska, site of our field project. The fourth and fifth sections respectively describe the Mount Carmel Cemetery and the Mount Lebanon Cemetery. The final section presents a comparison of data from the two cemeteries along with the historical and socio-cultural conclusions which can be drawn from this study.

Investigative Model and Techniques

The focus of this ethnoarchaeological study is on mortuary behavior as reflected in social patterns and material culture spanning a century from the 1880s to the 1980s. Although the term and explicit integrative techniques of ethnoarchaeology are relatively recent in the literature, the methodology is compatible within the domain of traditional holistic anthropology (cf. Stanislawski 1973; Adams 1977; Binford 1978; Gould 1978). In this study we follow the definition of ethnoarchaeology provided by William Adams (1977: viii) in his study of Silcott, Washington:

> Ethnoarchaeology is defined here as the study of a known group of people (ranging from a family to a community) through the synergistic combination of historical, archaeological, and ethnographic methodologies. Ethnoarchaeology is related to, but distinguished from, ethnohistory, historical archaeology, living archaeology, and ethnographic analogy. Ethnoarchaeology employs a continuous model by utilizing the direct historical approach.

The archaeological dimension here is drawn out from the analysis of material cultural remains. Archaeologists study human behavior primarily from the basis of material portable objects and structures. In this case study, the artifacts consist of gravestones while the structural element is provided by the organization and geographic settings of the two cemeteries. The "ethno" portion of the term ethnoarchaeology emphasizes the data to be obtained from, and integrated with, other information pertaining to known human behavior. The latter is observed in the role of an ethnographer studying contemporary society; it is also ascertained, for the relatively recent past, through the analysis of published documents and other archival sources. Ethnoarchaeology can serve systematically to interpret past behavior patterns and to elucidate, if not explain, those of the present. The utility of employing data from historic cemeteries in understanding ongoing human behavior patterns has been extensively demonstrated in previous studies of Christian cemeteries in the United States (Dethlefsen and Deetz 1966; Dethlefsen and Jensen 1977; Deetz 1977; Dethlefsen 1981; Nutty 1984). The specific application here involves an analysis of data from Jewish cemeteries.

Four principal avenues of investigation have been pursued in this study. First, we examined archival documents. The sources in Lincoln included deeds and other legal instruments pertaining to the two cemeteries, personal correspondence, and family records, in particular those entered in family prayerbooks and *yahrzeit* or death-anniversary books. In order to obtain background and comparative information relating to Jewish cemeteries and mortuary customs, we perused published and manuscript sources.[3] Second, we collected oral historical data via open-ended interviews with several members and officers of Lincoln's Jewish congregations and cemetery associations.[4] Third, we obtained information on contemporary burial practices among Jews. Interviews were conducted with the funeral directors representing the two mortuaries which handle the majority of Jewish burials in Lincoln. A participant in Lincoln's *Chevra Kadisha* or Holy Burial Society was interviewed. Personnel from Lincoln's two cemetery monument companies were contacted and an analysis was made of the written materials (Figure 4) they use in selling stone memorials to Jewish families.[5]

The fourth and most extensive investigative technique consisted of the field observation and recording of data from every mortuary monument and marker in the Mount Lebanon and Mount Carmel cemeteries.[6] The total inventory comprised 857 stones as of August 1985: 537 at Mount Carmel and 320 at Mount Lebanon. In each cemetery a sketch map was drawn showing the spatial relationships of all monuments, markers, and other features such as benches, plant containers, and decorative shrubs and trees. This procedure was employed since (a) the official cemetery plat maps were not available for use in the field, and (b) the plat maps show cemetery lot ownership rather than where individual stones have been erected. As each gravestone was mapped in, it was assigned a field number on the basis of its location by row and position within that row. For the purpose of data analysis, consecutive case numbers were subsequently assigned to the gravestones in each cemetery. Documentation of the gravestones also included the taking of field photographs. The field recording of specific data for each gravestone was facilitated by the use of a standardized form developed for that purpose. Our data categories pertaining to factors such as gravestone form and size, social unit represented, epitaphs, language of inscriptions, and symbols were adapted from the field-recorded variables and values utilized by Coleen Nutty (1984) in her study of pioneer cemeteries in Story County, Iowa. The resulting information was subsequently processed and analyzed with the use of a microcomputer. To gain a comparative perspective beyond our review of the literature, we have also made general observations in Jewish cemeteries in other communities.[7]

While the bulk of the data can be gathered in an objective manner, we are intentionally exploiting the subjective experiences we had in Jewish congregations while growing up in Lincoln. Although we have not lived extensively in Lincoln as adults, we visit our home town often since both our families still reside there. In recent years, as participant observers, we have had the sad but instructive duty of burying family members who have died in Lincoln. We are thus utilizing the networks of kinship and friendship we still have in that city—among the living of the community and the deceased at Mount Lebanon and Mount Carmel.

General Background

The earliest Jewish settlers in what is now the United States were primarily Sephardic Jews of ultimate Spanish-Portugese background. Following the Iberian Inquisition, many of these Sephardic Jews settled in other Mediterranean countries in addition to Holland, England, and Germany. Arriving in the United States in the mid-seventeenth century, these Sephardim became residents of communities under Dutch and English jurisdiction (Blau 1976; Fishman 1973; Grinstein 1980; Handlin 1954; Learsi 1954; and Levinger 1944). Although explicit religious freedom was not immediately universal, congregations were soon formed and they organized various vital operations including arrangements for the burial of the dead within grounds which had been consecrated according to Jewish religious tradition.

The first Jewish cemetery in North America was established in 1656 by the Dutch Sephardic Jews in what is now New York City (Pool 1952: 8–9). Although the exact location of that cemetery cannot be documented at the present time, its mere existence is historically significant. According to David de Sola Pool (1952: 6–7):

> In Jewish life, to a greater degree than is commonly found elsewhere, the establishment of a common consecrated burial ground is a significant sign of permanent settlement. In medieval Germany the secular authorities would sometimes name and classify Jewish communities by the cemeteries which they used. The cemetery served as the permanent geographic nuclear unit of community organization. At least it was immovable property, while the living Jew, the quarry of many a brutal man hunt, for his own protection had to be a movable chattel of the local feudal prince. . . . So when the Jews of New Amsterdam in 1655 applied for permission to own a cemetery, they showed beyond all doubt that they intended to remain in this part of the New World and throw in their lot with the new colony.

In 1656 The Jews of Curacao, in the Antilles, also established a cemetery. Meanwhile, in North America, Congregation Yeshuat Israel in Newport, Rhode Island, purchased land for a cemetery in 1677 (Gutstein 1936: 295). Back in New York City in 1682, a second cemetery was established in the New Bowery by Congregation Shearith Israel (Pool 1952: 8–9). Today this cemetery is located just off Chatham Square. Within the next century, Jewish congregations in other eastern and southern communities purchased land for cemeteries.[8] Here and there in early American history, however, there were prohibitions against the establishment of Jewish cemeteries. In seventeenth and eighteenth century Boston, for example, Jewish merchants and businessmen were welcomed or at least tolerated; but it was not until the 1840s that permits were granted for Jewish burial grounds in that city.[9]

During the eighteenth century Sephardic Jews, including those from the Levant, continued to immigrate to America. They were outnumbered, however, by the Ashkenazic Jews from European countries north of the Mediterranean. During the early and middle nineteenth century, these Ashkenazim were primarily from Western and Central Europe. In contrast, from the middle of the nineteenth into the twentieth century, the major influx of Ashkenazic Jews was from Eastern Europe. The dynamics of immigration of Ashkenazim are significant beyond the specific countries of origin. In general, the different waves of immigration brought people of somewhat differing theological orientations and ritual practices (Bamberger 1971; Handlin

1954). By the 1880s, the Jews who had come from Western Europe and Central Europe generally followed the principles and practices of Reform Judaism, a movement which began in Germany (Philipson 1967; Philipson 1936; Schwartzman 1971; Schwartzman 1962; Silverman 1970). On the other hand, the Ashkenazim from Eastern Europe brought with them the long-established theology and practices of Orthodox Judaism. Within the United States a third "branch", Conservative Judaism, emerged during the nineteenth century (Davis 1963; Gordis 1978; Parzen 1964; Sklare 1972). Conservative Judaism provided a middle-ground for many Jews who found Orthodoxy too traditional if not "separatist" and also those who viewed Reform as too liberal if not "assimilationist".

Lincoln, Nebraska, As a Specific Setting

The Nebraska Territory was created in 1854 and a year later the territorial capital was established in Omaha. Nebraska statehood was ratified in 1867. The capital was then removed to the town of Lancaster which was subsequently renamed Lincoln. Prior to the 1860s—with the exception of California during the era of the Gold Rush—most Jewish citizens had settled in the eastern United States. After that time, however, Jews started to settle in communities located in what are now the midwestern and western states of America. During Nebraska's Territorial days in the late 1850s and early 1860s, for example, some Jewish traders were among the inhabitants of Omaha (Auerbach 1927; Gendler 1968; Levitov 1976; and Rosenbaum and O'Conner-Seger 1981). Settlement of the area by Jewish families increased following the admission of Nebraska as a state. Although the history of Jews in Nebraska has not yet been fully documented, it is known that during the 1870s and 1880s members of the Jewish faith established themselves in several cities and larger towns and were primarily engaged in business and commercial enterprises.

Available sources conflict as to the time of earliest Jewish pioneers in Lincoln (cf. Auerbach 1927; Hayes and Cox 1889; and Sawyer 1916). It is known, however, that Jewish people had indeed settled in Lincoln prior to the 1880s, and most probably as early as the late 1860s. According to available information these citizens of Jewish faith held religious services in private homes. Historical sources indicate that two separate congregations were formed during the 1880s: Congregation B'nai Jeshurun was incorporated in 1884 and Tifereth Israel Congregation was established in 1885 (Hayes and Cox 1889; Newmark 1981; Sawyer 1916). B'nai Jeshurun, also known today as the South Street Temple, was founded on the principles of Reform Judaism. In contrast, the original members of Tifereth Israel were essentially Orthodox although the synagogue soon came to incorporate Conservative as well as Orthodox Judaism. The original members of B'nai Jeshurun were predominantly Western Ashkenazim; they came mostly from Germany, Austria, Alsace-Lorraine, and France. On the other hand, most of the early members of Tifereth Israel were Eastern Ashkenazim; they came largely from Russia, Poland, and Lithuania. During the 1880s the Nebraska state legislature deeded lots to congregations of various religious denominations in an attempt to encourage the construction of houses of worship in the state's capital city. In 1885 two lots on the northwest corner of 12th and D Streets were deeded to Congregation B'nai Jeshurun (see Figure 1). Their temple building was constructed on those lots in 1893. In 1924 Congregation B'nai Jeshurun built a new temple at 20th and South streets; they continue to meet there at the present time. Tifereth Israel Congregation built a synagogue at 13th and T streets in 1903 (see Figure 1). In 1913 they constructed and moved to a second house of worship at 18th and L streets. Tifereth Israel presently meets at a synagogue which was built at 3219 Sheridan Boulevard in 1954. During the course of Lincoln's history other Jewish congregations have existed for short periods of time.[10] In essence, however, the main outline of the history of Jews in Lincoln from an institutional point of view can be followed through congregations B'nai Jeshurun and Tifereth Israel. Lincoln's Jewish population in recent years has been estimated between 1,000 and 1,200 people. Tifereth Israel, once the smaller of the two congregations, presently has approximately 200 family members while B'nai Jeshurun has about 90 family members (Raglin 1978). There are, of course, other Jews in Lincoln who are not affiliated with any religious institution. Nonetheless, most of Lincoln's Jews still identify as being members of "the Temple" or "the Synagogue".

Over time the social significance of these facts extends beyond demographic data pertaining to country of origin and the mere labels of sub-denominational branches of Judaism. The early members of Tifereth Israel brought with them, and continued, the theological orientation and liturgical practices of European Orthodoxy. Generally, in the Orthodox and Conservative tradition, religious adherents observe the Mosaic and rabbinical laws which regulate matters such as diet, ritual dress, priestly purity, and the specific forms of individual and group prayer (Blau 1976; Davis 1963; Sklare 1972). On the other hand, the founding members of B'nai Jeshurun came from the heritage of the European Reform movement which was transplanted to the

United States and elaborated during the early and middle decades of the nineteenth century under such leaders as Max Lilienthal, Isaac Mayer Wise, David Einhorn, and Kaufmann Kohler (Schwartzman 1971: 173–180, 195–208). The principles and practices of American Reform Judaism were established at the Philadelphia Conference of 1869 and further codified at the Pittsburgh Conference of 1885. Reform leaders formally declared their intention to "accept as binding only the moral laws and maintain only such ceremonies as elevate and sanctify our lives" in their practice of Judaism (Schwartzman 1971: 215). Reform practices which overtly rejected a number of specific Mosaic and traditional rabbinical laws included the equal participation of women in religious worship and education, the use of a choir and musical instruments in addition to or instead of the ritual chanting of a cantor, rejection of the absolute obligation to follow kosher dietary laws, and the optional rather than required wearing of religious paraphernalia such as the yarmulke or skull cap, the tallis or prayer shawl, and the tefillin or phylacteries (Schwartzman 1971: 214–218). Of particular interest to our study of the material aspects of Jewish mortuary behavior are several specific theological planks in the Pittsburgh Platform upon which, as noted above, Congregation B'nai Jeshurun was founded. First was the disavowal of the hope for a return to Zion—that is, a homeland in Palestine. Rabbi Isaac Mayer Wise, in fact, once proclaimed "America is our Zion" (Philipson 1936: 15). Another plank of the Pittsburgh Platform specified that the principles of Prophetic Judaism would be observed rather than the rituals mandated by traditional Rabbinic Judaism. Thus the social and ritual prerogatives of the priestly castes, the Kohanim and the Levites, were not recognized. A third part of the American Reform Jewish practices codified at Philadelphia and Pittsburgh called for the use of vernacular languages (i.e., English and German) as well as Hebrew in religious services. Trilingual prayer books in Hebrew, English, and German from this period are explicit artifacts of this change in ritual practice and theological orientation.

Oftentimes the institution of Reform practices in American congregations did not come about without animosity or even open violence. For example, in 1840 the introduction of organ music at Beth Elohim Congregation in Charleston, South Carolina, was the principal catalyst for the withdrawal of a conservative faction. The latter group formed a separate congregation known as Shearith Israel and further signified their disassociation from Beth Elohim by building a wall around their section of the Jewish cemetery in Charleston (Elzas 1903: 94).[11] While the pioneer Jews in Lincoln, Nebraska, may not have engaged in such overt disagreements, the founding members of B'nai Jeshurun and Tifereth Israel no doubt eyed one another with at least some of the same concerns and discontents as their co-religionists' factions did in Charleston. We do not have documentary evidence to substantiate that point; but having grown up in Lincoln in the mid-twentieth century, we are not unaware of the circulating stories about friction between members of the two congregations.

Perhaps today members of B'nai Jeshurun and Tifereth Israel interact in more common realms than they did fifty or one hundred years ago. They have, for example, a joint fund drive for the United Jewish Appeal and they sponsor mutual programs for youth and for senior citizens. Nevertheless, saying one belongs to "the Temple" or "the Synagogue" is, in a sense, a cognitive code for expressing some degree of social distance, differing philosophical orientations or world views, and varying observances of specific religious rituals. From an ethnoarchaeological perspective, we note that this non-material, bipartite code has been manifested materially for a century in the maintenance of two separate cemeteries, Mount Lebanon and Mount Carmel.

Mount Carmel (Chebra B'nai Jehuda) Cemetery

The earliest identified Jewish gravestones in Lincoln date from the late 1880s. Several are contained within the burial ground known today as the Mount Carmel Cemetery. This cemetery is located on North 14th Street, north of the business district and State Capitol, in Belmont, which was a separate and primarily residential community in the late nineteenth century. Today Belmont lies immediately within Lincoln's northern corporate limits (see Figure 1). Deeds on file in the Recorder's Office at the Lancaster County Court House reveal that on August 17, 1886, the property comprising the cemetery was sold by Grant A. Bush and Mabel A. Bush to S. Polwosky for the sum of $300. On September 15, 1886, this land was transfered by S. Polwosky and Rachel Polwosky to the Chebra B'nai Jehuda Cemetery Association in consideration of $350 to cover the cost of the mortgage undertaken in the original land acquisition. The earliest extant gravestone is that of a Mrs. Levy who died in January of 1888. Rachel Polwosky died in 1892; she is interred along with other early burials in the first row of graves facing east onto North 14th Street.

Particularly striking when one views the Mount Carmel Cemetery is the fact that it is a carefully enclosed and explicitly Jewish space (Figure 2). The perimeter of the cemetery is bounded by tall pine

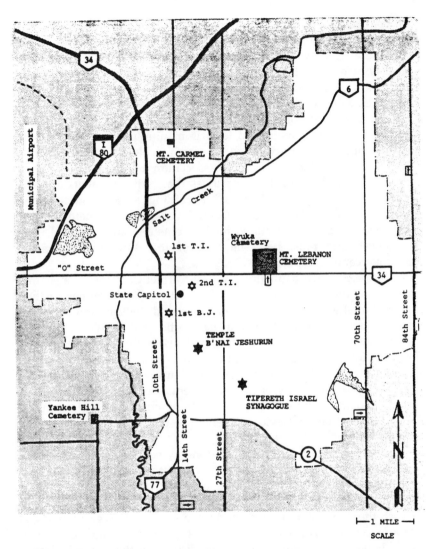

Figure 1. Map of Lincoln, Nebraska, showing locations of Mt. Carmel Cemetery, Mt. Lebanon Cemetery (in Wyuka Cemetery), Tifereth Israel Synagogue, and Temple B'nai Jeshurun.

trees, thick shrubs, and an iron fence. A large entrance arch exhibiting a Star of David and the words "Mount Carmel Cemetery" demarcates this space as a Jewish burial ground. Two six-pointed stars also embellish the locked gates—a material symbol of the mandate in Deuteronomy (11:20) to abide by the words of the Lord and remember the commandment that "Thou shalt write them upon the doorposts of thy house and upon thy gates . . ." It should be noted in this regard that Hebrew cemeteries have traditionally been referred to as *bet olam,* House of Eternity, and *bet chayim,* meaning House of Life (Ydit 1971: 272). Within the gates of Mount Carmel Cemetery are buried Lincoln's Orthodox and Conservative Jews although this cemetery is a legal corporation separate from Tifereth Israel Synagogue. Restriction of the cemetery to Jews is manifested in a deed on file at the Lancaster County Court in which a plot is granted by the Chebra B'nai Jehuda Cemetery Association to Louis Orlofsky on January 18, 1901. This deed stipulates that "All interments must be made according to Jewish rites." According to Sheldon Kushner, President of the Mount Carmel Cemetery Association, there are only two requirements to be buried in this cemetery: an individual must be Jewish and must be a member of the Association (personal communication, August 17, 1982).

Inside the well-maintained Mount Carmel Cemetery is a central, tree-lined, road which separates the northern and southern halves of the burial ground. The road curves around the southern perimeter of the cemetery to facilitate vehicular traffic. Initially we had several strong visual impressions standing just inside the central gates and looking into the area of the gravestones. First, there seemed to be a good number of gravestones and the burial area looked somewhat crowded. Second, many of the monuments were red or pink granite. Third, Judaic symbols—writing in Hebrew characters and/or motifs such as the Star of David or menorah—characterized most of the stones.

Analysis of our data collected stone-by-stone indicates that these initial impressions are correct. Furthermore, there are other significant factors in the data base. Selected quantitative and qualitative date for Mount Carmel Cemetery are summarized in Figure 5 and Figure 6. At the time of our field study there were 537 gravestones at Mount Carmel. The majority (63%) of these are monuments—that is, relatively large stones set perpendicular to the ground surface, while the minority (37%) are markers—relatively small stones set parallel to the ground surface. As in other American cemeteries, monuments can be used as separate memorials to designate the grave of one or more individuals. Monuments also can be used to designate individuals or other social units (families, spousal pairs, siblings etc.) in conjunction with separate markers which specify the particular graves of the husband, wife, or other kinfolk. As indicated, markers can be used in conjunction with monuments; or they can be employed separately to indicate individual graves. Specifically at Mount Carmel,

Figure 2. View of Mount Carmel Cemetery from North 14th Street. Note bound space enclosed by trees, shrubs, and fence; gates with Stars of David. Photograph by David Gradwohl.

46% of the stones are monuments only, 16% monuments associated with markers, 7% markers only, and 31% markers associated with monuments. As shown in Figure 7, the forms of gravestones at Mount Carmel reflect those which one would expect to find in late nineteenth and twentieth century cemeteries throughout the United States (Nutty 1984; Dethlefsen 1981). Nearly two-thirds of the gravestones are horizontal blocks followed in frequency by vertical blocks or compound vertical-horizontal blocks, wedges, columns or gabled obelisks, tablets, and other forms which include a cylinder, heart-shaped stones, two ledger-like slabs, and two angels carved in the round. In regard to our initial visual impression—beyond the actual number of stones— the higher percentage of monuments to markers accentuated the apparent density of graves. Adding to this impression, perhaps, is the fact that there are more vertical blocks at Mount Carmel than at Mount Lebanon (see Figure 5). In addition it is interesting to note that the 537 gravestones at Mount Carmel represent 534 people. Of that total, 62.5% of the individuals are represented by monuments only, 6.5% by markers only, and 31% by a combination of monuments and markers. Regarding the materials from which the memorials are manufactured, 47% of the gravestones at Mount Carmel are of red or pink granite. We note that this frequency is nearly four times greater than that at Mount Lebanon. At the present time, however, we have no satisfactory explanation of this difference.

As would be expected in a cemetery where Orthodox and Conservative Jews are buried, the placement of Hebrew inscriptions and Judaic art motifs on gravestones at Mount Carmel is very frequent. In terms of meeting this need, Lincoln's cemetery monument companies have brochures from which Jewish symbols can be selected (see Figure 4). Customers purchasing monuments and markers are thus offered a number of choices in terms of gravestone forms and

Figure 3. View of Mount Lebanon Cemetery from the West. Note open space at top of photograph bordered by curving driveway. Photograph by David Gradwohl.

the kinds of artistic embellishments they wish to be cut into the memorials for their deceased family members. The monument companies also have templates from which Hebrew letters, as well as different styles of English letters, can be put together for the names and vital statistics of the deceased or for epitaphs if such are desired. For the purposes of accuracy, the rabbi of Tifereth Israel (or less frequently the rabbi of B'nai Jeshurun) usually prepares the draft of the templates for the Hebrew inscriptions and then proof-reads them before they are cut into the stone (Richard Tomandl, personal communication, August 16, 1982; Max Speidell, personal communication, May 22, 1986). Of the 537 gravestones at Mount Carmel, 72% contain Hebrew inscriptions and/or Judaic symbols. In some instances, individual stone markers may contain no Hebrew lettering or Judaic symbols; rather, those elements are carved into the monument with which the markers are associated. In that perspective, the explicit Judaic identification of individuals buried at Mount Carmel is even more striking. Of the 534 people represented in this cemetery, 91% are associated with Hebrew inscriptions and/or Judaic art symbols.

As indicated above, at Mount Carmel many gravestones contain inscriptions in Hebrew, most often in conjunction with inscriptions in English. Within the total inventory of gravestones, 1% are in Hebrew only; 65.9% in English and Hebrew; 32.7% in English only; 0.2% bilingual in English and in Yiddish with Hebrew characters; and 0.2% which have not yet been inscribed. According to Orthodox tradition, Jewish gravestones typically contain certain specific information pertaining to the deceased. This information, usually written in Hebrew, includes the full Hebrew name of the deceased, the Hebrew name of his or her father, the date of death (and sometimes the date of birth) according to the Jewish calendar, and—if the deceased was a male, his status as a Kohen, Levite, or Israelite (Lamm 1981: 188–192; Trepp 1980: 338–339; Klein 1979: 295–296). Traditionally there could be no reference to a woman's relationship in the priestly castes since membership in the Kohanim and Levites is a male status which is inherited patrilineally. However, the priestly status of a deceased woman's father was usually stated on her gravestone. Generally two additional letters in Hebrew are placed at the top of the inscription (see Figure 4). These letters represent an abbreviation of the phrase *Po Nikaver [et]* meaning "Here is buried" or "Here lies". At the end of the inscription are typically placed five Hebrew letters standing for the phrase *Tehee nafsho[h] tzerurah bitzror ha-hayim* meaning "May his [her] soul be bound up in the bond of eternal life."

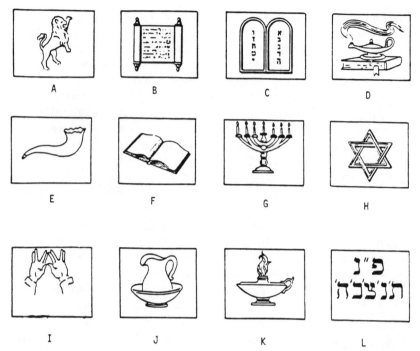

Figure 4. Jewish symbols from pamphlet, "How to Choose Your Monument," printed by Rock of Ages Monument Company. (A) Lion of Judah; (B) Torah, Scroll of the Pentateuch; (C) Ten Commandments, Mosaic Decalogue; (D) Bible and Lamp—Light of the Soul; (E) Shofar; (F) Bible, book, knowledge; (G) Menorah; (H) Star of David, shield, divine protection; (I) Kohanim hands raised in priestly benediction; (J) Pitcher and bowl, symbol of the Levites; (K) jahrzeit lamp, remembrance; (L: upper) "Here lies"; (L: lower) "May his/her soul be bound up in the bond of eternal life."

The above epigraphic formula is found on the majority of gravestones, both monuments and markers, in the cemetery. Also at Mount Carmel two other formulaic abbreviations in Hebrew are frequent (Suri Jacknis, personal communication, August 15, 1985): The first, often found at the top of monuments, is translated as "For Eternal Memory"; the other, usually found within the inscription after the name of the deceased, stands for the phrase "May His [Her] Memory Be A Blessing." As is typical of gravestones in Christian cemeteries at the turn of the century (Nutty 1984), some of Mount Carmel's older monuments contain long epitaphs. Some of these are derived from biblical passages; others extol the virtues of the deceased. Adjectives often employed are: dear, famous, praiseworthy, righteous, modest, pious, generous, simple, upright, and virginous (Suri Jacknis,

Figure 5. Comparison of selected quantitative characteristics of the Mount Carmel and Mount Lebanon cemeteries.

	Mount Carmel		Mount Lebanon	
Number of Gravestones	537		320	
Monuments	337	(63%)	75	(23%)
Markers	200	(37%)	245	(77%)
Memorial Unit				
Monument only	249	(46%)	21	(6.5%)
Single family				
monument with markers	88	(16%)	43	(13.5%)
Two or three family				
monument with markers	0		11	(3.5%)
Markers only	35	(7%)	62	(19.5%)
Markers with monuments	165	(31%)	183	(57%)
Gravestone Form				
Horizontal block	351	(65%)	287	(89.7%)
Vertical block	105	(19.4%)	23	(7.2%)
Wedge	36	(7%)	1	(0.3%)
Column/gabled obelisk	25	(5%)	0	
Tablet	11	(2%)	2	(0.6%)
Other	9	(1.6%)	7	(2.2%)
Materials				
Red/pink granite	250	(47%)	39	(12%)
Gray granite	227	(42%)	269	(84%)
Marble	54	(10%)	9	(3%)
Bronze	6	(1%)	3	(1%)
Language of Inscription				
Hebrew only	5	(1%)	0	
Hebrew and English	354	(65.9%)	7	(2.2%)
English only	176	(32.7%)	312	(97.5%)
English and Yiddish	1	(0.2%)	0	
English and German	0		1	(0.3%)
Not inscribed	1	(0.2%)	0	
Jewish Symbol and/or				
Hebrew Inscription				
Present	384	(72%)	23	(7%)
Absent	153	(28%)	297	(93%)
Place of Birth and/or Death Inscribed	1	(0.2%)	10	(3.2%)

Figure 5. (continued)	Mount Carmel		Mount Lebanon	
Number of Individual People	534		278	
Represented by monument only	334	(62.5%)	32	(11.5%)
Combination of marker &				
monument	165	(31%)	183	(66%)
Marker only	35	(6.5%)	63	(22.5%)
Individuals Associated with Jewish				
Symbol and/or Hebrew Inscription				
Present	486	(91%)	29	(10.4%)
Absent	48	(9%)	249	(89.6%)

personal communication, August 15, 1985). Other endearing phrases are also present, for example "apple of our eye," and "crown of our head". Titles (Mr. and Mrs.) are used frequently. The term "reb" appears often as an honorific title rather than designating a rabbi per se. In one case, a woman who was indeed the wife of a rabbi, is referred to as the *rebbetsen*. Many inscriptions at Mount Carmel include not only the date of death in the Jewish calendar, but also, if appropriate, reference to the fact that the deceased died on the Sabbath, a religious holiday, or the High Holy Days. In addition to the Sabbath, special days so noted on Mount Carmel gravestones include *Yom Kippur* (Day of Atonement), *Succos* (Festival of Booths), *Pesach* (Passover), *Shavuos* (Pentecost/Festival of Weeks), and *Rosh Hodesh* (the New Moon). Many of the references are even more specific, for example, stating that a person died on *erev* (the evening of) *Rosh Hodesh* or on the sixth day of *Pesach*. One epitaph entirely in Hebrew is typical of this pattern we have been discussing. In translation (Suri Jacknis, personal communication, 15 August 1985) the inscription reads: "Here lies the woman, Esther, the daughter of Isaac, the Kohen, the wife of Abraham J. Bricker, who died in her thirtieth year, the last day of *Pesach*, 680" [5680 in the Hebrew calendar or 1920 in the Gregorian calendar].

The inscriptions in English are typically brief and limited to the deceased's name, date of birth and death in the Gregorian calendar, and perhaps an affinal (husband or wife) and/or consanguineal (mother, father, daughter, son, grandmother, or grandfather) kinship term. There are several cases of three-generational kinship terms— for example, "husband, father, and grandfather". Epitaphs in English are rare and generally short. For example, one inscription reads: "A beloved man who will live forever in the hearts of all who knew him." Interestingly enough, several of the longest epitaphs in English

Figure 6. Comparison of selected qualitative characteristics of the Mount Carmel and Mount Lebanon cemeteries.

	Mount Carmel	Mount Lebanon
Location	At edge of city	Within center of city
Site Characteristics	Separate cemetery; closed (bound) space	Within state/municipal cemetery; open (unbound) space
Boundary Markers	Fence, locked gates, closely-spaced coniferous trees and shrubs; large sign with Stars of David	Curving roads, row of widely-spaced deciduous trees; small metal markers
Small Pebbles on Gravestones	Present (rare)	Absent
Information Included on Gravestones:		
Dates in Hebrew Calendar	Present (frequent)	Absent
Dates in Gregorian Calendar	Present (frequent)	Present (exclusively)
Symbols of Kohanim & Levites	Present	Absent
Titles and Honorific Labels	Present (frequent)	Present (rare)
Reference to Jewish Holidays	Present	Absent
Symbol of Jewish Sodality	Rare (1 case)	Absent
Masonic Symbol	Rare (1 case)	Present (3 cases)

date to the 1960s and 1970s. One monument (representing 0.2% of the inventory of Mount Carmel) refers to the fact that the deceased person was born in Mannheim, Germany. As discussed subsequently, references to the place of birth of the deceased are more frequent at Mount Lebanon. Gravestones provided by the U.S. government to former servicemen usually include data pertaining to the deceased's rank, military branch and unit, and period of service or participation in a specific war. There are eight such stones at Mount Carmel; all of them exhibit Stars of David.

Artistic embellishments on gravestones at Mount Carmel include the repertoire of non-religious motifs which one can find generally in other cemeteries in Lincoln, and, indeed, throughout the United States. The most frequent design consists of flowers including roses, lillies, daffodils, tulips, and stylized blooms. Oak leaves, ivy leaves, combinations of leaves and flowers, and combinations of leaves and geometric designs are also common. Monograms, banners, urns, fruit (especially grapes), trees and birds are also represented. Single occurrences include a lamb (associated with the stone of a child), snowflake, pinecones, and crossed rifles. Admittedly these motifs may be intended to have some symbolic meaning—for example, the rose depicting love, oak leaves representing strength, or an urn standing for the idea of destiny (Nutty 1984: 61–66). However, it is more probable that customers purchasing gravestones are unaware of these symbolic associations and, rather, select memorials with these designs because they are aesthetically pleasing. In fact the memorials which the monument companies have on hand often have these motifs already carved upon them. Thus the customer can simply have the name of the deceased and appropriate vital statistics added to the stone. On the other hand, there are specific Judaic symbols on many gravestones at Mount Carmel. It is likely that these motifs are selected with a good deal of care and awareness. The most frequent Judaic symbols at Mount Carmel are the Star of David, menorah or candelabrum, lamp (representing the *yahrzeit* light or *ner tamid*, the everlasting light), scroll (the Torah or Pentateuch), book (the Bible), and tablets (the Ten Commandments). Stars of David are typically associated with males while the menorah is correlated with females. Women, it will be recalled, are the kindlers of Sabbath candles. More specific are the insignia of the priestly castes. The symbol of the Kohanim consists of two hands, with the middle fingers parted, raised in priestly benediction (see Figure 3). The Levites who traditionally, as temple attendants, washed the hands of the Kohanim prior to religious services, are symbolized by a pitcher or by a ewer and basin. At Mount Carmel there are six monuments with the insignia of the Kohanim and one with the symbol of the Levites. In cases where a single gravestone serves as the monument for a Kohen and his wife, the blessing hands symbol is placed by the husband's inscription while another motif (usually a menorah) decorates the woman's side of the stone. Not all Kohens and Levites at Mount Carmel Cemetery are memorialized by the insignia of their castes.

Figure 7. Selected Gravestones from Mount Carmel Cemetery. Photographs by David Gradwohl.

A. General View. Note all gravestones with Judaic symbols (Stars of David and/or epitaphs in Hebrew).

B. Gravestone with menorah motif and the symbol of the Kohanim (hands raised in priestly benediction).

C. Gravestone with pitcher and basin motif (symbol of the Levites).

In most cases, however, the priestly status of these individuals is indicated within the Hebrew inscriptions on their gravestones. Symbols on two monuments signify two sodalities: a Masonic emblem and the crest of B'nai B'rith. Two other monuments which memorialize children contain carvings of angels in the round. Photographs of the deceased are attached to several other monuments in the Mount Carmel Cemetery. While we initially thought this practice would be contrary to the Orthodox tradition which abhors graven images, we have observed the use of photographs on gravestones in a number of Orthodox and Conservative cemeteries throughout the central and eastern United States. Further research, we suspect, will show the derivation of this practice from Eastern Europe where it occurs in both Jewish and Christian cemeteries. Similarly, the presence of small pebbles left on some tombstones at Mount Carmel is a practice we have observed in other Orthodox and Conservative cemeteries in the United States and Europe. This ritual is of long standing in European Jewish cemeteries and may represent a vestige of the times when mourners actually helped fill the gravepit over the coffin of the deceased (Bocher 1976).

Mount Lebanon Cemetery

Until the late 1890s, Lincoln's Reform Jews were buried at the Yankee Hill Cemetery located to the southwest of the city limits (see Figure 1). A deed in the Recorder's Office at the Lancaster County Court House shows that the property for this cemetery was acquired on April 12, 1864, by the Mount Pleasant Class of the Methodist Church on Salt Creek Mission, Nebraska Conference. During the period of the Nebraska Territory, the community established in this locality was known as Saline City. As Nebraska approached statehood, there was a good deal of speculation and political maneuvering to have Saline City, rather than Lancaster (as Lincoln was called in those days), designated as the state capital. Lincoln, however, became the state's capital city and greatly overshadowed Saline City, later known as Yankee Hill. On April 13, 1892, two and one-half acres of the Yankee Hill Cemetery were purchased for $600 by the trustees of B'nai Jeshurun for use as that congregation's burying ground. That portion of the Yankee Hill Cemetery was called Mount Lebanon Cemetery. It is probable that the action taken by B'nai Jeshurun in April of 1892 was precipitated by the sudden death of Paul D. Mayer, infant son of Charles and Estelle Mayer, on March 27 of that year.[12] Three years later the *Nebraska State Journal* (April 16, 1895) commented that "Mount Lebanon cemetery in Yankee Hill precinct, the property of the Bnai Jeshurem [sic] congregation of this city, is undergoing great changes at the hands of a landscape gardener. Walks and driveways are being laid out and the grounds otherwise beautified." As of 1898, fourteen burials had been interred at Mount Lebanon in Yankee Hill.

On February 4, 1899, a group of men acting as trustees of the Mount Lebanon Cemetery Association met with the trustees of Wyuka Cemetery which had been established in 1869 as a state and municipal cemetery (Minutes of the Board of Trustees, Wyuka Cemetery, February 4, 1899). Wyuka Cemetery is located near the present center of Lincoln's metropolitan area (see Figure 1). The Mount Lebanon Cemetery Association petitioned for permission to purchase one acre of land in Wyuka Cemetery for the sum of $500. The request was approved, and the deed was signed on April 19 of that year (Book 95 of Deeds, page 449). An item in the *Nebraska State Journal* for April 24, 1899 noted that "The remains of Simon Friend were yesterday removed from the receiving vault at Wyuka and interred in the new Jewish cemetery. Rev. Abram Simon, rabbi of Temple Israel at Omaha, officiated at the funeral services." Simon Friend had died more than a month earlier, on March 14. There are still some unresolved questions as to why Mount Lebanon Cemetery was established at Yankee Hill in the first place and then why it was moved to Wyuka. One explanation was offered in the *Nebraska State Journal* for May 16, 1899:

> The Hebrew cemetery, which has heretofore been at Yankee Hill, has recently been moved and hereafter, a plot of ground, to be known as Mt. Lebanon annex to Wyuka, will exist. The change in the situation was made because of the greater accessibility of Wyuka cemetery and of the better conveniences for keeping the grounds in fine condition during the summer. Fourteen bodies have been moved from Yankee Hill to Wyuka. The ground selected consists of an acre and a half in the cemetery; situated a little northeast of the G.A.R. plot. It is to be the cemetery of the members of the reformed Hebrew sect in this city, the orthodox Hebrews having a cemetery on North Fourteenth street.

On March 13, 1904, the trustees of Mount Lebanon Cemetery Association deeded over the Wyuka property to B'nai Jeshurun Congregation for the sum of one dollar (Book 118 of Deeds, pages 456–458). The Temple has been in charge of Mount Lebanon Cemetery since that time.

Wyuka Cemetery comprises in area of 200 acres. Its outside boundaries are marked by a fence, but there are no internal fences enclosing separate internal divisions of the cemetery. In fact, Wyuka was designed as a landscape park in the manner of the English garden school (Chatfield 1982). Curving avenues wind through the gently sloping terrain. These horizontal rather than vertical elements demarcate the different sections of the cemetery. Wyuka Cemetery, now included on the National Register of Historic Places, serves as the burial ground for the majority of Lincoln's citizens of various Protestant denominations and there are special "soldiers' circles" for veterans of the Civil War, Spanish American War, and more recent wars. Particularly striking when one views the present Mount Lebanon Cemetery is the fact that it is an open space without immediately obvious visible indications that it is a Jewish burial ground (see Figure 3). On three sides the boundaries of Mount Lebanon consist of Wyuka's paved, curving avenues. The fourth side of Mount Lebanon coincides with a row of widely-spaced deciduous trees which may be remnants of a former property line along what were the previous eastern limits of Wyuka Cemetery. To the east of these trees is Section 39, a non-denominational section of Wyuka which permits only small memorial markers. When we started our research project in 1982, there were no signs specifying the locus of Mount Lebanon. Now there are several small, inconspicuous metal markers with the words "Mt. Lebanon" stuck into the ground near the corners of this section—like the small markers which label Wyuka's other sections by their numerical designation. The markers are so small that they are easily ignored.

As at Mount Carmel, we had strong visual impressions at Mount Lebanon when we initially stood off and attempted to view the cemetery as outside observers. First, within the open space of Mount Lebanon, there appeared to be fewer and more widely-spaced gravestones than at Mount Carmel. Second, the majority of gravestones were of gray granite; and third, there was a paucity of Hebrew inscriptions and Jewish art motifs.

Again, our stone-by-stone analysis of the monuments and markers at the Mount Lebanon Cemetery validated these initial impressions and revealed some more subtle factors. Salient data for gravestones in this cemetery are summarized in Figure 5 and Figure 6. At the time of our field study there were 320 gravestones at Mount Lebanon. Here, contrary to Mount Carmel, 23% are monuments while 77% are markers. More specifically, 6.5% are individual monuments only; 13.5% are one-family monuments associated with markers; 3.5% are two- or three-family monuments associated with markers; 19.5% are markers only; and 57% are markers associated with monuments. As just indicated, at Mount Lebanon there are 11 monuments which are shared by two or three related families. The Ackerman and Frank families, for example, share a common monument which exhibits both family names on the same side of the stone. On other stones the different names and their associated markers may be on separate sides of the monument. For example, the related Mayer and Schlesinger families share a monument; "Mayer" is carved on the east side of the monument and the Mayer markers are east of the monument; "Schlesinger" is carved on west side of the monument and the Schlesinger markers are west of the monument. Finally, the related Nathan, Sanders, and Samuels families share a monument; the Sanders and some Nathans are buried on the west side of the monument; the Samuels and more Nathans are buried on the east side of the monument. There are, it should be noted, no monuments of this type at Mount Carmel. The presence of large family plots at Mount Lebanon certainly reflects strong familism which characterizes Ashkenazic Jews. We suspect from our general observations, however, that this particular practice is derived from Christian cemeteries in the United States rather than from Jewish cemeteries in Europe. The deceased at Mount Carmel unquestionably had kinship ties which were equally strong if not stronger than those of their co-religionists at Mount Lebanon; but in Lincoln the Orthodox burial pattern followed the Jewish antecedents from Europe.

Regarding the forms of Mount Lebanon gravestones (see Figure 8), 89.7% are horizontal blocks; 7.2% vertical blocks; 0.6% tablets; 0.3% wedges; and 2.2% other forms including scroll-like shapes and compound monuments. In regard to our initial impression regarding Mount Lebanon, there are indeed fewer gravestones than at Mount Carmel. The impression of a lower density of stones at Mount Lebanon was further accentuated by the higher proportion of markers to monuments, the smaller percentage of vertical monuments, and the total absence of columns or gabled obelisks. We also note with interest that the 320 gravestones at Mount Lebanon represent 278 people. Of that total, 11.5% of the individuals are represented by monuments only; 22.5% by markers only; and 66% by a combination of monuments and markers. As mentioned above, the stone-by-stone tabulation of Mount Lebanon's gravestones reveals that 84% of the memorials are of gray granite as opposed to the predominance of red or pink granite at Mount Carmel. Our initial impression—now a descriptive fact—is intriguing; but, at present, the historical and/or social significance of this material preference is wanting.

Our third preliminary visual impression at Mount Lebanon, contrary to Mount Carmel, suggested that there were fewer gravestones which could be unquestionably identified as representing

Jewish people on the basis of Hebrew epitaphs or symbols. Again, our stone-by-stone analysis of the field data bears out this impression. Of the 320 stones, only 7% contain Hebrew inscriptions and/or Judaic symbols while 93% of the inventory have none. The Judaic art symbols represented at Mount Lebanon include Stars of David, menorahs, eternal lights, and a scroll. Most of the Stars of David occur on markers issued to military veterans by the U.S. government. Two of the eleven government-issued markers at Mount Lebanon, however, do not have the Star of David; by contrast, all of the government-issued markers at Mount Carmel exhibit this motif. Insignia specific to the Kohanim and Levites are entirely absent at Mount Lebanon, although some Reform Jewish men could, if they wished, trace their descent from those priestly castes. By 1885, however, Reform Jews had disavowed the castes in the Pittsburgh Platform; consequently, one would not expect to find the insignia of the Kohanim and Levites at Mount Lebanon. Considering this matter from the perspective of people rather than gravestones, of the 278 individuals represented at Mount Lebanon, 10.4% of the population are associated with Hebrew inscriptions and/or Judaic art symbols. In this matter, then, the statistics from Mount Lebanon are almost exactly the reverse of those from Mount Carmel.

In regard to non-religious art motifs, the gravestones at Mount Lebanon are not unlike those at Mount Carmel. Approximately three fourths of the stones, however, are not embellished beyond the general shaping of the stones or perhaps a simple line border around the area of an inscription. Again, the most frequent motifs are floral designs including roses, irises, daffodils, poppies, and morning glories. Leaves combined with flowers, flowers and/or leaves combined with geometric patterns, and separate geometric patterns are also relatively common at Mount Lebanon. Monograms and fruit (especially grapes) are also observed. One monument has a bas relief of tall, footed torches; this motif could also be considered a variation of the eternal light motif. Masonic emblems are noted on three gravestones representing 1% of the memorials at Mount Lebanon.

As indicated above, Hebrew inscriptions are rare at Mount Lebanon. Within the total inventory of gravestones, 97.5% are in English only; 2.2% in English and Hebrew; and 0.3% in English and German. The German inscription consists of the dates of birth [Geboren] and death [Gestorben] and an epitaph which translates as "Deeply mourned and not forgotten." The Hebrew inscriptions are highly abbreviated compared to those of Mount Carmel. Two refer only to the names of the deceased; three employ the shortened letters representing the epitaph "Here lies" and/or "May his [her] soul be bound up in the

A

B

C

Figure 8.   Selected Gravestones from Mount Lebanon Cemetery. Photographs
by David Gradwohl.
A. Family monument surrounded by markers of individual family
members.
B. Double marker (husband and wife) with abbreviated use of
Hebrew.
C. Double monument (husband and wife) exhibiting exclusive
use of English in addition to the places of birth and death of
the deceased.

bond of eternal life;" one inscription translates as "For Eternal Memory" and the other as "May his memory be for a blessing" (Suri Jacknis, personal communication, August 15, 1985). At Mount Lebanon there are no references to death on Sabbath, the High Holy Days, or holidays. Except for the military information placed on government-issued markers, inscriptions in English are nearly all limited to the name of the deceased, dates of birth and death, and kinship status. Very few longer epitaphs were observed. One reads "It was his lot to die at the prime of life and far from his loved ones. Rest in peace;" another states "Death separates but it also unites. It reunites whom it separates."

Ten individuals representing 3.2% of the sample had stones with inscriptions which specified their place of birth; in four cases, this was coupled with an indication that the individual died in Lincoln. Places of birth included Alsace-Lorraine (4 cases); France (Phalsbourg, Eppernay, and Mettingen); Vienna, Austria; New York City; and Valley Falls, Kansas. As noted above, at Mount Carmel the place of birth (Mannheim, Germany) was specified for only one person. All of these birth places, it should be noted, are in Western Europe or the United States.

Discussion and Conclusions

In Lincoln, the gravestones in both Jewish cemeteries are essentially those forms which have been available to and used by the general populace during the last century. This pattern is also seen in Europe (cf. Bloch 1953; Cohn 1931; Davidovitch 1971; Grotte 1941; Grunwald 1902; Herman n.d.; Kohler 1906; A. Levy 1923; Lion 1960; Wischnitzler-Bernstein 1931; and Wolf 1922) and in the eastern United States during the seventeenth to nineteenth centuries (cf. Elmaleh 1962; Gutstein 1936; B. Levy 1983; Mendes 1885; Stern 1895; and Temken 1971). This pattern also appears to hold true for the Caribbean and South America (cf. Emmanuel 1957; Enciclopedia Judaica Castellana 1949; Shilstone 1956; and Wolff 1976) although the Sephardim there—as in Europe and in Colonial America—had a preference for horizontal ledger slabs instead of vertical monuments. On the other hand, Lincoln's Jewish cemeteries—like those elsewhere in the United States and in Europe and South America—are separated to some degree from non-Jewish burial areas. In addition, the gravestones—particularly those of the Orthodox and Conservative Jews—exhibit inscriptions and religious symbols which are not found in non-Jewish cemeteries.

The location and structure of the Mount Carmel Cemetery reflect a notable degree of separateness and exclusiveness vis-a-vis the general population in Lincoln. Boundary-maintaining mechanisms include the location of the cemetery on the northern periphery of Lincoln, the bordering conifer trees and thick shrubs, the surrounding of the graveyard by an iron fence with locked gates exhibiting Stars of David, and the elements on the gravestones. In addition to the consistent use of Jewish symbols and Hebrew inscriptions, specific insignia designate the priestly roles of the Kohanim and the attendant roles of the Levites. Insignia pertaining to secular sodalities are extremely rare on the stones. It might be added, however, that some stones at Mount Carmel are accompanied by separate, small metal markers from the American Legion and other military organizations. One Masonic insignia is present. Members of the Jewish faith, it should be observed, have been involved in Masonry since the American Colonial Period (Gutstein 1936: 169; Kusinitz 1984). The Masonic emblem, for example, is present in the cemetery of Congregation Yeshuat Israel in Newport, Rhode Island. Given the original Eastern European constituency of the Orthodox and Conservative Jews in Lincoln, it is significant that the one monument with Yiddish inscriptions occurs at Mount Carmel. With the exception of English, however, other vernacular languages are not represented on the stones.

On the other hand, the placement and structure of Mount Lebanon Cemetery reflect different historical and theological trends among Lincoln's Reform Jews. The movement of the cemetery from Lincoln's periphery at Yankee Hill to a centric position at Wyuka is, perhaps, instructive. Nonetheless, Mount Lebanon is *integrated within* Wyuka which is both a state and municipal cemetery. The area of the Reform Jewish cemetery is open rather than bounded. In a sense, this spatial placement is a sort of paradigm for the relatively early and rapid integration of the German Reform Jews into American society. The one monument with a German epitaph takes on a historical significance in this regard as a material index of the Western European origins of the members of B'nai Jeshurun. Inscriptions and embellishments on the gravestones reflect basic tenets of Classical American Reform Judaism. First, one notes the use of the vernacular language almost to the exclusion of Hebrew. Second, the disavowal of the rights, duties, and obligations of the Kohanim and Levites is reflected in the total absence of symbols pertaining to those priestly roles. Third, the presence of inscriptions relating to the deceased's place of birth and death may, in our opinion, be related to the fact that Classical American Reform Judaism repudiated the idea of an eventual return to Zion (Israel) and rejected the Orthodox concept that Jews outside the Holy Land were living in exile in the Diaspora. Hence citizenship was a matter to be explicitly expressed. On the other hand, one notes that Sephardic Jews in the Antilles and the maritime communities of the eastern United States also frequently signified the place of birth on their tombstones. Thus, this factor may be more a matter of general customs (minhagim) than religio-political significance. Finally, the smaller number of specific Jewish symbols and insignia at Mount Lebanon can be correlated with the fact that Classical American Reform Judaism emphasizes cognitive principles and ideas beyond certain material and ritual forms which obtain in Orthodox and Conservative Judaism. From an exclusively materialist point of view, the Mount Lebanon Cemetery is barely distinguishable from the Christian sections of Wyuka. But the geographic space is well defined to the members of B'nai Jeshurun as a cognitive domain superimposed on the land. Fundamental beliefs and identifications are certainly not lost at Mount Lebanon as witnessed by the rituals and ceremonies associated with burials and yahrzeit anniversary observances there. Beyond that, the mere fact that Reform Jews choose to be buried in the Mount Lebanon section of Wyuka, rather than in one of the other sections of that cemetery (or, indeed in Lincoln's other cemeteries) is a powerful statement in itself. In essence, the non-material aspect of space is itself the principal identifying factor.

The data from this study, viewed in an ethnoarchaeological perspective, elucidate certain historical, socio-cultural, and intra-group variations among American Jews. In this instance the differing dimensions of doctrine and ritual practice among Orthodox, Conservative, and Reform Jews have operated as well as differences in national origin in Europe. Data from the graveyards, along with other information, tell us much not only about the pioneer experiences of Jews in the American midlands, but also about the ongoing strategies of survival among Jews and other people throughout the United States in the twentieth century.

Notes

1. We gratefully acknowledge support of an Iowa State University Research Grant and a National Endowment for the Humanities Travel Grant which underwrote portions of our archival investigations and archaeological field-work during the summers of 1985 and 1986.

2. In this essay, the English spelling of institutions with Hebrew names follows the transliteration employed by those organizations, for example, Chebra B'nai Jehuda Cemetery, Congregation B'nai Jeshurun, and Congregation Yeshuat Israel (the first congregation in Newport, Rhode Island). Since Lincoln's Jewish population is derived historically from Ashkenazic roots, the spelling of all other Hebrew words follows the traditional Ashkenazic transliteration rather than the Sephardic or modern Hebrew form.

3. Appreciation is expressed to Dr. Jacob R. Marcus and Mrs. Fannie Zelcer for their assistance at the American Jewish Archives in Cincinnati, Ohio, and to Dr. Nathan Kaganoff and Dr. Bernard Wax for their help at the American Jewish Historical Society in Waltham, Massachusetts. Other archives utilized in this study were the Nebraska State Historical Society, the Omaha Jewish Community Center Library, and the New York City Public Library.

4. The following individuals were of particular help in our project: Fannie Ellinger, Bernard S. Gradwohl, Elaine Mayer Gradwohl, Sheldon Kushner, Hymen Rosenberg, Ilse Speier Rosenberg, Eva Speier, and Paula Storch Williams.

5. We acknowledge with gratitude information provided to us by Max Speidell and Richard Tomandl (Speidell Monuments Inc.), Max Roper (Roper and Sons Mortuary), and Leroy Butherus (Hodgman-Splain-Roberts Mortuary). Especially appreciated was the assistance of Sheldon Kushner, member of the Chevra Kadisha and also president of the Mount Carmel Cemetery Association. We also thank Jack M. Meyer (Herman Meyer and Son Funeral Directors) of Louisville, Kentucky, for sharing with us his extensive knowledge of Jewish mortuary customs.

6. Our thanks are extended to Marsha S. Miller and Nancy M. Osborn who worked with us in the recording of field data in Lincoln's Jewish cemeteries; translations of selected Hebrew inscriptions were provided by Suri Jacknis; Dorothy Kushner and Ruth Burke assisted in translating the Yiddish epitaph at Mount Carmel Cemetery.

7. We acknowledge the help of Bernard Kusinitz in gaining access to the Yeshuat Israel (Old Touro Synagogue) Cemetery in Newport, Rhode Island; Elizabeth Weinberg conducted our visit to the Jewish Section of Springdale Cemetery and the Old Jewish Cemetery on Wilson Avenue in Madison, Indiana; Florine Ney escorted us through the Beth El Cemetery in Harrisonburg, Virginia; and in Albany, New York, Walter Zenner took us to visit the Cemetery of the Benevolent Society of Albany and the Congregation Beth Abraham-Jacob Cemetery. We have also made comparative observations in other communities: Kansas City, Missouri (Jewish Section of Elmwood Cemetery); St. Joseph, Missouri (Adath Israel Cemetery); Des Moines, Iowa (Emanuel Jewish Section of Woodland Cemetery, and the Jewish Glendale Cemeteries); Chicago, Illinois (Jewish Waldheim Cemeteries); Louisville, Kentucky (The Temple: Adath Israel-Brith Sholom, Keneseth Israel, Anshei Sfard, Adath Jeshurun, and the Agudas Achim cemeteries); Philadelphia, Pennsyl-

vania (Mikveh Israel Cemetery); Raleigh, North Carolina (Magnolia Hill Section of Oakwood Cemetery); and New York City (Chatham Square Cemetery). During the summer of 1984 we also had the opportunity to observe gravestones in Frankfurt, Germany (the extant Frankfurt Judischer Friedhof) and Selestat, France (Cimetiere Israelite de Selestat which serves a number of communities in western Alsace).

8. Congregation Mikveh Israel obtained ground for a cemetery on Spruce Street in Philadelphia in 1740 (Elmaleh 1962). In Charleston, South Carolina, land originally purchased by Isaac De Costa for a family burial plot was deeded over in 1764 to Congregation Beth Elohim to be used as a communal cemetery (Elzas 1903). In Savannah, Georgia, Mordecai Sheftall obtained land from King George III in 1762 and formally established the Old Jewish Burial Ground or "Sheftall Cemetery" in 1773 (Levy 1983: 15). Earlier in the history of Savannah, in the 1730s, General James Edward Oglethorpe had granted permission for the Colonial Jews of the community to be buried within a section of the town's common.

9. Boston's first Jewish cemetery was founded in 1844 by Congregation Ohabei Shalom (American Jewish Historical Society 1981: 15). This event reflected the growing immigration of Ashkenazim to the United States in addition to a greater toleration of Jews in New England. Prior to the 1840s, Boston's Jews had to be buried in Albany, Newport, or New York.

10. For example, Talmud Torah Congregation was formed as a separate group in 1903; but it merged with Tifereth Israel in 1910. During the late 1940s and 1950s, a group split off from B'nai Jeshurun, called itself the American Jewish Reform Congregation of Lincoln, and held services in private homes. Today that congregation no longer exists, its members having either died or moved away.

11. In 1850 Rabbi Isaac Mayer Wise was himself discharged from Congregation Beth El in Albany, New York. The controversy brewed over one congregational faction's discontentment with Wise's prayer book, *Minhag America*, and culminated with the irritation aroused by the rabbi's public disavowal of a belief in the coming of a personal Messiah (Schwartzman 1971: 178–180). At the urging of his faction, Rabbi Wise entered the synagogue to conduct the Jewish New Year services. As he approached the Ark to remove the Torah scroll, he was physically struck by the president of the congregation. The police were summoned to establish order among the ensuing combatant congregation members, and the synagogue was subsequently closed down for the day. This brouhaha resulted in the immediate formation of the Anshe Emeth Congregation by Wise's followers who quickly implemented many radical reforms including an organ and family pews where men and women could worship together.

12. The gravestone of Babette Speir (or Spear) is dated September 13, 1886. It is likely, however, that she died and was buried elsewhere prior to being interred at Yankee Hill.

References

Adams, William H.
1977   Silcott, Washington: Ethnoarchaeology of a Rural American Community. Reports of Investigations, No. 54. Laboratory of Anthropology, Washington State University.

American Jewish Historical Society
1981   On Common Ground: The Boston Jewish Experience 1649–1980. Waltham, Massachusetts: American Jewish Historical Society.

Auerbach, Ella Fishman
1927   Jewish Settlement in Nebraska: General Survey. Unpublished typescript, Nebraska State Historical Society.

Bamberger, Bernard J.
1971   The Story of Judaism. New York: Schocken Books.

Binford, Lewis R.
1978   Nunamuit Ethnoarchaeology: A Case Study in Archaeological Formation Process. New York: Academic Press.

Blau, Joseph L.
1976   Judaism in America: From Curiosity to Third Faith. Chicago: University of Chicago Press.

Bloch, Joseph
1953   Le Cimetiere Juif de Hagenau. Paris: Durlacher.

Bocher, Otto
1976   Der Alten Juden Friedhof in Worms. Neuss: Gesellschaft Buchdruckerei.

Chatfield, Penelope
1982   Wyuka: A "Rural" Cemetery in Lincoln, Nebraska. Nebraska History 63 (2): 183–193.

Cohn, Gustav
1931   Grab und Grabstatten. Encyclopaedia Judaica: Das Judentum in Geschichte und Gegenwart 7: 609–614. Berlin: Verlag Eshkol A-G.

Davidovitch, David
1971   Tombstones. Encyclopedia Judaica 15: 1218–1233. New York: Macmillan.

Davis, Moshe
1963   The Emergence of Conservative Judaism: The Historical School in Nineteenth Century America. Philadelphia: Jewish Publication Society of America.

Deetz, James
   1977   In Small Things Forgotten: The Archaeology of Early American Life. Garden City, New York: Doubleday Anchor.

Dethlefsen, Edwin S.
   1981   The Cemetery and Culture Change: Archaeological Focus and Ethnographic Perspective. *In* Modern Material Culture: The Archaeology of Us. R. A. Gould and M. B. Schiffer, editors, pp. 137–159, New York: Academic Press.

Dethlefsen, Edwin and James Deetz
   1966   Death's Heads, Cherubs, and Willow Trees: Experimental Archaeology in Colonial Cemeteries. American Antiquity 31 (4): 502–510.

Dethlefsen, Edwin and Kenneth Jensen
   1977   Social Commentary from the Cemetery. Natural History 86 (6): 32–39.

Elmaleh, L. H.
   1962   The Jewish Cemetery, Ninth and Spruce Streets, Philadelphia. Philadelphia: Congregation Mikveh Israel.

Elzas, Barnett A.
   1903   The Old Jewish Cemeteries at Charleston, S.C.: A Transcript of the Inscriptions on Their Tombstones 1762–1903. Charleston, S.C.: Daggett Printing Co.

Emmanuel, Isaac Samuel
   1957   Precious Stones of the Jews of Curacao: Curacaon Jewry 1656–1957. New York: Bloch Publishing Co.

Enciclopedia Judaica Castellana
   1949   Lapidas Funerarias. Enciclopedia Judaica Castellana 6: 518–521. Mexico, D.F.

Fishman, Priscilla
   1973   The Jews of the United States. New York: Quadrangle.

Gendler, Carol
   1968   The Jews of Omaha: the First Sixty Years. Master's Thesis, University of Omaha, Omaha, Nebraska.

Gordis, Robert
   1978   Understanding Conservative Judaism. New York: The Rabbinical Assembly.

Gould, R. A. (editor)
   1978   Explorations in Ethnoarchaeology. Albuquerque: University of New Mexico Press.

Grinstein, Hyman B.
   1980   A Short History of Jews in the United States. London: Soncino Press.

Grotte, Alfred
1941   Tombstones. Universal Jewish Encyclopedia 10: 265–267. New
       York: Universal Jewish Encyclopedia, Inc.

Grunwald, M.
1902   Portugiesengraber auf Deutscher Erde. Beitrage zur Kultur und
       Kunstgeschichte. Hamburg: Alfred Janssen.

Gutstein, Morris
1936   The Story of the Jews of Newport: Two and a Half Centuries of
       Judaism 1658–1908. New York: Bloch Publishing Co.

Handlin, Oscar
1954   Adventure in Freedom: Three Hundred Years of Jewish Life in
       America. New York: McGraw-Hill Book Co.

Hayes, A. B. and Sam D. Cox
1889   History of the City of Lincoln, Nebraska. Lincoln: State Journal
       Company Printers.

Herman, Jan
ND   Jewish Cemeteries in Bohemia and Moravia. Brno: Council of Jewish
       Communities, Czech Socialist Republic (ca. 1980).

Klein, Isaac
1979   A Guide to Jewish Religious Practice. New York: Jewish Theo-
       logical Seminary of America.

Kohler, Kaufmann
1906   Cemetery. The Jewish Encyclopedia 3: 637–642. New York: Funk
       and Wagnalls.

Kusinitz, Bernard
1984   Masonry and the Colonial Jews of Newport. Rhode Island Jewish
       Historical Notes 9 (2): 180–190.

Learsi, Rufus
1954   The Jews in America: A History. Cleveland: World Publishing
       Co.

Lamm, Maurice
1969   The Jewish Way in Death and Mourning. New York: Jonathan
       David Publishers.

Levinger, Lee J.
1944   A History of the Jews in the United States. Cincinnati: Union of
       American Hebrew Congregations.

Levitov, Betty
1976   Jews, The Exodus People. *In* Broken Hoops and Plains People:
       A Catalogue of Ethnic Resources in the Humanities—Nebraska
       and Thereabouts. pp. 291–336, Lincoln: Nebraska Curriculum
       Project.

Lion, Jindrich
1960 The Old Prague Jewish Cemetery. Prague: Artia.

Levy, Arthur
1923 Judische Grabmalkunst in Osteuropa. Berlin: Verlag Pionier.

Levy, B. H.
1983 Savannah's Old Jewish Community Cemeteries. Macon, Georgia: Mercer University Press.

Mendes, A. Pereira
1885 The Jewish Cemetery at Newport, R.I. Rhode Island Historical Magazine 2 (6): 81–105.

Newmark, Maurice A.
1981 Beginnings of the Pioneer Congregation of Lincoln, Nebraska. Western States Jewish Historical Quarterly 14 (1): 45–49. [Original 1918].

Nutty, Coleen Lou
1984 Cemetery Symbolism of Prairie Pioneers: Gravestone Art and Social Change in Story County, Iowa. Journal of the Iowa Archaeological Society 31: 1–135.

Parzen, Herbert
1964 Architects of Conservative Judaism. New York: Jonathan David Publishers.

Philipson, David
1967 The Reform Movement in Judaism. New York: KTAV Publishing House, Inc. (Revised edition edited by Solomon B. Freehof).
1936 Personal Contacts with the Founder of the Hebrew Union College. Hebrew Union College Annual 11: 1–18.

Pool, David de Sola
1952 Portraits Etched in Stone: Early Jewish Settlers. New York: Columbia University Press.

Raglin, Jim
1978 Jews Found a Home, Better Life in Lincoln. Lincoln (Nebraska) Sunday Journal and Star, May 21, 1978.

Rosenbaum, Jonathan and Patricia O'Conner-Seger
1981 Our Story: Recollections of Omaha's Early Jewish Community 1885–1925. Omaha, Nebraska: Omaha Section of the National Council of Jewish Women.

Sawyer, Andrew J.
1916 Lincoln—The Capital City and Lancaster County, Nebraska. Chicago: S. J. Clarke Publishing Company.

Schwartzman, Sylvan D.
1971 Reform Judaism Then and Now. New York: Union of American Hebrew Congregations.

1962   Reform Judaism in the Making. New York: Union of American Hebrew Congregations.

Shilstone, Eustace M.
1956   Monumental Inscriptions in the Burial Ground of the Jewish Synagogue at Bridgetown, Barbados. Bridgetown: Barbados Museum and Historical Society.

Silverman, William B.
1970   Basic Reform Judaism. New York: Philosophical Library.

Sklare, Marshall
1972   Conservative Judaism: An American Religious Movement. New York: Schocken Books.

Stanislawski, M. B.
1973   Ethnoarchaeology and Settlement Archaeology. Ethnohistory 20: 375–392.

Stern, Myer
1895   The Rise and Progress of Reform Judaism—Embracing a History Made From the Official Records of Temple Emanu-El of New York With a Description of Salem Field Cemetery (Its City of the Dead With Illustrations of its Vaults, Monuments, and Landscape Effects). New York: Myer Stern, Publisher.

Temken, Sefton D.
1971   Cemetery—In the United States. Encyclopedia Judaica 5: 276. New York: Macmillan.

Trepp, Leo
1980   The Complete Book of Jewish Observance. New York: Behrman House, Inc.

Wischnitzler-Bernstein, Rahel
1931   Grabsteinformen. Encyclopaedia Judaica: Das Judentum in Geschichte und Gegenwart 7: 631–634. Berlin: Verlag Eshkol A-G.

Wolf, Sandor
1922   Die Entwicklung des Judischen Grabsteines und die Denkmaler des Eisenstadter Friedhofes. IN Die Grabinschriften des Alten Judenfriedhofes in Eisenstadt, by Bernhard Wachstein, pp. 19–67, Wien: Adolf Holzhausen.

Wolff, Egon and Frieda
1976   Sepulturas de Israelitas, San Francisco Xavier, Rio de Janeiro. No. 3. Sao Paulo: Centro de Estudios Judaicos.

Ydit, Meir
1971   Cemetery. Encyclopedia Judaica 5: 271–276. New York: Macmillan.

12 Jews and Judaica: Who Owns and Buys What?

Samuel Heilman

People are often known through the objects which they possess and display. Samuel Heilman, an ethnographically oriented sociologist, uses this truism in an analysis of objects which are sold in Jewish gift and book stores. He utilizes the classification of sacred objects in Jewish law, in order to differentiate between those who practice a Torah-centered way of life and those who use these objects to show some attachment to the Jewish people, which has been called "symbolic ethnicity." There are similarities between his approach and that of the Gradwohls. Both studies show how different types of Jews display their underlying identities through material manifestations.

In his now classic study, *Peddlers and Princes,* Clifford Geertz argued that in Modjokuto, a rural Indonesian town he observed, the "traditional market [was] at once an economic institution and a way of life" (1963, p. 30). What went on in the buying and selling was more than merely commercial activity but something "reaching into all aspects of Modjokuto society, and a sociocultural world nearly complete in itself" (Geertz 1963 p. 30). Indeed, in the actual buying and selling, one could also discover reflections of the social and cultural system. And these were unmistakable to insiders. To put the matter perhaps most simply, shopping both reflected and supported a "moral order" (Geertz 1963 p. 128). Although Geertz was describing a relatively primitive society, the principles laid out in his study go far beyond the boundaries of the little Indonesian town of Modjokuto. They suggest, as Mary Douglas and Baron Isherwood later confirmed, that "consumption is the very arena in which culture is . . . licked into shape" (1979, p. 57).

As it is for the people in the Modjokuto market, so it is as well for Jews in Judaica shops. Just as one can discover elements of Javanese culture and society in the Modjokuto market, so one can decipher certain elements of Jewish life in the Judaica shop because goods are an information system, "the visible part of culture" (Douglas & Isherwood 1979 p. 66). Here, as the careful observer discovers, "the choice of goods continuously creates certain patterns of discrimination. . . ." (Douglas & Isherwood 1979, p. 66). Different kinds of people buy and possess different kinds of things. And those choices are by no means arbitrary. Rather they are informed and guided by society and culture. This is because, as John Hicks has argued, for the consumer, "the commodities which he purchases are for the most part means to the attainment of objectives, not objectives themselves" (1965, p. 166). Or, put more simply, "one knows [and displays] who one is by the objects one owns [and buys]. . . . ," (Csikszentmihalyi and Rochberg-Halton, 1981, p. xi).

And why? Because "there are no 'people' in the abstract, people are what they attend to, what they cherish, [buy,] and use" (Csikszentmihalyi and Rochberg-Halton 1981, p. 16). Among Jews, a person who has or buys a megillah, a scroll of Esther handwritten on parchment, is by virtue of that act and fact different from the one who does not. And the act of buying or possessing that megillah confirms the Jewish identity associated with it. As both merchants and buyers implicitly realize, culture and moral order enter the marketplace. Indeed, one might even go so far as to argue that in the course of buying and selling at least the latent objective of both merchants and buyers may be to demonstrate their awareness of and attentiveness to these 'background' matters. What seems at times to be simply the exchange of goods may turn out to be as well cultural performance and informational exchange on matters of significance in the realm of social reality. What I buy or own displays who I am. And thus an ethnography of Jewish material culture would do well to "treat the goods as markers, the visible bit of the iceberg which is the whole social process," (Douglas & Isherwood 1979, p. 74).

The purpose of this paper is to do just that, to provide an ethnography of Judaica acquisiton and possession as a way of tracing something of the moral and social order of Jewish life. By seeing who buys and possesses what, one can decipher something of the lines of cleavage as well as the threads of continuity among a people that is multiplex in its religious observance. In the Judaica shop, certain relationships among Jews and between them and their material culture can be traced. That is, "the clue to finding real partitioning among goods must be to trace some underlying partitioning in society," (Douglas and Isherwood 1979 p. 97).

Sources of the Data

To do this I observed buying behavior in a variety of Judaica shops in metropolitan New York and several shops in the Jewish communities in and around the Boston area. Over a period of several months, I went into these shops, wandering among patrons while watching and listening. To those who might perhaps argue that such a design by no means exhausts the possibilities, particularly if the shops and customers observed happened to be atypical, I would answer, again quoting Geertz, "seeing heaven in a grain of sand is not a trick only poets can accomplish" (1973, p. 44). From my own experience as an insider and from the impressions of other natives against whom I gauged my observations, the places and behavior I observed were rather typical. Moreover, to add to my data, for two months I also observed Judaica shops in Jerusalem (both those downtown and those in the Orthodox neighborhoods around Mea Shearim). To be sure, there are differences between Jerusalem and the other places—particularly when one compares Americans with Israelis—and even within Jerusalem there are variations between shops in one neighborhood and another. However, since so many of the shoppers in the Jerusalem Judaica shops I observed during the summer tourist season were Americans, there remained sufficient similarities to what I had found in the American scene that I included these observations here.

Finally, I surveyed a sample of over 100 Jews to discover what Judaica they owned. The respondents were randomly selected from three major sources: (1) a variety of synagogue membership lists—ranging from Orthodox through Conservative and Reform in their affiliation, (2) the student bodies of a two residential yeshivas—one in New York and another in Jerusalem, and (3) Jewish students at Queens College. The first group was meant to provide a sample of affiliated synagogue Jews, the second a sampling of those who are most involved in traditional Jewish life and norms—this is the community often referred to in Hebrew as the Haredi or ultra-Orthodox, and the third those who are young and often unaffiliated. To be sure, some of the Queens College students were affiliated. They, however, provide the most marginal Jews in my sample.

To offset the problems inherent in surveying the relatively young students in categories two and three, respondents were asked to answer not only about what they possessed but also about what their families owned. Thus, even a young respondent could provide information about a more established Jewish home. The total number of people surveyed with the questionnaire was 121. All questionnaires were administered in person. And all field observations were carried out by the writer. Thus the report that follows is essentially based upon field observations and survey sampling carried out in America and Israel during a period of three and a half months of 1986.

What is Judaica?

Before reporting what I found, some definitions are in order. Although the term "Judaica" has a variety of connotations, here it shall be used to denote those objects which in their origins are ineluctably associated with Jewish cultural and religious life.

Judaica objects are not all of a single type. Jewish law or *halacha* defines several categories. First come *klay kodesh* and *tashmishey kedusha*. There are, respectively, sancta of the highest order and their associated accoutrements—objects endowed with inherent sanctity that must, according to Jewish law, be treated with the greatest care and circumspection and handled only in specific ways. Although strictly speaking, tashmishey kedusha attain their utmost sanctity only when in use, while klay kodesh, regardless of whether or not they are actively in use for the purpose for which they were intended, remain forever *kadosh*, sacred, both types of objects are in practice ("practice" here refers to customs among the Jewishly knowledgeable) commonly treated as constantly holy. To qualify as klay kodesh an object must have one or more of the many names of God written upon it, while tashmishey kedusha are those items which service, enclose, or activate the use of the klay kodesh. According to Druk, "Everything made in honor of the Torah Scroll, even though it does not touch upon the essentials of the Torah scroll, is called tashmishey kedusha. . . . , (1986a, p. 72). Generally, consistent and constant accoutrements of klay kodesh would qualify as tashmishey kedusha.[1]

In addition to these sancta there are *tashmishey mitzva*. These are objects which in and of themselves do not have sanctity but which—while they are being used in the fulfillment of some religious ritual act—share a measure of veneration, although they do not have to be treated with the same care and circumspection as the sancta. To qualify for inclusion in this category, the objects must be required for the fulfillment of the ritual act. In a sense tashmishey mitzva are liminal—as indeed to some extent tashmishey kedusha are as well— in that they are betwixt and between the sacred and the profane. That is probably why there has been so much rabbinic debate about how they are to be treated. While they may be required for the carrying out of some act, they may on some occasions be optional; while they may be disposed of after use and lose their ritual and religious importance once the occasion for their use is past, users often (but not always) continue to associate them with the sacred and are reluctant to treat them differently from tashmishey kedusha. Tashmishey mitzva thus may be considered as "para-sacred" objects. Not endowed with inherent sanctity nor its accoutrements, they are nevertheless not altogether profane. They are rather parasitic sharers in a charisma not altogether their own. Indeed, so successful has the attachment between tashmishey mitzva and ritual life become that not only in practice but in certain halachic interpretations as well, the difference between them and tashmishey kedusha has become blurred (see, for example, *Shulchan Aruch/Mishneh Brura* 21:1).

Finally, in addition to objects that are more or less sacred and those that are para-sacred are those whose status may be described as "quasi-sacred." These are items that have some association with Jewish religious and ritual life but have according to Jewish law no inherent sanctity nor are they absolutely required for the fulfillment of some religious or ritual act. They may embellish the performance of that act and add to the sense of ceremony associated with an occasion but they are not (yet) sacred, or at least not as far as the dictates of Jewish law are concerned. They are what may be called, *r'shoot*, optional Judaica.

Rabbis have engaged in myriad debates about the degrees of sanctity with which one or another object is endowed. But while these halachic virtuosi may disagree about the precise hierarchy of the sacred, there remains a kind of practical knowledge among the laity as to what is "more holy" and what less so. The broad outlines of this knowledge are—as shall be seen—displayed in the moral order of the Judaica marketplace. While this knowledge parallels the religio-legal order of prominence, there are differences. To the extent that the popular order corresponds to relio-legal one, one may say that the moral order of the marketplace reflects the halacha. But where there is a difference, one must say that another moral order is at work.

While the rabbis may determine the definition of the sacred in the theoretical domains of Jewish law, in the realm of culture which depends more on practice than theory, the majority—even if they are religiously ignorant—have the power to define the situation. In fact, one might say that the taxonomy of Judaica that Jewish law defines only partially explains the taxonomy and moral order that emerges from the practical knowledge of the large body of Jewish people.

Yet, while there is a divergence between the law and practice in categorizing particular objects, and ignorance abounds, people do distinguish—either on the basis of religiously informed or some form of practical knowledge—among the Judaica they buy and possess. And they do recognize that some items are "more sacred" than others. Or put another way, as shall be shown below, echoes of the halachic distinctions still reverberate, however faintly, in the collective consciousness of Jewry.

From all of this three hypotheses emerge: *first, that not all people buy or own the same sorts of objects; second, that while the significance of certain objects varies from person to person, there is a moral and cultural order that informs their choice; and third, there is a hierarchy of who buys and owns what—those who are more observant of ritual will possess more items, specifically sancta of a higher order, than those who are less observant.* All of this is underpinned with a native understanding of where to buy different sorts of things. So, the possession and especially the buying of Judaica becomes a way to show what kind of a Jew one is, what one knows about Jewish life and how one goes about living it. And "any choice between goods is the result of, and contributes to, culture," (Douglas and Isherwood 1979, p. 76).

The Objects

What are the objects of Judaica? In fact, as already suggested, the objects including those which are optional, are largely shaped by the corpus of Jewish law and custom that engenders their use. Although over time and throughout history there have been alterations in style and the aesthetic elements associated with such objects, the kinds of things included in these categories vary relatively little. Indeed, in my observations, I discovered no more than sixty-one such objects, of which more than half (thirty-three) were in the realm of the optional.

What has changed is the knowledge of ritual. As Jews moved away from traditional religion and their knowledge of it decreased, objects that were once a standard and recognizable part of their environment became less so. Things that once had meaning because of their use in a ritual context no longer hold the same meaning for the context is no longer intact. And, thus while today because of the processes of mass production and the improved economic condition of Jews anyone may in principle buy anything he or she wants on the open market, wants are still shaped by moral, cultural, social and religious consciousness. With these points in mind, here is a list of all the Judaica I found on sale.

As becomes abundantly clear from even the most cursory examination of the list, the largest number of objects available are in the domain of the optional.[3] All of these are in fact what may be called "enhancers." That is, they enhance the occasion on which

Table 1

Klay Kodesh

Torah scroll, mezuza contents, Passover haggadah, prayer book, teffilm, Megillah, Talmud, Bible, and other holy books

Tashmishey Kedusha

mezuza case, t'fillin bag, *yad, tas,* Torah cover, and crowns

Tashmishey Mitzva

tallit, Sabbath/holy day candelabrum, *shofar,* wine goblet, menorah, *havdala* candle, Passover *seder* plate, *challah* cover, matza cover, *kittel,* skull cap, *tallit katan*

R'shoot

ornamental wedding ring, amulet, magen David & hamsa charms, Hanukkah top, spice box, *etrog* case, *lulav* holder, *pirsumay nissa, havdala* candle holder, *havdala* saucer, *shalach manot* plate, charity box, toy Torah scroll, *ma'im achronim* cup and saucer, *challah* cutting board and knife, *tallit* bag, silver cover for holy book, *netilat yada'im* cup and towel, holy day honey pot, decorative *tichel,* decorative kosher dish towels, prayer plaques, festive table crumb cleaner, decorative Passover pillow case, *s'firat ha'omer* counter, Sabbath light switch cover, hymnal holders, *mizrach* plaque, Purim noisemaker[2]

they are used. And if that enhancement is not ritually mandated, it is nevertheless clearly in the spirit of the occasion. As earlier noted, the ritual and religious demands of Judaism demand the possession of relatively few objects, but for those who wish to enlarge upon these, there are many possibilities. What remains now, then, is to see who buys and owns what and to suggest some reasons why.

The Ethnography

To begin with, let us look at the survey results. Keeping in mind that the acquisition and possession of certain goods is a clear indication, both symbolic and instrumental, of one's religious identity, outlook, and persuasion, one discovers a clear connection between levels of Jewish observance and objects. A look at Table 2 below is revealing with regard to who owns what. Respondents were asked to identify themselves religiously as Haredi, Orthodox, Conservative, or Reform and then asked which of the following items they or their families possessed. To be sure, this table represents a preliminary and pilot sampling. Although the sample of 121 is relatively small (and weighted towards the Orthodox), the relationships among the various elements support the basic thesis that *there is an association between religious persuasion or outlook and objects possessed.*

If we consider first who owns what, we notice first that in general, the more observant one is, the more likely one is to own Judaica. That is, Haredi and Orthodox respondents (essentially the population of those most engaged in Jewish ritual observance and which makes heaviest use of the items in question) more often possessed objects on the list than did those who identified themselves as (the relatively less observant) Conservative, and they in turn owned proportionately more than Reform Jews. To those cases which are exceptions, I shall return below.

Nevertheless, there still are echoes of the moral order of Judaica established by the halacha. That is, Jews of all stripes are more likely to own that which Jewish ritual law considers more important. With regard to sancta of the highest order (excluding objects such as a Torah scroll and its associated accoutrements which are normally possessed by communities rather than individuals), nearly 65% of the objects are possessed by a majority of the respondents in each religious category. With regard to the para-sacred, about 50% of the objects are owned by a majority of the respondents in each religious category. Finally, with regard to the quasi-sacred items, in no case did a majority of respondents in all the categories report their possession.

When we look to see which objects are most likely to be owned by all Jews, regardless of sectarian affiliation, the results are also quite revealing. The most ubiquitous is the mezuza. On average, 94% of Jews of all persuasions claimed to have one. This is no surprise since the mezuza on the door (or in some cases around the neck—the questionnaire made no distinction) is perhaps the single most important sign of Jewish identification in America. The next two items which on average were most often possessed by all Jews were a Hanukkah menorah (89%) and a Passover haggadah (83%). The reasoning here seems based on the outstanding importance which these two holy days have for American Jewry. In contemporary times, Hanukkah and Passover have become among the most popular of Jewish holy days for Americans (Cohen and Ritterband, 1984). The menorah and the haggadah seem to have become the outstanding symbols of this celebration. Indeed, for many Jews these two items may have become more than symbols of these particular ritual observances; they (and particularly the menorah) have become as well emblems of general Jewish identification. Accordingly, the material culture reflects the emphasis among American Jewry of these

Table 2

Klay Kodesh

Object	Haredi	Orthodox	Conservative	Reform
Torah scroll	7%	17%	28%	0
mezuza contents	100%	89%	96.5%	92%
haggadah	100%	91%	83%	58%
siddur (without trans.)	100%	83%	69%	25%
siddur (with translation)	n.a.	89%	76%	42%
t'fillin[4]	100%	83%	76%	42%
Purim megillah	27%	51%	10%	8%
Talmud	93%	83%	31%	25%
Bible	100%	74%	65.5%	75%

Tashmishey Kedusha

Object	Haredi	Orthodox	Conservative	Reform
mezuza case	87%	89%	90%	83%
t'fillin bag	100%	85%	79%	42%
yad (Torah pointer)	7%	17%	3%	0
Torah breast plate	0	1.5%	0	8%
Torah covers	7%	8%	3%	0
rimonim (Torah crowns)	0	6%	0	0

Tashmishey Mitzva

Object	Haredi	Orthodox	Conservative	Reform
tallit	100%	80%	76%	50%
Sabbath candelabrum	87%	86%	76%	50%
shofar	60%	41.5%	24%	8%
wine goblet	100%	86%	69%	58%
Hanukkah menorah	100%	88%	76%	92%
havdala candle	100%	83%	17%	8%
Passover seder plate	93%	65%	52%	67%
challah cover	100%	71%	41%	25%
matza cover	80%	66%	45%	25%
kittel	87%	37%	7%	0
kippa (skull cap)	100%	68%	48%	58%
tallit katan	100%	58.5%	17%	0

R'Shoot

Object	Haredi	Orthodox	Conservative	Reform
ornamental wedding ring	80%	18.5%	24%	0
amulet contents	33%	5%	14%	0

Object	Haredi	Orthodox	Conservative	Reform
amulet case	0	14%	17%	0
Hanukkah top	73%	81%	59%	8%
spice box	87%	85%	21%	8%
etrog box	67%	61.5%	17%	0
lulav holder	n.a.	38.5%	7%	0
pirsumay nissa (menorah case)	60%	12%	7%	0
havdala candle holder	67%	41.5%	14%	8%
havdala saucer	67%	38.5%	7%	0
shalach manot plate	27%	29%	7%	0
charity box	100%	89%	41%	8%
toy Torah scroll	53%	51%	21%	8%
ma'im achronim set	87%	43%	7%	0
challah board & knife	67%	72%	28%	17%
challah plate	47%	49%	17%	8%
tallit bag	100%	68%	34%	17%
silver bound holy book	33%	43%	34%	8%
hamsa charm	13%	85%	10%	8%
Star of David charm	13%	35%	41%	41%
chai charm	n.a.	37%	34%	25%
laver	93%	65%	7%	0
holy day honey pot	53%	54%	10%	0
netilat yada'im towel	27%	29%	7%	0
meat & milk decorated towels	33%	21.5%	7%	0
prayer plaques	27%	9%	0	0
festive crumb cleaner	20%	20%	7%	8%
Passover pillow case	27%	29%	10%	0%
sefirat ha'omer counter	13%	31%	3%	0
Sabbath light switch cover	33%	14%	3%	0
hymnal holders	47%	6%	0	0
mizrach plaque	40%	21.5%	3%	8%
Purim noisemaker (gragger)	60%	72%	41%	8%
N=	15	65	29	12

holy days over others. Even the Sabbath candelabrum is on average possessed by fewer Jews (75%) than the Hanukkah lamp.

Looking at the top five objects owned on the average by all Jews in my sample, one discovers an echo of the halachic order of priority. The most frequently owned objects are either among the sacred or para-sacred. These include: (1) mezuza [94%], (2) Hanukkah menorah [89%], (3) Passover haggadah [83%], (4) Bible [78½%], and (5) wine goblet [78%]. Here in brief is the moral order of American

Jewish ritual observance: a mezuza on the door or neck, a celebration of Hanukkah and of the Passover seder,a Bible or other holy book in the house, and a goblet for Passover, Sabbath or any other holy days. Moreover, each of these items also has its decorative side and can, as shall be discussed below, serve as an *objet d'art*—a factor which may also account for its popularity.

What about the notable exceptions? Looking down Table 2 one discovers the coincidence between level of observance and Judaica possession markedly disturbed in the following cases: Torah scroll and its associated accoutrements, megillah, Bible, menorah, seder plate, skull cap, wedding ring, amulets and charms, and s'firat ha'omer counter. The first two of these can be accounted for by the fact that these objects are in many cases associated with the synagogue and communal ownership, a factor that interferes with the relationship between object and person.

In the cases of the para-sacred Hanukkah menorah, Passover seder plate and skull cap where more Reform than Conservative Jews claim to possess the objects, this apparent anomaly may be explained by the relatively small number of Reform Jews surveyed. Or one might speculate, for the less observant, ownership of these icons of Judaica may serve as an iconographic replacement for observance and hence the object becomes paradoxically more important and more ubiquitous.

As for s'firat ha'omer counter, such calendars are unnecessary to the Haredi yeshiva students whose life is immersed in the Jewish calender nor are they of use to the non-Orthodox who fail to count the days of the omer between Passover and Shavuot.[5] Only the Orthodox, who maintain the count but are not always immersed in the counting need and use such calendars.

It is, however, in the area of optional Judaica that the relationship between religious outlook and objects becomes most complex. In most cases, here too the more Orthodox one's outlook, the more likely is one to possess these Judaica objects. Thus, for example, the Orthodox and Haredi were far more likely to own an etrog box than the non-Orthodox Jews. And while certain items were owned by few Jews—*shalach manot* plates, for example—even here, the Orthodox and Haredi were more likely to have them than the other types of Jews. To be sure, in many instances, non-Orthodox Jews did not even know what many of the objects listed were, much less have them.

But what about the exceptions here, cases in which those who were less traditionally observant were more likely to own a Judaica object? If we look even more closely at these exceptions and compare the non-Orthodox with the Orthodox (i.e., considering them as a single category), we detect that only with ornamental rings, amulets, and charms are the least traditionally observant sometimes more likely to possess an object than their more ritually observant counterparts. Why?

In a way, this finding confirms the basic thesis as much as the other cases. Consider for example, the Star of David charm. Non-Orthodox Jews are more likely to own this than Orthodox and Haredi ones. Similarly, the chai charm does not significantly distinguish among Jews. In many ways, we may suggest that these objects, and others like them, which have little if any association with ritual activity or a particular holy day, have become almost free-floating symbols of Jewish identification. They are associated with no ritual obligations. Accordingly, those Jews whose religious outlook tends to be rather more liberal and free-floating might therefore be as much or even more attached to these context-free object-symbols, which nevertheless have symbolic and iconographic significance.

Context and Ecology

Ethnographically, one may speak of objects as being in or out of context, as being tuned, in Geertz's terms, "to an envisaged cosmic order," (1973, p. 90). In the case of Judaica, things that are acquired and used for the purposes for which they were originally intended, in the line with the demands of Jewish law and custom may be thought of as being in context. On the other hand, Judaica items which are treated as objets d'art or souvenirs of Israel and thereby become primarily articles of aesthetic or keepsake value may be said at times to be out of context. Buying and owning the latter may symbolize an attachment, however vague, to things Jewish but not necessarily to the religious ritual associated with the object. Hence, a Jewish person may buy a seder plate, menorah, an embroidered skull cap or even a decorated or illuminated haggadah because he is a Jew but also because he considers the thing as an art collectible rather than for use in its original function.

Ornamentation clearly plays a key role here. As noted earlier, decoration can turn the optional into something that almost seems sacred. But it can also take the sacred and make it move beyond a strictly religious definition. Indeed, for generations, the ornamentation of Judaica has broadened its appeal beyond its strictly religious and ritual use. And as the auctioneers at Sotheby's and Christie's have discovered, that appeal has waxed rather than waned in recent years.

Without question, the decoration and ornamentation of Judaica objects is a way of lifting them from their original context and moving them to another. In a sense as objets d'art, Judaica becomes far more accessible to many more people. To want and possess it you do not necessarily have to use it in its primary incarnation. Those who could not see themselves using Judaica in its context can see themselves possessing it as art.

But how is one to decide whether an object is in or out of context? Generally, one must admit that to properly interpret the ethnographic meaning of objects one must be aware of the whole pattern of culture. This is because, as Douglas and Isherwood explain, the choice of goods not only creates patterns of discrimination but also overlays and reinforces others: "all goods carry meaning, but none by itself," (p. 72). Thus, knowing about where a person lives, his religious orientation and other aspects of his existence—in short knowing the context of his life—enables one to properly comprehend his choice of objects as well as the meaning he attaches to these possessions. That is, looking *only* at objects is a risky way of determining the cultural and social attachments of the possessor. But does that mean that the objects themselves and their acquisition cannot be sociologically revealing? Not necessarily.

The concept of center and periphery is useful here. The center might be defined as the tradition and the established meanings it has ascribed to various objects. The periphery, on the other hand, might be defined as the new and contemporary associations that have become identified with the objects. Jews may likewise be described as being closer to the center or the periphery, attached more to the tradition and stability or to innovation and change.

In line with this continuum running from the center to the periphery, one might suggest (and my field observations confirm) that those close to the center tend to buy their Judaica in context, at the traditional time and for the established purposes while those at the periphery have given new meanings to their Judaism and accordingly to the objects by which they represent and display it.

In the last hundred years, and especially since Israel has grown in importance as an icon of Jewish existence, decorative Judaica has taken on additional meaning: as a souvenir of the Holy Land. Or, put more simply, holy (or quasi-holy) objects turn out to be ideally suited mementos of a trip and hence an attachment to Israel. Indeed, there are even people who, although they have not been to Israel, will buy some Judaica from there as a way of associating themselves with the Jewish homeland and ergo, the Jewish people. These Jews often care little about the specific context or meaning of the items as long as "they are Jewish" or "Israeli."

For these Jews, who exist on the periphery of tradition from whence many of these objects originate, the more decorative an object, the more ornamental, the further it seems from its primary context and the more it appears conceivable as a collectible. A silver-covered prayer book from Israel can be owned even by someone who would otherwise have no use for or interest in a prayer book. Since the economy of Judaica requires making objects attractive to the largest audiences, one should not be surprised to discover that the most Judaica shops are heavily stocked with objects that are decorative and relatively context-free collectibles.

Reflecting this reality, Israel's hotels have begun to stock decorative sancta in their Judaica shops. It is thus not unusual to find a silver-covered prayer book, a colored tallit, or shofar in these shops—along with a wide array of para- and quasi-sacred items from menorahs and etrog cases to skull caps and challah covers. The understanding is that someone who would not normally want to buy a prayer book or tallit might nevertheless choose to own a decorative one as a memento of the visit.

In the case of Israeli goods, there is more than just souvenir collection going on here. This accumulation of Judaica from Israel may be said to define a kind of sanctification of the profane. Indeed for some Jews, for whom Israel is the be-all and end-all of their Jewish identification, these mementos of Israel, whether actually acquired there or gotten secondhand through a dealer or local shop, are often the great treasures of their Jewish life.

In recognition of this fact many Judaica shops have taken to carrying many decorative Judaica items from Israel and Jewish objets d'art, many of which turn out to be quasi-sacred. Moreover, the sancta they merchandise are also ornamental. The reasons are obvious. First there are increasing numbers of Jews for whom the Israel connection is what counts most. And second, there are fewer Jews who buy Judaica in context, since these days there are fewer Jews who themselves may be said to be in context. Objets d'art, on the other hand, are for everyone.

In contrast, when one looks into the shops that service the precincts of most traditional Orthodoxy—for example some of those in the Haredi sections of Brooklyn or the back alleys of Jerusalem's Mea Shearim—there one discovers fewer objets d'art and more holy books and other sancta. Like the shoppers, the shops are tuned "to an envisaged cosmic order," (Geertz 1973, p. 90). Judaica shops in Orthodox communities are thus more likely to be filled with holy books and those items that cannot be easily ornamented or otherwise lifted out of context.

And what about those shops that service both kinds of communities? The shopkeeper who serves both an observant and non-observant clientele must be careful to keep in stock objects that can appeal to both Jews of the center and those of the periphery. Consider, for example, a Judaica store in Kew Gardens, New York that serves both those who are in and out of context. The careful observer will notice that here there are in fact two shops: the first, commonly placed in front and near the door or displayed in the window is filled with the ornamental or the decorative, including gift books written in English and appealing to those who do not or cannot read Hebrew. Here, in prominent display, were the Hanukkah menorahs, the Bibles, the silver-bound gift books and charms—everywhere charms, almost as if the shop were primarily concerned with jewelry. But there is a second Judaica shop in back. This is the one filled with holy books and other sancta. Indeed, in one shop I visited, some of the tashmishey kedusha and mitzva were kept in the basement where only community insiders knew where to find them. The reasons for these differences are fairly clear once one realizes the different communities these shops serve.

In Jerusalem, the division was even more marked: The souvenir shops that stocked the menorahs and other general-appeal Judaica were in the downtown shopping district while the stores that stocked a wide variety of sancta and the para-sacred were in the more Orthodox neighborhoods around Mea Shearim. But even in the latter there was a front, loaded with general-appeal Judaica, and a back supplied with sancta.

As one observes the ecology of the Judaica shop, one discovers a matching human ecology as well. That is, customers divide themselves with the more Orthodox getting further into the shop (both physically and metaphorically) as they move toward the sacred and the para-sacred objects. Others, in contrast, remain near the door, hovering around the charms, wine goblets, and menorahs. And thus, a look at the placement of people around the shop reveals a kind of moral order of the Jewish community. The separation in the worlds outside the shop, beyond the realm of material Judaica is reflected inside the store: different worlds, different corners of the store. Commonly the non-decorative, context-specific objects are in the back and there too one finds the Jews of the center, while the periphery and the peripherals stand in the front near the door. The symbolic nature of this division seems unmistakable. Insiders get deep inside (where they are often perusing holy books or trying on sacred garb) while the outsiders, the tourists, remain at the edge. The insiders come in at the right season and ask for things on time; the others can come at any time but are likely to ask for souvenirs, charms, and amulets as well as decorative or highly ornamented objects.

Presumably, as one moves more deeply into Jewish life one may also move more deeply into the shops. And indeed, it is curious to discover the new explorers, the *baalai t'shuvah* or returnees to traditional Judaism when they make their first tentative forays into the inner sanctum of the Judaica shop as they make their ways toward the sancta stored there.

Indeed, although I asked shoppers coming into a Judaica shop to classify their religious persuasion so as to discover whether or not there was an association between what they bought and who they were, it was soon quite clear to me (as it long had been to experienced merchants) that patrons could be easily identified and classified by the goods they were interested in buying. Thus, for example, those who came in to buy a tallit katan, the fringed garment that Jewish law demands all males wear as part of their normal attire, signaled thereby their association with traditional observance. Few if any non-observant Jews would be interested in this article for it has little if any use beyond the fulfillment of the ritual obligation of wearing fringes, a commandment that neither they nor those for whom they shop observes. It cannot be lifted out of context. Thus in most Judaica shops, the talit katan was always stored in the back or out of sight—except in shops which served only the Orthodox; there it was prominently displayed in front.

On the other hand, the marginally observant, gave themselves away often by buying items out of context. They asked for the most ornamented objects. They bought menorahs and Passover plates at all seasons—often at the 'wrong' time of year. And those selected were often chosen for their aesthetic value rather than whether or not they conformed to the demands of the mitzva, the religious ritual. So objects can signal differentiation, if one knows something about them and how they may be used.

As is clear from the case of the menorah, timing can also be crucial for interpretation. To borrow once again from Douglas and Isherwood: the consumption of goods is "used for notching off . . . intervals," (p. 66). When something is acquired or used tells a great deal about its meaning for the buyer and user. In the Jewish world, certain objects are purchased primarily at particular seasons of the year. The purchase of these items is an important way for both buyer and seller to indicate an awareness of and involvement in the concerns of the season.

Indeed the same pattern emerged at other important intervals of the year. Although stocked throughout the year, haggadahs and other Passover-related objects become particularly popular items around that festival. Similarly, people buy a megillah more commonly around the Purim holiday on which it is recited; so too at Sukkot when the etrog is used, etrog boxes likewise become a ubiquitous feature on the Judaica shop shelves. But for people on the periphery, this calendar was unknown or irrelevant.

Comparably, Jewish life cycle events are often marked by the acquisition of various objects that mark the change in status through which a person passes. Thus, upon toilet training an Orthodox young boy may get a tallit katan to wear, at bar mitzvah time he may purchase phylacteries as well as a tallit, at marriage he may receive a kittel, upon moving into one's own place one may acquire a mezuza and so on. With regard to Judaica then, acquisition of these objects in the right time of the calendar year or life cycle (the time in which the objects may be assumed to be acquired in order to be used in line with their original purpose) may be culturally understood as a way of marking off time as well as aligning oneself with a particular group and order.

To be sure, objects in the list of the quasi-sacred are harder to interpret because a number of them, as already indicated, are context free. While ornamental wedding rings, Hanukkah tops, etrog cases, lulav holders, pirsummay nissa, graggers, shalach manot plates, holy day honey pots, Passover pillow cases and s'firat ha'omer counting calendars all are associated with specific festivals and holy days and when bought around these times can be interpreted accordingly, the timing of the acquisition of other objects appears more difficult to decipher. Consider for example amulets and charms; a decorative tichel; decorative towels for milk and meat dishes; festive table crumb cleaners; havdala saucers, candles and holders; mizrach and prayer plaques; toy Torah scrolls; after-meal lavabos or challah boards and knives. All these objects in fact *do* have their life-cycle contexts. Some have to do with the setting up of households; others are used for marking changes in personal status. And thus, the buying of these objects can also be understood as in or out of context. Here, however, one needs to know the personal life-cycle context of the buyer in order to understand the occasion of acquisition.

Conclusion

Looking at the acquisition and possession of Judaica one cannot but be impressed with the expressive meaning of things, as "a means of individual *differentiation,*" (Csikszentmihalyi and Rochberg-Halton 1981, p. 33). The moral and religious order to which one belongs guides the choice of what to buy. Those close to the center and the tradition buy sancta and other Judaica at the right time and for the traditional reasons. Those on the periphery shop where a different moral order is in effect. Where the souvenir and art buyers linger, time is suspended, and that which is decorative and aesthetically appealing takes precedence over that which is ritually and temporally appropriate to the season. And the shopkeeper, knowing that both types of Jews come into his shop has set aside place for both.

But Judaica does not only differentiate; it can also provide "symbols of social integration" (ibid., p. 36). As the survey demonstrates there still is a sense across the board of Jewish life that some objects are the *sine qua non* of being an identified Jew. Whether one buys or possesses a mezuza for hanging on the doorpost in line with Jewish law or simply to express a symbolic attachment to being a Jew or even as a souvenir of an attachment to Israel, that mezuza serves to link one with all others who have one. The same might be said about menorahs, haggadahs, wine goblets, or many of the other items on the Judaica list. For the Jew who acquires, keeps, and attends to Judaica does so, albeit at various levels of meaning and in a variety of contexts, to reaffirm some attachment to Jewish life. With these things in hand, Jewish life is never too far away.

Notes

The writing of this paper was made possible by a grant from the Research Foundation of C.U.N.Y. No. 6–66230. Thanks are also due to Moshe Kahan for help in data collection.

1. According to Rabbi Eliahu, the Gaon of Vilna, as cited in the Code of Jewish Law of Moses Isserles (ch. 154), "anything that comes into contact with [objects which are] sacred, even if only to enclose or protect it, is called *tashmishey kedusha.*"

While in principle all sancta within each of these sub-categories share a similar sacred status, some of these objects are 'more equal' than others. Thus, for example, while both a printed Bible and a handwritten Torah scroll contain the same text, the former is according to Jewish law not considered to be as sacred an object as the latter. Or, a coverlet made for a Torah scroll is considered to be "more holy" than one made for a Purim megillah.

2. All the items listed under the first three categories in Table 1 qualify as Judaica whether or not they are decorative, but in the case of the optional, decorativeness may play a definitive role. Thus, for example, whether or not the contents of a mezuza are printed in an elegant hand or on a large or a small piece of parchment, they qualify as sancta (although to be sure differences in parchment size and the quality of writing are reflected in cost). However, a box to be used to hold spices which are part of the ceremony marking the end of Sabbaths and holy days is an item of Judaica only if it is decorative. Otherwise it is just a box.

3. Although all objects of Judaica have undoubtedly been affected by the changing context of Jewish life, the greatest change by far has occurred in the domain of what has here been called "optional Judaica," the quasi-sacred. This is because so much of this material is associated with custom and changing tradition and because these are affected more easily by the impact of acculturation. While a kind of historical catalogue of those items which have come in and gone out at the "optional" fringe is beyond the scope of this paper, it is safe to say that many of the objects which today are to be included among Judaica would not have been so catalogued at another time and it is not inconceivable that others will yet enter in the future while other objects will fall into disuse and become curios of a bygone era.

4. The figure includes males and females together. Leaving out females, the percentage jumps to 100% for haredi, 87% for Orthodox, 87% for Conservative, 50% for Reform.

5. The *omer* is a forty-nine day period between Passover and Shavuot which, according to Jewish law, must be counted without interruption.

References

Cohen, Steven M. & Paul Ritterband, "The Social Characteristics of the Jews of Greater New York," *American Jewish Yearbook*, 1984: 128–161.

Csikszentmihalyi, M. & Rochberg-Halton, *The Meaning of Things* Cambridge: Cambridge Univ. Press, 1981.

Douglas, Mary and Isherwood Baron, *The World of Goods: Towards an Anthropology of Consumption*, New York: W. W. Norton 1979.

Druk, Zalman, *Mikdash Me'at*, Jerusalem, 1986a, second edition.

Druk, Zalman, *Mikraey Kodesh*, Jerusalem, 1986b, second edition.

Geertz, Clifford, *Peddlers and Princes: Social Change and Economic Moderni-zation in Two Indonesian Towns*, Chicago: University of Chicago Press, 1963.

Geertz, Clifford, *The Interpretation of Cultures*, New York: Basic Books, 1973.

Hicks, John, *A Revision of Demand Theory*, Oxford: Oxford University Press, 1963.

Glossary

Most of the terms in this glossary are those which pertain to Jewish cultures as described in this book, but a number of other technical terms are also defined. Several definitions are based on those in Harvey Goldberg (1987): Judaism From Within and Without, Albany: State University of New York Press.

I have also opted to allow each author to use his/her own transliteration (with minor modification) rather than imposing a single system on them. Different pronunciations, transliterations, and the like represent the plurality of perspectives found among both Jews and social scientists. For instance, use of Ashkenazic, rather than the Israeli "Sephardic" pronunciation of Hebrew words represents an ideological position vis-à-vis Zionism.

W.P.Z.

Agudath Israel, an Orthodox Organization founded in Kattowitz in 1911 devoted to the strengthening of Orthodoxy in the world. It tended to take a separatist view towards the non-Orthodox and to be hostile or lukewarm (at best) to the Zionist movement. Agudath Israel functioned both in Eastern and Western Europe, in Israel, and in the United States.

Ahavas Yisroel (Heb.), love for one's fellow Jews.

aliyah (Heb.), the ritual honor of being called up to recite the blessings before and after a section of the Torah is read in the synagogue.

alte heym (Yid.), literally "the old home," referring to European birthplace of immigrants.

anshey (Heb.), literally, "people of," term followed by name of town or city of origin in Europe designating a religious congregation.

Ashkenazim (Heb.) (pl. form of Ashkenazi, from Ashkenaz), the name of a place/people in the Bible (Gen. 10), which medieval Jews applied to

281

the Rhineland. The term was then applied to Germany and to all Jews from Central and Eastern Europe who spoke Yiddish and/or followed "Ashkenazic" customs.

Austritt (German for secession), term applied to Samson Raphael Hirsch's concept that Orthodox Jews must withdraw from their local Jewish communities if the latter are dominated by Reform Judaism. The Orthodox were expected to form separate communities of their own.

ba'al teshuvah (Heb., f. ba'alat teshuvah; pl. baalei teshuvah, m; ba'alot teshuvah, f.), literally "master of repentance." Refers to one who has repented of deviation from Torah and who has committed him/herself to Jewish observance. Used today to describe those who have become radically more traditionally Jewish or orthopraxic.

bar mitzvah (Heb.), literally "son of the commandments"; a Jewish boy who has reached the age of thirteen and consequently has acquired religious obligations and privileges of an adult. A synagogue ceremony marking a boy's attainment of bar mitzvah has been part of Jewish practice since at least the Middle Ages.

bat mitzvah, literally "daughter of the commandments"; a Jewish girl who has reached the age of twelve, and consequently acquires certain religious obligations and privileges. A synagogue ceremony marking a girl's attainment of bat mitzvah is a twentieth century innovation, and usually takes place at age thirteen to parallel the male bar mitzvah ceremony. (Heb.)

bimah (Heb.), the elevated platform in the synagogue on which the Torah is read during services.

b'nai mitzvot, plural of bar/bat mitzvah.

bobbeh (Yid.), grandmother. It is used affectionately by many American Jews of East European descent. *Zeyde* (grandfather) is used similarly.

bris, berit (Heb. covenant), name used for the ceremony in which males are ritually circumcised. It thus commemorates the covenant between God and Abraham. Except for special cases, it is performed on the eighth day after birth and usually accompanied by a celebration.

cemetery marker, a gravestone or tombstone, normally small in size, which is set horizontally in relationship to the ground surface.

cemetery monument, a gravestone or tombstone, normally medium to large in size which is set vertically in relationship to the ground surface.

challah (hallah), (Heb. rolled, rounded loaf), generally refers to bread for the Sabbath or festivals, usually in twisted loaves. Also refers to portion of dough which was originally taken off bread and offered to the Kohen, but which orthopraxic Jews today will burn as symbolic of the gifts to priests.

Chevra Kadisha, (Heb., burial society), (see khevre).

Conservative Judaism, a branch of American Judaism which takes a middle path between Reform and Orthodoxy. It officially tends to view the Torah as authoritative, but recognizes the need for change, based on both modern needs and critical scholarship.

Dayan (Heb.), judge in a rabbinic court.

d'var Torah (Heb.), an orally presented commentary on a section of the Torah. A sermon.

epitaph, an inscription on a gravestone in memory of the person buried there.

ethnoarchaeology, the study of patterns of material culture among living people as an aid to interpreting human behavior of the past; combines historical, archaeological, and ethnographic methodologies.

etrog (Heb.), citron, used during Sukkot with *lulav.*

evrei (Russian), from *'ivri* (Hebrew) meaning Hebrew. The polite term for Jew, as opposed to *zhid* (kike) used perjoratively.

Gemeinde (German for community), a community, specifically used by German Jews to refer to the Jewish community. In Europe this generally meant the single legally-recognized community in each town. In America it could also refer to specific congregations.

genizah (Heb.), a synagogue storeroom for sancta. Sacred texts and any document bearing God's name cannot be destroyed. Therefore these texts are generally stored in a synagogue before ultimate burial.

gragger (Yid.), Purim noisemaker. They are used during the synagogue reading of the Book of Esther and are used to drown out mention of Haman, the villain of the story.

haftorah (Heb.), a reading from the prophetic books of the Bible which supplements the section from the Torah (five books of Moses) read on a particular Sabbath or holy day.

haggadah (Heb., lit. narration), a text for the *seder* (Passover table service), the story and commentaries that accompany the *seder.*

halacha, halakhah (Heb.), Jewish law, stemming from Pharasaic-rabbinic-Talmudic interpretation of the Torah and encompassing ritual, ethical, civil, and criminal law. Orthodox Jews view this corpus as binding.

halachic, pertaining to Halacha.

hamal (Turkish), porter or stevedore. A common occupation among Sephardic Jews in the Ottoman Empire and Balkans.

Hamentashen (Yid.), special triangular pastries, which are said to resemble the ears of the villain Haman (see biblical Book of Esther) and are eaten during the holiday of Purim.

hamsa (Arabic), an amulet in the shape of a five-fingered open hand. It is a Muslim and Jewish talisman against the evil eye.

Hanukkah (var. Chanukkah, Chanuko) (Heb.), "Feast of Dedication." It is an eight day holiday commemorating the rededication of the Second Temple of Jerusalem after its desecration by Hellenists and the victory of Judah Maccabee over the Hellenistic Jews and their Syrian supporters in 164 B.C.E. The festival begins on the twenty-fifth day of the Hebrew month of Kislev (in December) and is marked by the lighting of candles.

Hasid (khosid) (Heb., Yid.), pious. Refers today primarily to adherents of Hasidic sects.

Hasidista (Yid.), a Hasidic woman.

havdala (Heb.), separation ceremony, marking the end of Sabbaths or holy days.

Havurah (Heb.), small group. Term used for small, often experimental, prayer and study groups in North America. These may be independent or affiliated with synagogues and with a havurah movement.

High Holidays (also High Holy Days), the New Year and Day of Atonement. The most common holidays on which Jews attend services. These Holidays are also called *yamin nora'im* (Heb., days of awe).

Kaddish (Aramaic), a prayer in Aramaic glorifying the name of the Holy One. In the traditional prayer services, it is recited at several points to mark the end of a portion of the service. The final *Kaddish*, recited at the end of a service is called the mourners' kaddish and is recited by those whose immediate kin (parents or children in particular) died within the past eleven months or on the anniversary of their death (jahrzeit). It is also recited by mourners prior to burial. Traditionally it can only be recited if there is a quorum of ten men present.

kadosh (Heb.), sacred.

Kashruth, the state of being kosher (ritually fit food).

Kehilla, the traditional Jewish term for the organized Jewish community. In the pre-modern world, the kehilla combined functions usually associated with a religious body (hiring clergy, upkeep of houses of worship, and religious education) and those more commonly associated with local government (taxation, regulation of Jewish commerce, etc.). Traditionally, every Jewish community, no matter what the size and number of synagogues, had a single local kehilla.

khai; chai (Heb.), lit. life. The two Hebrew letters, the *'het* and the *yod* which form this word also represent the number *18* and are used in necklaces for good luck, which also signify being *Jewish*.

khevre; chevra (Heb., Yid.) a voluntary society or association performing a specific Jewish communal function. One of the most common was the khevre kadisha, holy society, or burial society which prepared the dead for burial.

kippa (Heb.), skull cap, sometimes called a *yarmulke* or *kappeleh*.

kittel (Yid.), a white surplice and shroud, worn by males on Yom Kippur, Passover one's wedding and in death.

Klal Yisrael (Heb.), the collectivity of the Jewish people.

klay kodesh and *tashmishey kedusha* (Heb.), respectively, sancta of the highest order and their associated accoutrements.

Kohen (Heb., priest, p. Kohanim), a member of the priestly class, putatively descended from Aaron, Moses' brother, in the male line. In ancient times, kohanim had ritual duties and rights associated with the Temple service, and they retain several ritual privileges in traditional Jewish worship. They are additionally restricted from being polluted by dead bodies and from marrying divorcees and proselytes.

kosher (Heb., proper), the laws of kashrut mark what foods, both meat and dairy, may be eaten. It specifies which animals' meat may be consumed, how they are to be slaughtered and other conditions necessary for consumption.

landslayt, Yiddish plural term referring to people hailing from a common birthplace. Singular is *landman*, "compatriot."

landsmanshaft (Yid., pl. landsmanshaftn), societies formed by immigrants for a variety of purposes on the basis of local ties in Eastern Europe.

l'chaim, l'khayim (Heb. for life), the traditional Jewish toast.

Levi (Eng. pl., Levites; Heb. pl. Leviyim), a descendant of the biblical tribe of Levi. The Levites served as assistants to the priests (see *kohen*) in the Temple service, and continue to have minor ritual duties and privileges in this regard.

lulav, palm branch, used at the Sukkot holy days.

maim achronim (Heb.), after-meal laving during which, by ablutions, hands are made ritually pure for the subsequent recitation of grace.

matza (Heb.), unleavened bread, eaten throughout Passover.

Megillah (Heb.), handwritten parchment scroll of Esther, read on the Purim holy day.

menorah, (Heb.), a seven branched candelabrum generally symbolizing Judaism; for the festival of Hanukkah, an eight-branched menorah with a ninth arm for the lighting candle is used.

mezuza, (Heb.), hand-inscribed biblical verses used in talisman placed on door posts. Similar ones are used for necklaces.

mikveh (Heb.), a ritual bath used to purify people who have been ritually polluted. Most commonly, it is used by women after completing their menstrual cycle. It is also used by proselytes on their conversion to Judaism and by men, especially Hasidim.

minhag (Heb., custom) (pl. minhagim), in traditional Jewish law, an old and customary practice, not based on a passage in the Torah, but which became binding and sacred through the force of longtime observance. The term generally refers to local variations in observance of tradition, as between Sephardim, Ashkenazim, Yemenites, or Italians. Among Ashkenazim, there are also such variants, especially between German and Polish Jews. The term may also be applied more loosely to differences between Reform and Conservative and Orthodox Jews.

minyan (Heb.), prayer quorum. The minimum number of adult males needed for holding communal (as opposed to individual) prayer services is ten. Today Reform, Reconstructionist, and many Conservative Jews will count adult women in the quorum.

mitzvah (Heb.), commandment. Literally refers to divine commandments ordained by the Torah. Metaphorically extended in Yiddish to refer to good deeds.

mizrach (Heb.), east, for Western Jews, usually the direction of Jerusalem and thus the orientation of their prayers.

Mizrachi, the religious Zionist movement.

ner tamid, the Everlasting Light; a lamp, symbolizing the eternal presence of God, located above the Holy Ark in a synagogue; often seen as a symbol on gravestones in Jewish cemeteries.

netilat yada'im (Heb.), the ritual laving of hands before bread, normally done by spilling water from a cup over the hands.

Omer (Heb.), literally sheaf. Period of fifty days beginning with the second day of Passover and ending with Shavu'ot.

Orthodox Judaism, those Jews who believe that the Torah, both written (the five Books of Moses) and oral (including the Talmud) was divinely revealed and remains authoritative to this day. Orthodox Jews, however, remain divided by origins (eg, Ashkenazic, Sephardic) and by their own orientations to worldly activity and non-observant Jews.

One group believes that Jews may participate in the society at large as individuals while adhering to the law, while others (e.g., Hasidic sects and other groups) believe that participation in the society, including secular education and exposure to mass media must be limited.

Passover (Pesah), is one of the three major festivals of the Jewish year, commemorating Israel's deliverance from enslavement in Egypt 3,200 years ago, as recounted in Exodus. On the evenings of the first (and for more Orthodox Jews), the second nights of Passover, a Seder or ritual service is held.

pirsumay nissa (Heb.), glass and brass case for a menorah, enabling its placement outdoors during Hanukkah.

Pittsburgh Platform, statement of principles made at a conference of Reform rabbis in Pittsburgh, Pennsylvania in 1885. It affirmed the Reform view that Mosaic legislation pertaining to most ritual matters was foreign to moderns and therefore not binding. It also rejected the doctrine of bodily resurrection and a view of Jews as any kind of national entity with political aspirations. These views were considerably toned down and in statements of principle made from the 1930s on. Those who continue to adhere to the Pittsburgh Platform are often referred to as "classical Reform Jews."

Purim (Heb., "lots"), Jewish holiday celebrated on the fourteenth day of the month of Adar (in March). It commemorates the defeat of Haman, who plotted to kill the Jews in the Persian empire, according to the Book of Esther in the Bible. The holiday is marked by noise-making with *graggers* (see above) and feasting.

rebbe (pl. rebbes) (Yid.), the charismatic or hereditary leader of a Hasidic dynasty.

rebbetzin (Yid.), rabbi's wife.

Reform Judaism, one of the three major movements of American Jews. It originated in Germany but flourished in the United States. It views Scripture as divinely inspired, not divinely revealed. The *Torah*, both written and oral, is not authoritative. Reform Jews continue to perform those traditional rituals that they believe can promote a Jewish ethical, God-oriented life.

rimonim (Heb., literally pomegranates), ornamental crowns placed on Torah scroll staves.

Rosh Chodesh (Rosh Hodesh) (Heb.), the new moon—traditionally marked as a "minor" holy day.

Rosh Hashanah (Heb.), New Year. Celebrated on the first two days of Tishri. This is a generally solemn festival.

r'shoot (Heb.), optional Judaica—not required by halacha.

Seder (Heb., order), referring to the ritual order appropriate to a celebration. The seder par excellence means the domestic celebration which takes place on the first night of Passover in Israel and the first two nights in the Diaspora. The seder includes reading and discussing a narration of the exodus from Egypt, singing of psalms and hymns, and a festival meal.

Sephardi, Sepharadi (Pl. Sephardim). Sepharad, a biblical place name which was applied to the Iberian peninsula by medieval Jews. As a result of the expulsions from Spain and Portugal in the fifteenth Century, Spanish and Portuguese Jews became dispersed throughout the Mediterranean lands and to Northwest European lands and their colonies in the New World. Today, the term Sephardi may refer narrowly to Jews who speak Judeo-Spanish (Ladino or Judezmo) and/or can trace their descent to the Iberian peninsula. More broadly, the term refers to Jews who came under the influence of these emigres and who accepted Sephardi law, liturgy and customs and thus has come to include most non-Ashkenazi Jews, especially from the Middle East.

S'firat Ha'omer (Heb.), the forty-nine days counted between the second night of Passover and the Shavuot, the next holy day. Some people have a counter or calender for keeping track of the time.

Shabbos zeiger (Yid.), Sabbath clock, a timer used by orthopraxic Jews to turn lights on and off on the Sabbath. Turning electricity on and off manually is prohibited.

Shabbat Shalom, the Hebrew form of the greeting for the Sabbath, meaning Sabbath of peace. See Gut Shabbos.

Shabbatones (Heb., Eng.), Sabbath get-togethers for baalai tshuvah hosted by Hasidim.

shalach manot (Heb.), dispatched edibles sent during the Purim holy day among friends and neighbors. Usually includes hamantash sweets, dried fruits, and nuts.

shamash, sexton in a synagogue. Sometimes has liturgical functions as well as caretaker functions.

Shavu'ot (Heb.), the Feast of Weeks. Together with Passover and Sukkot, it is one of the Three Pilgrimage Festivals. It takes place fifty days (seven weeks plus a day) from the second day of Passover. By tradition, it is the day on which the Torah was revealed to the Israelites on Mount Sinai. It is also known as the Pentecost and the Feast of First Fruits (Hag BaBikkurim).

shofar (Heb.), a ram's horn that is blown during the Jewish New Year (Rosh Hashanah) and the end of Yom Kippur (Day of Atonement).

shohet (Heb.), a slaughterer following Jewish law for slaughter.

shtetl (Yid., pl. shtetlakh), small town. The term generally refers to the small market towns of Eastern Europe from which most East European Jewish immigrants arrived. Like the term, ghetto, in the nineteenth Century, it is used as a shorthand term for the Jewish community and culture of that region.

siddur (Heb.), prayer book.

simcha, simkhe (Heb., Yid.), a happy occasion; a time for rejoicing.

sodality, a voluntary association or club, such as the *Chevra Kadisha* or Masons.

Sukkot (Heb., booths), the Feast of Booths (or Tabernacles) which begins on the fifteenth day of Tishri (Sept./Oct.) on or after the autumnal equinox. As other festivals, an extra day (ninth day) is celebrated in the Diaspora. Sukkot is a joyous holiday following the solemn High Holy Days. The last day of the holiday is known as "Simkhat Torah" and is particularly joyous in celebrating the end and beginning of the cycle of reading the Torah in the synagogue.

talis (talit) (Heb.), a prayer shawl, usually of wool or silk, bearing fringes on each of its four corners (tzitzit). It may be worn as an undergarment by orthopraxic Jews.

tallit katan (Heb.), is the small fringed four cornered garment worn as an undergarment by orthopraxic males.

Talmud, the term most commonly and comprehensively used to include both the Mishnah and Gemara which developed in the period between the first and sixth Centuries (C.E.). The Talmud, written in Hebrew andAramaic, contains authoritative interpretations of *halacha* (Jewish law) and derives practice from verses in the Torah.

tas, ornamental breast plate for Torah scroll.

tashmishey mitzvah, objects which in and of themselves do not have sanctity but which—while they are being used in the fulfillment of some religious ritual act—share a measure of veneration, although they do not have to be treated with the same care and circumspection as the sancta.

tefillin (Heb.), Phylacteries, which are worn by men during the daily morning service. The tefillin consist of small leather boxes, containing passages from the Torah which are strapped on to the left arm and head.

tichel (Yid.), a married woman's head covering, commonly a kerchief.

Torah, the five books of Moses; the first five books of the Bible. The term, Torah, is also used more generally to include the "oral Torah" and its products including the Talmud, commentaries on both Torah and Talmud, codes of law, and other sacred lore.

tzedakah (Heb.), literal meaning, righteousness. It generally means "giving" or "charity" today.

Va'ad Harabbanim, rabbinical council (generally an Orthodox rabbinical council) of a locality.

yad (Heb., hand), pointer used in synagogue during reading of Torah scroll to mark the passage being read (chanted). It is in the form of a hand.

yahrzeit, (Yid.; jahrzeit in German) the anniversary of a person's death date; traditionally observed by mourners with rituals including the lighting of a memorial candle at home, recitation of the *kaddish* in the synagogue, and often a visit to the grave of the deceased family member or other loved one.

yarmulke (Yid.), see kippa.

yeshiva (Heb.), a school or academy for teaching Talmud to advanced students. It prepares them to be rabbis in the traditional sense of judges. In the United States the term also is used for Orthodox Jewish day schools, whether elementary or secondary.

Yeshiva world, the milieu dominated by the heads of the major institutes of higher Talmudic learning characterized by a rigorously Orthodox viewpoint dominated by a concern for the observance and study of traditional Jewish law.

Yiddish, a Germanic language spoken by Ashkenazic Jews. It first developed in the Rhineland and was carried by German Jews to Eastern Europe.

Yiddishkeit (Yid.), Jewishness. This quality may be interpreted differently by different varieties of Jews, whether religiously or in a secularist manner.

yikhus; yikhes (Yid.), pedigree; genealogy, may also include achieved status in the community, such as university degrees and income. In Eastern Europe the Jewish community was stratified through a complex system of status including degrees of descent, wealth, and learning.

Yizkor; yisker (Heb., "He will remember"), prayer service recited in the synagogue on Yom Kippur, Shemini Atzeret (eighth day of Sukkot), on the eighth day of Passover, and on the second day of Shavu'ot in which the dead are remembered. It is named for one prayer within that portion of the service which opens with the word, *yizkor*.

Yom Kippur (Heb., also Yom HaKippurim), Day of Atonement. This holy day is marked by abstinence from food, drink, sexual activity, and wearing of leather for twenty-four hours.

zhid (Russian), "kike"; derogatory term for Jews.

Contributors

JANET S. BELCOVE-SHALIN was born and raised in Chicago. She received her M.A. degree from the University of Chicago, and she has recently defended her Ph.D. thesis on the Hasidim of Boro Park at Cornell University. She has written on tradition and social change and on the methodological issues of ethnographic field work.

DINA DAHBANY-MIRAGLIA is a linguistic anthropologist. She received her Ph.D. from Columbia University in 1983 and has been teaching courses in anthropology, sociology, women's studies, English as a second language and in interdisciplinary studies at CUNY and elsewhere since 1976. She is working on a manuscript of verbal expressions of Yemenite Jewish ethnic identity and has published articles on Yemenite Jewish ethnic identity, immigration, traditional poetry and ethnolinguistics.

JACK GLAZIER received his Ph.D. in anthropology in 1972 from the University of California at Berkeley following field research in East Africa. After two additional periods of fieldwork there, he turned his attention to American Jews when he began research in Indianapolis in 1980. He has published widely in his two major research areas. He is currently professor of anthropology and chairman of the department at Oberlin.

DAVID MAYER GRADWOHL and HANNA ROSENBERG GRADWOHL both grew up in Lincoln, Nebraska. They attended the University of Nebraska. David pursued graduate work at the University of Edinburgh in Scotland and received his Ph.D. from Harvard University; Hanna attended graduate school at Boston University and has an M.S.W. from the University of Iowa. Hanna is a school social worker with the Heartland Area 11 Education agency and David is a Professor of Anthropology at Iowa State University.

SAMUEL HEILMAN, Professor of Sociology at Queens College and the Graduate Center of the City University of New York, is author of *A Walker in Jerusalem, The Gate Behind the Wall, The People of the Book, Synagogue Life;* and (with Steven M. Cohen) *Cosmopolitans and Parochials: The Many*

Faces of American Modern Orthodox Jews [forthcoming]. He has published major studies on Jewish unity and disunity, the contemporary Jewish family, and the ethnography of Jewish education, as well as numerous articles and reviews.

HANNAH KLIGER is Assistant Professor in the Department of Judaic and Near Eastern Studies and the Department of Communication at the University of Massachusetts, Amherst. She is currently broadening her research on Jewish immigrant associations in America by examining ethnic organizations in Israel and by focusing on Jewish women's participation and leadership in these groups.

STEVEN M. LOWENSTEIN is Isadore Levine Professor of Jewish History at the University of Judaism in Los Angeles. He received his Ph.D. from Princeton University. He has written numerous articles on the social and cultural history of German Jewry, especially during the nineteenth century. His book, *Frankfurt on the Hudson: The German Jewish Community of Washington Heights, 1933–1983, recently came out, and he is now working on a social history of the Berlin Jewish Enlightenment, 1756–1823.*

FRAN MARKOWITZ received her Ph.D. from the University of Michigan in Ann Arbor in 1987. She was Study Director of a survey of Soviet Jewish immigrants in New York City. Currently she is conducting research on Soviet Jews in Israel. A number of her articles are currently in press. Her interests include urban anthropology, the cultures of Eastern Europe, and comparative Jewish cultures.

DAVID SCHOEM is Assistant Dean for Freshman/Sophomore Curriculum at the University of Michigan. He is a Lecturer in Sociology, teaching "Blacks and Jews: Dialogue on Ethnic Identity". His forthcoming book is tentatively titled *Ethnic Survival in America: An Ethnography of a Jewish Afternoon School.* He is co-editor of *Students Talk About College: Essays From the Pilot Program.*

STUART SCHOENFELD is associate professor of sociology at Glendon College of York University (Toronto). He has conducted research on a variety of topics related to Jews, ethnicity and religion. He is editor of *The Changing Jewish Community* and the author of numerous articles. Recently he has been doing research on the links between bar/bat mitzvah and Jewish institutions and identification.

MYRNA SILVERMAN is in the Department of Health Services Administration, University of Pittsburgh's Graduate School of Public Health, where she teaches and conducts research on aging and long-term care. Her book entitled *Strategies for Upward Mobility: Family Kinship and Ethnicity Within Jewish Families in Pittsburgh* is forthcoming.

Contributors   **293**

WALTER P. ZENNER is Professor of Anthropology at the State University of New York at Albany. He received his B.A. from Northwestern University and his Master of Hebrew Letters from the Rabbinical School of the Jewish Theological Seminary of America. He has done fieldwork among Jews and Arabs in Israel, Syrian Jews in Jerusalem, New York, and Manchester (England) and with new immigrants and state employees in Albany (NY). He is coeditor and contributor to *Urban Life: Readings in Urban Anthropology* and *Jewish Societies in the Middle East*. He is editor of the Anthropology and Judaic Studies series for SUNY Press.

Index

American Indians, Native Americans, 9, 27, 64, 80, 99, 106
Antopol, 144, 146
Arenas, 137–141
Anthropological study, 3–7, 19–23, 24–26, 39–40, 45–46, 50, 225–227, 260–261; see also ethnography
Ashkenazim, Ashkenazic, 5, 24–26, 40, 43–62, 71–76, 139, 228–229; see also Yiddish, Soviet Jews, German Jews, East European Jews
Assimilation and acculturation, 8, 9, 16, 24–26, 41, 46–48, 57–60, 66–67, 112, 197–200

Ba'alei teshuvah, 6, 40, 117, 191–193
Bar mitzvah, bat mitzvah, 14, 17, 89, 91, 96, 104, 117–135, 276
Barth, Frederik, 8
Benedict, Ruth, 4, 5, 6, 194
Bialystok, 144, 146, 150
Bible, 107, 268, 269
Blacks, 16, 18, 25, 66, 67, 69, 70, 71, 74, 217
Bobover, 21, 185, 186, 195
Bosk, Charles, 188, 189, 190
Burial societies and services, 146, 213, 214, 226, 232, 234, 244, 245

California, 15, 16, 20, 192, 229
Canada, 11, 13, 15–16, 17, 137, 198
Cemeteries, 14, 138, 140, 213, 214, 223–259
Center and periphery, 271–277

Ceremonial objects, Jewish, 263–277; see also Passover, Purim, Hanukkah, Sabbath
Christian fundamentalism, 6
cemeteries, 238, 244, 250
identity, 72–73, 102
religion, 25
Cohen, Steven, 8
Community center, Jewish, 19, 28, 55, 84, 88, 89, 137
Configurationism ("Boasian Culture and Personality Approach"), 4, 5, 6, 19, 185, 194; see also shtetl
Conservative Judaism, 20, 47, 83, 96–116, 117, 122, 138, 167, 179, 217, 224, 229, 244, 251, 252, 262, 266–271, 279
Consumers, Jews as, 14–15, 91, 236–237, 260–279
Csikszentmihalyi, Mihalyi, 261, 277
Czestochowa, 144, 146, 155

Demography, 10–11, 47–48, 166–169, 217
Diamond trade, 12
Dietary laws; see Kashrut
Douglas, Mary, 19, 28, 260–261
Duker, Abraham J., 24–25, 27
Durkheim, Emile, 118–119, 132, 187–188

Eastern Europe, 144; see Poland, Soviet Union
East European Jews, 50, 51–54, 143–164, 166–169, 170–171, 179,

295

183–200, 223, 228–229; *see also*
    Ashkenazic, Soviet Jews, Yiddish
Elderly, 17, 168, 213
Ethnic identity, ethnicity, 8–9, 18, 19,
    39–41, 43, 44, 63–65, 79–81, 90–92,
    113, 172, 174, 195–197, 261; *see also*
    stigma, interethnic strategies
Ethnoarchaeology, 225–227
Ethnography, 21–23, 45–46, 98,
    184–189; *see also* participation
    observation, ethnoarchaeology
Evolution, cultural, *see* modernization
    perspective

Family and kin, 8, 13–14, 17–18, 28,
    51–54, 83, 149, 152, 165–181,
    195–196, 198, 226, 227, 240
Family clubs, 8, 18, 149, 174
Fischer, Claude, 10–11, 27
Fraternal order, general, 157, 251
French in Quebec, 16
Functionalism, 6, 19, 187–188

Gadol, Moise, 58–59
Geertz, Clifford, 19, 188, 260, 262, 271
Gentiles, 18, 23, 24, 25, 26, 46–47, 137,
    184, 187; *see also* political behavior,
    ethnic identity, Christians
German, 231, 239, 248, 251
German Jews, 4, 11, 13, 18, 49, 50,
    138, 139, 166, 208–221
Germany, 209–212, 241
Gift and book shops, Jewish (Judaica),
    260–279
Glazer, Mark, 8, 18
Goffman, Erving, 22, 44–45, 64

Halakha, 263–265, 269–271, 275; *see
    also* Mishnah
Hanukkah, 25, 139, 174
Hanukkah menorah, 266, 267, 268, 269,
    270
Haredi, 262, 266, 267, 268, 271,
    273–277; *see also* orthodox Judaism,
    Hasidism, Hirsch
Hasidism, 11, 12, 13, 15–16, 18, 21,
    22–23, 25–26, 72, 75, 140, 183–207,
    208, 215, 217

Havurot, 18, 20–21, 25–26, 40, 131
Hebrew, 101, 108, 109, 123, 129, 176,
    231, 234, 237, 238, 239, 248, 251
Hebrew school, 24, 40, 96–115, 120,
    122, 138
Heilman, Samuel, 10, 14–15, 19, 21–23,
    185
Hirsch, Samson Raphael, 140, 208–212
Hirschian Orthodoxy, 208–221
Hispanics, 25, 67, 68, 69, 70, 217
Holocaust, 148, 155, 156, 186
Homogenization; *see* assimilation and
    acculturation

Immigrant associations (comparative),
    143, 145–146, 160; *see also*
    landsmanshaft
Indianapolis, 43–62
Individualism, 7–8, 18, 24, 118–119,
    121, 132; *see also* Schoenfeld
Interethnic strategies, 63–76, 79–92
Intermarriage:
    Ashkenazic-Sephardic, 51–54, 57;
    Ashkenazic-Yemenite, 74–75; Jewish-
    Gentile, 4, 54, 89
Isherwood, Baron, 260–261
Israel, 39, 65, 86, 100, 103, 146,
    153–154, 157, 252, 273; Americans
    in, 262; Israeli goods, 272–273;
    Israelis, 67, 68, 72, 76; *see also*
    Jerusalem
Istanbul, 24

Japanese-American, 99, 106
Jerusalem, 262, 274; *see also* Israel
Jewish Defense League, 16
Jewish Federation, Jewish philanthropic
    in Indianapolis, 48, 52–53, 55, 57,
    59–60; program for Soviet Jews,
    86–87, 215; in Lincoln, Nebraska, 232
Jewish fraternal orders, 148, 149, 157
Judaica shops, 14–15, 260–279

Kashrut, 9, 11, 14, 75, 76, 137, 214,
    216, 221, 231
Kehilla, 208–211
Klay kodash, 263, 268
Kranzler, George, 186–187, 188, 197

Kohen, Kohanim, 231, 237, 242, 251
Kugelmass, Jack, 17, 19–20
Ku Klux Klan, 46–47

Ladino (Judezmo), 40, 49, 50, 51, 56, 69
Landsmanshaft, 18, 55, 138, 143–163
Lawyers, 16–17, 175
Leichter, Hope, 8, 13–14, 17–18
Levite, 231, 237, 242, 251
Leyton, Elliott, 4, 13
Liberal-conservative-radical split, 15–18, 28
Lincoln (Nebraska), 43, 223–255
Local/cosmopolitan dichotomy, 16–17
Lodz, 144, 146, 150, 151, 152, 155
Lubavicher Hasisim, 185, 191–193, 194, 195–196, 200
Luckmann, Thomas, 118, 132

Marxism, 188, 189
Material culture (Judaica), 223–279
Mead, Margaret, 4, 6
Middleman minority theory, 27–28
Minsk, 144, 146
Mintz, Jerome, 185, 186, 193, 194, 198
Mishnah, 119–120, 210, 264
Mitchell, Douglas, 186, 191
Mitchell, William E., 8, 13–14, 17–18, 23
Modernization perspective, 7–9, 27, 117–119, 137
Music and dance, Hasidic, 194–195
Myerhoff, Barbara, 17, 19–20, 21–22, 195

New York City, 11, 16, 17, 19, 28, 64, 66, 82, 87–88, 147–148, 184, 187, 191, 198, 199, 200, 208–221, 261, 262, 273

Occupational structure, 1–14, 27–28, 46, 49, 56, 57, 58, 168–178
Orthodox Judaism, 5–6, 9, 11, 19, 26, 27, 72, 75, 81, 82, 83, 86, 87, 99, 106, 137–138, 139, 140, 167,

208–221, 224, 229, 234, 244, 250, 251, 252, 262, 266, 271–277, 278; *see also* Hasidim
Ottoman empire, 49, 65, 76
"Outsider doctrine", 21–23

Park, Robert E., 4
Participation-observation, 6–7, 21–23, 45–46, 76, 147–148, 184–187, 227
Passover, 85, 240; Passover seder, 14, 17, 25, 139, 174; Passover seder objects, 266, 267, 268, 269, 270–271
Peddling, 12–13, 28, 171
Pittsburgh, 166–178, 191, 192
Plotnicov, Leonard, 4, 64, 186, 191
Pluralism, 8, 65, 66–67, 75, 76, 110–112, 137
Poland, 147, 149; *see also* Antopol, Bialystok, Czestochowa, Lodz, Warsaw
Political behavior, 14–15, 27–28, 48, 198, 217–219
Poll, Solomon, 22, 184, 185, 188, 198
Prayerbook, 72, 101, 231, 254, 266, 268
Purim, 21, 85, 195, 269, 276
Purim play, Hasidic, 21, 186, 195

Rabbi, 20, 46, 60, 83, 84, 89–90, 97, 106, 120, 138, 240; rebbes (Hasidic), 189–191, 199, 208–219
Radicals, Jewish, 11, 15, 16, 17, 148, 149
Reconstructionism, 117, 169
Reform Judaism, 15, 20–21, 46, 55, 60, 86, 89–90, 99, 106, 117, 137, 138, 139, 209, 210, 211, 217, 224, 229, 231, 248, 251, 252, 262, 266–271, 278
Rochberg-Halton, Eugene, 261, 277
Rosh Hashanah, 85, 87, 96, 112, 240
R'shoot, 264, 268, 270–271, 277–278
Rubin, Israel, 188, 190

Sabbath, 23, 75, 88, 108, 109, 120, 123, 125–127, 137, 240, 244, 268–271, 278
Scrap metal industry, 12, 28
Secularization, 8, 88–89
Seder; *see* Passover seder
Sefirat ha-Omer, 270–271

Self-hatred, 18
Sephardic Jews, 8, 18, 22, 40, 43–62, 67, 227–229; see also Syrian Jews
Shaffir, William, 15–16, 185, 187, 189, 191, 192, 198
Shtetl, 5, 17, 24, 197, 198; see also East European Jews
Silverman, Myrna, 18, 64
Sociolinguistics, 64–65, 75–76, 185, 198–199
Sociology, 4–5
Southern Jews, 15
Soviet Jews, 18, 40, 43, 79–95, 138, 218
Soviet Union (U.S.S.R.), 81, 82, 85, 89
Spicer, Edward, 8–9
Spiro, Melford, 3–4
Star of David (Mogen David, "Jewish/Star"), 67, 87, 233, 234, 241, 242, 248, 266, 271
Steinberg, Stephen, 8, 58
Stigma, 26, 44–45, 50–54; see also ethnic identity
Suburb, 11, 98, 168, 173, 176, 197
Synagogues, 11, 15, 18, 19–21, 22–25, 45, 59–60, 72, 85–87, 117–135, 137, 138, 139, 146, 208–219, 224, 228, 229–232, 234, 254
Symbolic approach, 19, 20, 21, 188–189; symbolic interactionism, 188–189
Syrian Jews, 4, 13, 22, 23, 67, 139, 262

Tales, Hasidic, 185, 193–194
Tashmishey kedusha, 263, 268, 270–271, 277–278
Tashmishey mitzva, 263, 268, 270–271, 277–278
Technology, 7, 9, 11, 199
"Torah", attitude towards, 107, 192, 230–232, 271–277
Turner, Victor, 19, 20

United Jewish Appeal, 215, 232
Upper class, Jews in, 13–14, 28
Urban neighborhoods, 11, 16, 19–20, 27, 28, 50, 54, 57–58, 60, 87–88, 167–168, 169, 184, 185, 188, 197, 208, 212–221, 230

Warsaw, 144, 146, 150
Weber, Max, 188–189, 191, 196
Wedding, 14, 17, 89
Weinreich, Max, 25
Western European Jews, 223, 224, 228–229, 250
White Protestants, 13, 46–48; White Anglo-Saxon Protestant heritage, 106
Wirth, Louis, 4, 26, 27
Women; economic activity, 168; participation in synagogue, 117–135, 213, 242; participation in landsmanshaftn, 149–150, 152, 157; Hasidic, 194, 195–196, 199, 200; Yemeni, 70

Yemen, 64, 65
Yemeni, 18, 23, 40, 63–78
Yeshiva, 11, 185, 197, 198, 211, 215, 262
Yiddish, 23, 25, 50, 51, 56, 64, 71–74, 76, 82, 86, 91, 137, 143, 145, 147, 148, 150, 151, 152, 176, 198–199, 237, 239
Yom Kippur, 21, 86, 87–88, 91, 195, 240
Yugoslavia, 49, 56

Zborowski, Mark, 5, 17, 24, 197